The Crafting of Grief

Many books on grief lay out a model to be followed, either for bereaved persons to live through or for professionals to practice, and usually follow some familiar prescriptions for what people should do to reach an accommodation with loss. *The Crafting of Grief* is different: it focuses on conversations that help people chart their own path through grief. Authors Hedtke and Winslade argue convincingly that therapists and counselors can support people more by helping them craft their own responses to bereavement rather than trying to squeeze experiences into a model. In the pages of this book, readers will learn how to develop lines of inquiry based on the concept of continuing bonds, and they'll discover ways to use these ideas to help the bereaved craft stories that remember loved ones' lives.

Lorraine Hedtke, MSW, LCSW, PhD, teaches about death and bereavement throughout the US and internationally. She is a professor in counseling at California State University, San Bernardino, is on faculty at the Vancouver School of Narrative Therapy, and is an associate of the Taos Institute.

John Winslade, PhD, is a professor in counseling at California State University, San Bernardino. He is the coauthor of eleven books on narrative counseling and conflict resolution with translations into six other languages. He is an associate of the Taos Institute.

The Series In Death, Dying, And Bereavement

Robert A. Neimeyer, Consulting Editor

For a complete list of all books in this series, please visit the series page at: https://www.routledge.com/series/SE0620

Balk—Dealing With Dying, Death, and Grief During Adolescence

Beder—Voices of Bereavement: A Casebook for Grief Counselors

Berger—Music of the Soul: Composing Life Out of Loss

Buckle & Fleming—Parenting After the Death of a Child: A Practitioner's Guide

Davies—Shadows in the Sun: The Experiences of Sibling Bereavement in Childhood

Doka & Martin—Grieving Beyond Gender: Understanding the Ways Men and Women Mourn, Revised Edition

Harris—Counting Our Losses: Reflecting on Change, Loss, and Transition in Everyday Life

Harris & Bordere—Handbook of Social Justice in Loss and Grief: Exploring Diversity, Equity, and Inclusion

Harvey—Perspectives on Loss: A Sourcebook

Hedtke & Winslade—The Crafting of Grief: Constructing Aesthetic Responses to Loss

Jeffreys—Helping Grieving People – When Tears Are Not Enough: A Handbook for Care Providers, Second Edition

Jordan & McIntosh—Grief After Suicide: Understanding the Consequences and Caring for the Survivors

Katz & Johnson —When Professionals Weep: Emotional and Countertransference Responses in Palliative and End-of-Life Care, Second Edition

Kissane & Parnes—Bereavement Care for Families

Klass—The Spiritual Lives of Bereaved Parents

Kosminsky & Jordan—Attachment-Informed Grief Therapy: The Clinician's Guide to Foundations and Applications

Leenaars—Lives and Deaths: Selections from the Works of Edwin S. Shneidman

Leong & Leach—Suicide among Racial and Ethnic Minority Groups: Theory, Research, and Practice

The Crafting of Grief

Constructing Aesthetic Responses to Loss

Lorraine Hedtke and
John Winslade

Routledge
Taylor & Francis Group

NEW YORK AND LONDON

First published 2017
by Routledge
711 Third Avenue, New York, NY 10017

and by Routledge
2 Park Square, Milton Park, Abingdon, Oxon, OX14 4RN

Routledge is an imprint of the Taylor & Francis Group, an informa business

Library of Congress Cataloging in Publication Data
Names: Hedtke, Lorraine, 1957- author. | Winslade, John, author.
Title: The crafting of grief : constructing aesthetic responses to loss /
    Lorraine Hedtke and John Winslade.
Description: 1 Edition. | New York : Routledge, 2016. | Series: The
    series in death, dying and bereavement | Includes bibliographical
    references and index.
Identifiers: LCCN 2016002765| ISBN 9781138916869
    (hardback : alk. paper) | ISBN 9781138916876 (pbk. : alk. paper) |
    ISBN 9781315686806 (ebook)
Subjects: LCSH: Death—Psychological aspects. | Bereavement—
    Psychological aspects. | Memory.
Classification: LCC BF789.D4 H4193 2016 | DDC 155.9/37—dc23
LC record available at http://lccn.loc.gov/2016002765

ISBN: 978-1-138-91686-9 (hbk)
ISBN: 978-1-138-91687-6 (pbk)
ISBN: 978-1-315-68680-6 (ebk)

Typeset in ITC Giovanni Std
by Swales & Willis Ltd, Exeter, Devon, UK

Printed and bound in the United States of America by Publishers Graphics,
LLC on sustainably sourced paper.

Contents

Preface   viii

Series Editor's Foreword   xii

CHAPTER 1   Seeking Beauty in Grief   1

The Hardest Decisions   4

Focus of This Book   8

A Critical Edge   9

Grief as Natural   10

A Cultural Perspective   13

A Narrative Perspective   15

Crafting the Experience of Grief   17

An Ethical Task   19

Concern for the Self   20

Becoming   21

Agency   23

Power Relations   24

Asking Questions   25

CHAPTER 2   Reality Gains the Day   27

The Changing Conversation   31

Freud and Grief as an Illness   33

Melanie Klein and Object Relations Theory   36

The Trauma of Grief   37

Grief and Attachment   38

The Pathology of Normal   40

The Five Stages   42

Modern Grief Practice   45

The Tasks of Grieving   45

The Work of Grief   47

A Shifting Tide   50

CHAPTER 3   Re-membering   53

Membership   62

The Construction of Meaning   67

Memory   69

Postmodern Grief Psychology   72
Narrative Therapy and Grief   73
Re-membering Practices   77
Subjunctive Mood   79

CHAPTER 4   Becoming Bereaved   83
Suicide, Homicide, and Stories of Identity   85
Finding Agency in Suicide and Sudden Death   91
Shifting Verbs   94
Identity and Troubled Relationships   98

CHAPTER 5   Rescuing Implicit Meanings   102
The Turn to Meaning   102
Meaning and Discourse   103
Meaning Reconstruction   104
The Absent but Implicit   105
Double Listening   106
Distinguishing the Absent but Implicit   107
An Example of a Counseling Conversation   109
Collecting Treasures   113
Crafting Vitality   114
New Meanings   120
Inviting Audience Participation in Narrative Construction   123

CHAPTER 6   The Politics of Death   128
The Politics of the Therapeutic Relationship   132
Curiosity and Respect   135
The Politics of Knowledge about Grief   137
Social Forces That Exert Influence on the Practice of Grief   139
The Politics of Military Deaths   141
Disenfranchised Grief   144

CHAPTER 7   Elastic Time   147
Chronos and Aion   148
The Event of Death   148
What is Chronos?   151
What is Aion?   155
The Timelessness of Aion   159
Cultivating an Aesthetic Sense   161
Practice Implications   164
The Crafting of Grief   167

vi

CHAPTER 8   Embracing Fragility: The Gift of Damocles   169
The Imminence of Death   170
The Gifts of Relationship   172
Bestowing Legacy   174
Bequeathing Personal Qualities   176
Actualizing Vitality and Resisting Death   178
Intergenerational Legacies   180
Populating the Membership Club   182
The Fragility of Life Is the Mother of Beauty   190

CHAPTER 9   Reinvigorating Hope   194
What Is Hope?   195
Assumptions That Form the Foundation for the Crafting of Grief   196
An Aesthetic Approach   209

References   211

Index   221

vii

Preface

Grief psychology is awash with interpretive models. From Freud, through Kübler-Ross, to more recent dual process and two-track models, many examples exist. The assumption has been that professionals can help people chart a course through grief with reference to such models. Well-intentioned research into what people experience when a loved one dies has led to the proliferation of such models.

We have no desire to add another one. It is our suspicion that there lies a danger in models of grieving that they will be imposed on people who are susceptible to colonization, because they are vulnerable and struggling. Even when prescriptive models are helpful, they are built on a narrow range of epistemological assumptions and a simplistic account of reality, one of which is that the dead are often left behind.

Our purpose is different. We aim in this book to promote inquiry into what people find comforting, sustaining, and even invigorating in the presence of grief. We shall focus more on asking questions than on generating propositions. Our target audience is those who are engaged in counseling the bereaved, whether they are trained as physicians, psychologists, ministers, counselors, or funeral directors. We want to introduce some lines of inquiry that are different from those who research grief and seek to confirm the truth value of particular models.

We have written before (Hedtke & Winslade, 2004; 2005) about re-membering conversations in which an effort is made to mitigate the pain of loss by polishing the pieces of relationship that continue to live in the aftermath of death. This emphasis is still present in this book. However, we have sought to go a lot further here. We have deliberately drawn upon the philosophy of Gilles Deleuze in writing this book, for example in the discussion about time in Chapter 8, and in the emphasis on becoming while talking about identity in Chapter 4. We have also put Michael White's conception of the absent but implicit to new use in Chapter 5. The politics of death and grief have been implicit in our previous work. Here, in Chapter 6, they are addressed in a much more explicit way.

Through all of this, we have held to a belief that the best way through the pain of grief is not to follow a prefabricated model but to craft one's own responses. The concept of crafting is chosen carefully. It invokes skills and agency, learned in cultural contexts, and lies half-way between a science and an art form. If we take it seriously, it alters how we *do* counseling. To help people manage their own crafting, we need to develop lines of inquiry, rather than propositional models to squeeze into people's experience. Curiosity becomes more important than knowledge in what we are advocating. But curiosity still needs to be purposeful. Our aim in this book has been to suggest where curiosity might be directed when people are grieving and to show it in action.

The vision that has drawn us to write this book is that, if we give people the chance, if we are curious enough, many people can rise to the occasion into which death and bereavement calls them. Many people can find moments of significance in among the debris that death strews about the place. Many people can find moments of beauty among the moments of pain and loss. In our estimation, helping people find such moments of beauty is both therapeutic and what good counseling should aim to achieve. It is an ethic that should animate practice in the helping professions. It takes hard work, but it is possible, and we have tested it out in many conversations. Some of them are present in this book.

To show the approach we are advocating, each chapter includes ix at least one example of practice. These are mostly transcribed and edited conversations of actual counseling conversations. They feature the work of the first author and many of them were recorded in workshop contexts where Lorraine was teaching people how to conduct conversations based on this approach. They took place in several different countries and with people from a variety of cultural contexts. For all of these transcripts, the participants were offered the option of having their names and identities changed for confidentiality reasons. Interestingly, however, and perhaps as testimony to the practice, some of these people asked us to include their actual names. They were proud of what they had said and wanted to be named. In Chapter 8, the conversation with Megan and Paula features both mother and daughter. Paula died before the conversation was transcribed but she was explicit about wanting to be named in the transcribed conversation. For her, having her story in this book was a way of bequeathing a sort of legacy. Other participants' identities have been changed for their protection. We have honored their desires in this regard.

Chapter 1 features a story that is written by Waka Matsushita from Kyoto, Japan. It arose from a conversation with the second author, but it was written by Waka herself. Here, as with other stories, names or identifying information of other people mentioned in the text have been changed or omitted to protect their anonymity.

In Chapter 1, we lay out the major premises of the book and explain what we mean by an aesthetic approach to grief. It is contrasted with assumptions that emphasize grief as a natural response and leave little room for cultural differences. Chapter 2 traces the history of grief psychology from Freud's 1917 paper, "Mourning and Melancholia", to those who followed his lead: Melanie Klein, John Bowlby, Erich Lindemann, Colin Murray Parkes, Elisabeth Kübler-Ross. The more recent departures from the psychodynamic assumptions into social constructionist thought, beginning with the (1996) publication of *Continuing Bonds*, are also introduced in this chapter. In Chapter 3, the foundations for the approach in the rest of the book are laid. The subject is re-membering (the hyphen is intentional) and the social psychology of memory is examined before an introduction to the work of the anthropologist Barbara Myerhoff. Chapter 3 explores the bridge between Myerhoff's anthropological study and how her work was developed into the narrative practice of re-membering conversations. These first three chapters thus provide a theoretical and historical foundation for the rest of the book.

From here, the book addresses a series of particular issues, often very challenging and painful, to explore how an aesthetic approach crafts a purposeful response. The first of these found in Chapter 4 centers on stories of identity, which is conceived of as a fluid process of becoming, rather than as about fixed categories of who a person is. Chapter 4 also showcases how to craft responses to traumatic deaths, such as suicide, and conversations about troubled relationships, such as those marked by abuse. Chapter 5 highlights the value of Michael White's innovative concept of the "absent but implicit" to constructing and reconstructing meaning in grief, often picking up on the bits of beauty that might be left behind by grief. Chapter 6 turns toward the politics of death and grief. It addresses three main areas: professional power in therapeutic relationships; the power of knowledge control in grief psychology; and the social forces that impact differentially on people as they grieve. Chapter 7 breaks new ground in relation to the conceptualization of time. Drawing from the ancient Stoic distinctions between *chronos* and *aion*, as they are articulated by Gilles Deleuze, the case is made for the value of thinking in terms of *aion* for aesthetic conversations. Chapter 8 shifts focus to counseling conversations with those who are dying and offers an account of the search for the poignancy often born out of the urgency of the situation. Finally, Chapter 9 brings the major themes of the book together and suggests a new construction for doing hope.

Writing a book like this has been a lengthy process with many twists and turns. We owe a debt of gratitude to a number of people. We would like to thank the good people at Routledge, particularly Ms. Anna Moore, who had faith in what we were writing about, and the series editor, Robert Neimeyer, who has encouraged this work in many ways. We are grateful to Waka Matsushita who wrote her personal story for inclusion in Chapter 1 and for the series of people whose personal stories appeared in interviews in each chapter. Some of them are anonymous and some preferred to appear with their real names. For obvious reasons, we shall not spell out here which is which. There have been many who have trusted us with the care of their deceased loved one's stories. We have not taken this trust lightly.

Now the meanings to be made of what we have written lie in the hands of our readers. We wish you well in this journey. Our hope is that the significance of our thoughts will have an impact in people's living, and in conversations with those who are no longer alive, as well as in their practices and not just in their thoughts.

Lorraine Hedtke and John Winslade
Redlands, California, December 2015

Series Editor's Foreword

The dominant narrative of grief in the modern era, drafted by Freud at the height of WWI and elaborated by generations of theorists and popular writers, required mourners to grapple with the harsh reality of loss, confront a series of perturbing emotions, and ultimately withdraw investment from the deceased to "move on" without their loved one. Moreover, the terrain in which this ambivalent mission was to take place was essentially interior, in the heart and mind of the individual survivor. When successful, the bereaved was able to sever his or her "bondage" to the deceased and return to productive functioning, at best compensated by whatever comfort could be found in the private domain of memory. With variations specifying the presumed stages or tasks of such "grief work", often pursued under the watchful eyes of medical authorities, this model continued to hold sway through the end of the last century, and with surprising tenacity, continues into our own.

It is this narrative that Lorraine Hedtke and John Winslade contest and deconstruct in *The Crafting of Grief: Constructing Aesthetic Responses to Loss*. Drawing on anthropological, philosophic, and critical theory, they begin by re-visioning bereavement as a social process in which the "membership" of loved ones in the "club" of our lives is not canceled at the point of their deaths, but is instead conserved, and indeed extended as their stories are circulated through communities for whom their lives continue to matter. The implications of this alternative narrative are far-reaching, as it counterbalances the heavy emphasis on loss and stoic resignation in contemporary grief theory with the prospect of tapping into ongoing resources cultivated in relationship to the deceased and celebrated in the world of the living. Bonds therefore replace bondage, reconstruction replaces relinquishment, and participation in community replaces the privation of merely intrapsychic coping.

For me a distinguishing feature of this text was its consistent tacking between sophisticated theory and straightforward practice. Thus, at the former level, the authors wove together seamlessly Foucault's deconstruction of "regimes of truth" with Myerhoff's formulation of "re-membering" practices, found inspiration in Deleuze's philosophy of identity and White's narrative therapy, and undermined the presumed authority of *chronos*, the irreversible and inexorable march of the clock and calendar, by emphasizing *aion*, the timeless and immeasurable way in which the significance of lives extends backward and forward, linking past, present, and future without division. At the latter level of praxis, the text abounds with compelling case studies that feature the resourcefulness of real people meeting their own deaths with artistry, or accommodating with beauty and appreciation the deaths of others they love. Particularly helpful were the frequent transcriptions of counseling conversations demonstrating the freeing power of the subjunctive voice in conjuring the continued relevance of the deceased to the living, and the subtlety of "double listening" that reveals not only the painful acknowledgment of death, but also the poignant legacy of lives for those that follow. Far from adopting a "Pollyanna" optimism that turns aside from the harsher aspects of the human condition, Hedtke and Winslade unflinchingly reveal the relevance of crafting bereavement even in cases of suicide, homicide, perinatal loss, and troubled relationships. This coverage, relatively ignored in many contemporary treatises on grieving, makes clear that re-membering practices differ fundamentally from mere cognitive reframing.

In sum, *The Crafting of Grief* represents an artful act of resistance against the dominant narrative of grieving, one that opens up space for alternative stories of hope, inspiration, and meaning. At once subtle in its argumentation and simple in its presentation, it positions counselors to promote resourceful conversations with people who stand in the shadow of loss, as they seek beauty and vitality in the lives of others who have enriched their own.

Robert A. Neimeyer, PhD
Series Editor

Other Titles by the Authors

Lorraine Hedtke & Addison Davidove (2013). *My Grandmother is Always with Me: A Remembering Journey* (2nd Edn.). Lulu Press.

Gerald Monk & John Winslade (2013). *When Stories Clash: Addressing Conflict with Narrative Mediation.* Taos Institute.

Lorraine Hedtke (2012). *Breathing Life into the Stories of the Dead: Constructing Bereavement Support Groups.* Taos Institute.

John Winslade & Michael Williams (2012). *Safe and Peaceful Schools: Addressing Conflict and Eliminating Violence.* Corwin Press.

John Winslade & Gerald Monk (2008). *Practicing Narrative Mediation: Loosening the Grip of Conflict.* Jossey-Bass.

Gerald Monk, John Winslade, & Stacey Sinclair (2008). *New Horizons in Multicultural Counseling.* Sage.

John Winslade & Gerald Monk (2007). *Narrative Counseling in Schools: Powerful and Brief* (2nd Edn.). Corwin Press.

Lorraine Hedtke & John Winslade (2004). *Re–membering Lives: Conversations with the Dying and the Bereaved.* Baywood Publications.

John Winslade & Gerald Monk (2000). *Narrative Mediation: A New Approach to Dispute Resolution.* Jossey-Bass.

Gerald Monk, John Winslade, Kathie Crocket, & David Epston (1997). *Narrative Therapy in Practice: The Archaeology of Hope.* Jossey-Bass.

CHAPTER 1

Seeking Beauty in Grief

In 2009, Waka Matsushita[1] and her family were "living happily" in Japan when they were suddenly "thrown into an abyss" when her mother was diagnosed with cancer. Waka tells the story of what followed.

From the outset, the doctors assured us they could remove the renal cancer and that she would be just fine. However, during the initial surgery, the doctor found many cancer tumors and said that he could not continue. Her diagnosis was changed from renal cancer to metastatic cancer of the abdomen, which meant that her cancer had worsened to level four, the worst possible condition. This meant surgery was no longer an option and the doctor recommended chemotherapy.

His next words were crushing. Should the chemotherapy be unsuccessful, he told us, our dear mother would only have two more years to live. Then, he told us not to lose hope, with a hopeless expression on his face.

Worried, yet determined, we looked everywhere for answers and discovered one doctor who had seen great success with the same type of cancer. This doctor was famous in Japan. He had featured on TV as the doctor "with God's hands". We insisted on seeing

1

---

1 Waka Matsushita wrote this story for inclusion in this chapter. It is used with her permission but some others' names have been changed. Waka is a clinical psychologist in Kyoto, Japan, who has worked with many patients and families coping with mental health disorders.

him at whatever cost, and booked his next available appointment after a two-month wait.

During the examination, the doctor showed us diagrams and illustrations that boasted a post-surgery survival rate of five years for fifty percent of his patients. To us, these odds seemed far too low for our dear mother who we hoped would be with us for another forty years. The doctor did his best in an eight-hour operation; however, even the one "with God's hands" could only remove ninety percent of mom's cancer.

After the surgery, placing his hand on mom's swollen belly, he said, "Let's see what chemotherapy can do for the remaining cancer."

We had no idea what that meant. He told us to go to the chemotherapy room and our appointment ended.

Thus far, this story of cancer's intrusion into the life of a person and of a family might be typical of what happens many times over in different contexts. In what follows, however, Waka starts to tell a story of how, slowly and steadily, her mother and then her family began to craft their response to the shadow that death was casting over their lives.

Despite her condition, my mother showed that she did not fear death. On one particular day, a nurse asked me quietly, "Your mom doesn't know anything about her condition, right? Does she even know she has cancer?"

I replied, "Oh no, she knows everything. I mean everything."

"Are you serious?" the nurse replied. "Then, why does she look so calm and happy? Why do I hear laughing when you guys visit her?"

I just smiled and said in my heart, "That's my mom. That's us, my family."

The chemotherapy was tough. She experienced every side effect imaginable. We were at a loss to know how to best care for her, when a private practitioner in our neighborhood, Dr. Mishima, offered to make house calls. He was a kind man we had known since we were children. When mom couldn't eat, he gave her an IV. When she felt pain, he offered her relief. As mom's illness progressed, so did his visits, from once a week to twice and then three times.

Dr. Mishima was never far away. Whenever she suffered, he would rush to her side – often late at night. One night, when mom was in severe pain, we tried everything to help her, until finally, at around six in the morning, we called Dr. Mishima.

He immediately came and said, "Why didn't you call me sooner? I told you to call me any time."

These words filled our hearts with gratitude. He knelt beside her and gently took her hand and whispered, "You did an amazing job. I will take the pain from you now."

In early summer, Dr. Mishima produced a plastic bottle in which he had placed a small twig from a tree. As I looked closer, I could see tiny fireflies resting on the branch. In Japan, we gather by a river to watch the tiny fireflies (called hotaru), to celebrate the beauty of an early summer.

3

Mother could not leave the house to enjoy such pleasures, so Dr. Mishima found a way to bring summer to her. This made her smile and brought tears to our eyes. I felt joy to see my mother's smiling face, as she watched the glow of the tiny fireflies fluttering in rhythm with her own breath.

As winter arrived, Dr. Mishima's visits became more frequent. One day he brought a beautiful Christmas wreath. Mom was always so stylish and loved to decorate her house. She insisted that the wreath be hung in our entrance, so that every visitor could enjoy its beauty.

She discontinued her visits to the other doctor, and requested Dr. Mishima as her official practitioner. As her illness got worse, she did her best to fight back. I watched her suffer every day, but not once did I hear her complain. Never did she speak of self-pity. She would express gratitude for all the goodness in her life and of how blessed she was to be surrounded by caring loved ones.

As I listened to mom's request to change doctors, I realized that mom received hope to live not from the doctor with "God's *hands", but from Dr. Mishima. His daily visits offered much more than medicine – he also brought sincerity, care, and hope.*

It is worth pausing to notice some important aspects of professional practice here that go beyond what can be mapped onto charts and diagrams. Dr. Mishima makes no claim to have "God's hands", but he weaves into his care for Waka's mom and her family simple pieces of personal kindness. He respects the family's wishes, rather than imposing modern scientific knowledge onto them. And he draws from local cultural knowledge resources that help everyone find a moment of beauty through these events – the branch with fireflies above and the cherry blossom below. In these little ways, he invites the family to craft their own responses to the situation they find themselves in.

The Hardest Decisions

As winter drew to an end, Dr. Mishima spoke to us in private. He leaned forward and said quietly, "Do you want to care for her at home?"

It was his way of telling us to prepare; mom's final day was near. We all knew this moment would come but did not want to accept it. Our reply was instant: "We want to be at mom's side when she goes to heaven."

He said, "OK! Let's make it happen together!"

When cherry blossom trees were in full bloom, Dr. Mishima brought mom a beautiful cherry blossom branch. Cherry blossom viewing is a favorite tradition in Japan. Friends and family gather together to celebrate the coming of spring and to express gratitude and appreciation for being Japanese. It's a time to celebrate peace, health, and happiness.

Late April, my cell phone rang. My aunt had come to take care of mom for the day.

"Dr. Mishima said that she has only a week."

I asked my boss for the week off and headed home. For the next week we never left mom's side. My family came from far and

4

wide, and we all slept on the floor next to mom's bed, so that not a second would be wasted.

Mom suffered excruciating pain and violent vomiting, but still she never complained. She was weak, and lacked the physical strength to even turn in bed. There were moments of delusion, and the ability to speak waned. It was obvious that she knew her end was near. Still, she remained fearless.

One day, mom said, "Bring me all the scraps of lace in the house."

We looked at her, wondering why she would need such a thing.

"I want to choose a piece for my funeral. When I'm laid to rest, I want you to place it on my head. Let's have a rehearsal, so that I look beautiful at my own funeral."

Our mom had always wanted to be fashionable. We brought all the lace we could find, and in turn placed each piece upon her head. Looking in a mirror, she chose the piece she liked and proceeded to give precise instruction on how it should be placed. We even had a rehearsal, which made us all, including mom, burst into uncontrollable laughter.

5

Mother then asked if we'd prepared our mourning dresses for her funeral. She instructed us to get ready. In fact, I hadn't prepared my dress, because, deep inside, I felt that such preparation meant accepting that my mother would die. But, despite my hopes and prayers, it was time to accept the unacceptable. I found a dress on the internet and ordered it right away. When it arrived, I put it on and went to show my mom.

"How do I look?" I twirled for my mom in my new mourning dress, just like I would when going on an outing or a date.

Mom smiled.

My aunt, watching from the other room, became cross and gestured for me to stop.

My mom said, "I love that! It's a great choice. I'm relieved that you are good to go now. Have it ready on hand along with your accessories, so that you can go to the funeral at any time."

A few days later, watching the wedding of Prince William and Kate Middleton on TV, mom said, "Oh no! She stole my lace? I need it!"

Maybe she was a little delirious, or maybe she was joking. Either way, we just laughed and laughed. Mom was laughing too.

I said, "Mom, promise me you will stay by me, even after you are gone."

"Yes. Yes. I will always be with you. Don't worry. I will be always floating right above you." Then we laughed, imagining how funny it would be to see mom floating.

One day, mom spoke to each of us. "I've been really happy; I've had such a great life. Please forgive me for going to a better place first."

Then she took my brother, my sister, and me, in turn, by the hand, and gave us each a personal message of encouragement and blessing for our own lives.

After a short pause, mom cried out to dad who was being cared for in another setting, "Papa, I'm sorry for passing away before you. I always loved you so much and will love you forever."

We all burst into tears. Mom then closed her eyes and went to sleep. We did not know when, or if, she would wake again.

Many hours later, she awoke. She stared at us dazedly, opened her eyes wide, and said, "What! Am I still alive? Do I have to go through that all over again? I have already said everything I wanted to say."

After a second of silence, we all burst out laughing. Her calm attitude toward death saved us from falling apart.

One day before she passed, my sister and I told mom that we were going to see dad at his hospital. She was always pleased when we told her this and in the past, hurried us away. But on this day, she asked us not to go. She said, "I'm sorry. I don't want you to go – please forgive me – just this once – I want you to stay with me."

On May 2nd, at 6:00 am, my family and I, accompanied by close friends and our pastor, gathered around mom's bedside. We sang her favorite hymns and fought back tears. Her eyes were closed as she lay there hushed, barely breathing. Hugging one another and sobbing, we watched her chest moving up and down with each gasping breath.

At exactly 6:30 am, mom opened her eyes for the last time. Her eyes darted around the room in search of my brother, sister, and me. With her gaze fixed on her three children, a single tear trickled down her face. She didn't say a word, but, in that one instant, I felt a lifetime of love. Then she closed her eyes, and went to heaven.

At her funeral, we put the lace on her head just as she had wanted. She looked so restful and beautiful. I could imagine her saying to me, "Good job. Thank you . . . and wasn't the rehearsal hilarious?"

There are elements of Waka's story that many families will recognize. But there are also elements that are quite unique. These moments are not only sad and exceptionally hard, but are moments filled with love, strength, and even humor. They are the glimpses of what is unique to Waka's family and to those who are helping them. These are the moments when Waka's family crafts their responses to death. These are the moments when the presence of death in their lives requires that they put their own stamp on the event. Crafting these responses requires having an aesthetic sense of what is apt, and even beautiful, rather than just adherence to the right or the normal path.

There are also key moments, when Waka and her mother take up agency. They happen in the choice of the doctor who best suits the journey. They happen in the rehearsal for the funeral. They are there in the relational exchanges that are special to just this family. They pervade the moments of laughter, as well as the tears. They happen in the sorting of pieces of lace and through the link to a contemporary event, like the British royal wedding. We see them, too, in the physician's honoring of cultural traditions, like the bringing of cherry blossoms or the branch with the fireflies on it. They permeate the messages Waka's mom left as little legacies for each of her children.

The whole family, it seems, was left with a sense that they had done this well. It was painful and sad, but they had crafted a pathway that helped them through. Focusing on an aesthetic sense of death allows Waka's mom to play a significant role in this event, even though many who are dying are often left out of such conversations. Waka's mom had invited them to be with her in her dying, but she had also helped shape how they would live on with her memory, how the vibrancy of life would not be defeated by death, and how grief might be lived in consciousness of this sense of life. The moments of laughter were still powerful. The sense of family connection and relationship was still strong. The reality of death was not treated as more powerful than laughter, memory, cultural resonance, and personal relationship. Is this realistic? Perhaps not. But perhaps using creativity to craft a way through difficult events is more important than realism. It helps people fashion moments of beauty in among the pain. That is what this book will explore.

Focus of This Book

How might we respond to the presence of death in our own lives and in the lives of others? That is the focus of this book. Responding to this question includes, but is not restricted to, what is usually referred to as grieving. It also includes a focus on the experience of individuals and their loved ones who are approaching imminent death. We are most interested in how to work therapeutically with people in the circumstances of life that Waka and her family were encountering. We will explore how to create conversations that use the sweet moments, as well as the tough moments, to foster agency in the face of the unthinkable.

The concept of working therapeutically, however, should not be restricted to those who claim to be doing therapy. We use the term in a broader sense to refer to the kinds of conversation that people might experience as helpful, comforting, encouraging, and invigorating, whether they are holding such conversations with therapists, nurses, doctors, social workers, family members, or trusted friends.

To be therapeutic, an activity should help people make sense out of situations, overcome problems or difficulties, and find a pathway forward in life. It may involve the cure of what the ancient Greeks called "diseases of the soul". It may help a person find the wherewithal to put one foot in front of the other and carry on living through a challenging situation. It may help identify places of comfort that sustain a person through the less comfortable and more challenging moments that accompany death when it visits.

Not everything that may be called therapeutic fits within the boundaries of what is usually called therapy. For instance, going for a walk, listening to music, or looking at some cherry blossom may each be therapeutic but are not, in themselves, therapy. In the same way, we do not restrict helpful conversation with a person who is grieving to the formal therapy hour. Sometimes it may just be one question from a visitor that soothes, or opens up a new pathway for living. Many people can give comfort or help a grieving person to "know how to go on" (Wittgenstein, 1953, p. 151) in conversations of various kinds. Our interest is in the working assumptions that might govern such a helpful conversation or in the range of topics that might achieve this purpose. We shall refer in subsequent chapters to examples drawn from some counseling contexts, as well as from other kinds of conversations, but in no way do we intend to restrict the relevance of these ideas to formal counseling.

This book is driven by the idea that people can be invited into an active response to the challenges that death brings, much as Waka and her family sought to do. To be active in response means to be an agent in the construction of one's own life. Our assumption is that taking up such an active position in response to a significant life challenge is therapeutic in the sense mentioned above. It differs from having a feeling that one is being tossed about by the storms of fate or by what Shakespeare called "the slings and arrows of outrageous fortune" (*Hamlet*, III, I, 59).

And yet this feeling of being at the mercy of fate is common when we are grieving. We are cast, sometimes suddenly, into the middle of something that is bigger than us. Often we feel unprepared for it and our sense of knowing how to manage our lives is torn apart, particularly when the person who has died is, like Waka's mother, someone close. For this reason, we are interested in what inspires a sense of being able to respond as an agent. In its etymological roots, agency is connected to the ability to take action, but it can suggest also an entry point into meanings that can sustain grace in action through hard times. We are, therefore, concerned with the principles that might inform the taking of such action.

9

A Critical Edge

This book also has a critical edge. It is not so much that we want to criticize other approaches to grief counseling that many may have found helpful. When people are distraught, there are many practices in grief counseling that have offered comfort. We are concerned, however, about some professional prescriptions that could distance agency for the dying and the bereaved. These ideas can perhaps inadvertently make matters worse. Our aim is to distinguish a new way of walking alongside those who are dying and grieving that privileges their experiences and their knowledges.

This book also seeks to be critical in another way. It draws from a critical perspective on the taken-for-granted truths of psychology in general. In particular, we are influenced by the Foucauldian tradition of responding to, and in many instances challenging, the dominant discourses from our wider cultural world that have become incorporated into grief psychology. Such discourses often go unnoticed, unless they are deconstructed and their work as "regimes of truth" (Foucault, 1980, p. 131) made visible. By preference, we shall treat such perspectives as narratives that have become well known because they have cultural currency, rather than because they have immutable truth claims on the basis of their scientific strength.

The critical perspective we are speaking from is, therefore, based in the ideas that have emerged from social constructionist (Gergen, 1994; 2009a; 2009b; Burr, 2003) and poststructuralist (Foucault, 1980; 2000; Deleuze, 1990; 1994; Derrida, 1976) thinking. These movements of thought inform a fresh take on many of the conventional assumptions of the social sciences. They have been less extensively applied to forms of social practice, and even less to grief psychology, but where they have been, they have yielded extraordinary promise for producing helpful practices. We engage with them because they offer fresh ways to speak with people about many topics, including the experience of death and grief. Some of this potential has been borne out in the explicit application of these ideas in narrative practice. Hence, we have drawn extensively from the work on narrative therapy of Michael White and David Epston (1990; White, 2007), among others.

Grief as Natural

One specific place where we are critical is the apparent assumption in much grief psychology that grieving should be treated as a natural process and that, over time, it will follow a natural course toward some kind of healing. This assumption seems to have grown out of a medical model that treats grief like an illness with a point of onset, a middle course, and an endpoint of recovery. The goal of treatment should, therefore, be to help people return to a normal state of equilibrium or homeostasis, as might be expected after a viral infection. Perhaps this emphasis is not surprising, given that many of the most influential writers about grief have been medical doctors.

While death itself is, of course, part of the natural condition of human life, the manner in which we meet our own or a loved one's death is not necessarily natural at all, nor can it be squeezed into a one-size-fits-all response. It is shaped by all manner of cultural forces or discourses (Valentine, 2006; Walter, 1999). Waka's family experienced many things that were special to their family, their social context, and their cultural traditions. If we do not notice these moments, we potentially overlook resources out of which people can craft personal and intimate responses to death.

How we, and our loved ones, die is influenced by things like diet, economic systems, war, the quality of available healthcare, and the social and psychological events that affect the will to live. All of these forces also influence the experience of the bereaved. And yet, without sufficient consideration of the social process of the construction of experience, theories of grieving have fallen too easily into a naturalistic account. It is assumed that we can extract the elements of human nature from cultural forces and keep them separate in the cause of science.   11

Without critical thought, it is hard not to assume that what exists must be what is natural and that elements of human nature can be easily extracted from cultural forces by scientific inquiry. As a result, many discourses that dominate the cultural world in which a given theory is developed become naturalized into the account of death and grieving that masquerades as a force of nature. What is needed is an approach to science that equips us to make sense of social and cultural experience, not just to control for it and leave human nature exposed to view. In other words, we want to see a science of death and grief that takes more account of the effects of cultural discourses or the meanings that people make of their experiences of death in life. Such an account exists in a number of places but it has not been extrapolated into the design of therapeutic conversation as much as we would wish. We wish to fill this gap.

Our critical focus extends to approaches to death and grief that describe the stages of dying or the tasks of grieving as a sequence of natural moments of suffering. It is not so much that we find these stages always irrelevant and inaccurate. For many, they describe experience with a large degree of resonance and are found reassuring and helpful. The problem lies in the assumption of their universal applicability that removes context and requires compliance. We have been uneasy with the way they have been torn from the circumstances of their production and treated as discrete essences of truth. In the process, they have become more than descriptions as they have taken on the aura of prescription.

The idea of grief as a natural process leads to the notion that one needs to allow it to run its course, like a case of the flu. The best we can do is to resign ourselves to the suffering and accept it, so as not to make matters worse. After all, getting mad at the flu does not alter the course of a virus infection. Emotional responses do not worsen or ameliorate the effects of the illness. Treating grief in the same vein removes people's ability to act on their own behalf and assigns them to a path of passive suffering.

But grief is not like a virus. The course of suffering it brings does not produce antibodies in our immune system that lead to the eventual defeat of the microbial armies of grief in the bloodstream. We do not require a blood test to determine what kind of grief we are suffering from. Nor do we recover from grief in any natural way. Nor do we retain any grief antibodies in a way that guards against the next viral outbreak of grief. There is no vaccine to inoculate against grief's presence in our lives. Sometimes we never get over the death of a loved one. We imagine that such an assumption would sound disrespectful to Waka and her family and devalue the significance of her mother in their lives.

If the natural account of grieving were assumed, it would be understandably futile to stay in a place of denial, because natural processes ignore our refusal to acknowledge them. What is, therefore, encouraged in conventional trajectories of grief psychology, it seems, is often the acceptance of suffering as necessary and inevitable. The bereaved are rendered almost helpless in the face of grief, much as if it were equivalent to an earthquake or a hurricane that wreaks uncontrollable havoc and we are left devastated and without any answer to it.

We do not pretend that people who are grieving do not suffer. We do question, however, whether it is necessary for therapeutic practice to acquiesce in the face of such suffering and focus people on how to feel the emotions of loss and dwell on them. Often, in the name of therapy, people are encouraged to intensify feelings of loss and sadness in the belief that intensification of emotion will accelerate the course of grieving. For example, we recently heard of a grief counseling center in Southern California that requires clients to recount the story of a person's death as a requisite component to receiving services. The assumption is that intensification of emotion, most often sadness, will lead to its release and hence its dissipation. While helping people lessen painful feelings may be a worthy goal, it may not best be pursued by intensifying feelings of loss. The focus on feeling one's feelings more fully has sometimes seemed to be the object of what grief counseling has emphasized. This logic is too reliant on the naturalistic version of grieving.

A Cultural Perspective

Another problem with the idea of grief as a natural process is that it has directed the psychology of grieving to concentrate on the individual body as the site of grief – both for the bereaved and for the dying person. The impression that can be taken from much work in this field is that individuals grieve on their own or that grieving happens only inside the skin of a person.

While being thrown into grieving can often seem like an "act of God", our responses to this situation are never free from very human cultural influences. A natural emphasis obscures this cultural element. Grieving is not just a medical phenomenon. Neither are the medical processes that surround death free from social and cultural influences. They both have a large social component.

That human beings are social creatures is often overlooked. We interact with the world outside our skin. We are in constant conversation with others – actual conversations in which we participate and virtual conversations that we play out in our heads. We create rituals to mark our experience with social meanings and grieving is certainly a case in point. These rituals are born of thousands of conversations and social interactions, in only a small portion of which each individual has partaken. For example, there are ways in which Waka's story is particularly Japanese, for example in the appreciation of fireflies and cherry blossoms.

In the end, we do not grieve on our own (Valentine, 2006), nor do we make meaning about death in isolation. We do so in communities and in relationships with others. We are influenced by long-standing traditions of religious thought and grieving practices. And yet there are few models in the psychological literature of relational or community processes of grieving. Most of the process models that are well known focus on what happens inside the individual. A full understanding of the experience of grieving requires a greater focus on the cultural forces at work in the production of grief and not such narrow restriction to an individual perspective. Focusing on a relational connection might lead to more deliberate inquiry into what took place in the

13

conversations between Waka and her mother over funeral "rehearsals", rather than a narrow focus on the meaning of the rehearsals for the bereaved individual.

The inclusion of more cultural perspectives makes the field more complicated, because we have to deal with diverse cultural differences. A universal emphasis on the "natural" human experience of grieving is tidy and easily grasped. Being tidy is not good enough, however, if it is often not applicable. The natural account starts to break down in the face of the multiple cultural influences that give shape to individual experience. In other words, cultural diversity of all kinds contributes as much to personal experience of grief as does universal human nature. Grief, therefore, needs to be considered in terms of the cultural forces that give shape to human experience much more than has been acknowledged and valued in the past.

Furthermore, pieces of psychological knowledge are themselves products of culture. Michel Foucault (1980) demonstrated clearly that knowledges are products of discourse or "regimes of truth" (p. 131). Not only do they emerge out of the cultural conditions of a particular context, but they also start to shape and affect that context in subtle, and sometimes not so subtle, ways. Knowledge about death and grief is no exception.

In grief psychology, for example, the perspectives and worldviews of Elisabeth Kübler-Ross's cancer patients in a Genevan cancer ward have had an extraordinary influence on people's experiences of dying and of grieving in many quite different contexts. Kübler-Ross's (1969) stages of dying are so well known that it is not uncommon for people to calibrate their experience against expectations drawn from Kübler-Ross's work. While she did not write specifically about grief in her earlier research, her model has been extrapolated to include grief and loss of all kinds for professionals and lay people. Professionals routinely speak about "patients" as "being in denial". Lay people approach counselors with concerns that they cannot escape the "anger" stage, or have not experienced enough sadness yet, or, after ten years, cannot understand why they have not reached "acceptance".

Kübler-Ross's original descriptive studies are thus often treated as norms against which to measure emotional progress. As a result, they now produce effects in people's lives, as if they were a set of ethical instructions on how to grieve correctly, rather than simply describing a "natural" course of events.

The challenge then is to articulate an approach to death and grief that does not fall back on a naturalistic account of the process of suffering and recovery. We want to avoid offering yet another model that could be taken up as a rigid prescription. How, therefore, might we speak about the experience of grieving without universalizing it and keep in mind the different cultural forces that make us human? Beyond that, how might we respond to the grieving of others in ways that respect their cultural preferences and their desire to have agency in their own lives? Even better, how might we respond to death and grief in our own and others' lives in a way that is comforting, invigorating, sustaining, and (dare we say it) even at times beautiful, rather than focused on merely surviving suffering? These are the questions this book will endeavor to address.

A number of ventures into this territory have been made in recent decades. We shall document these and acknowledge their contributions. Let us endeavor to lay out some principles that we want to assert and promote. Perhaps the example above of Dr. Mishima might give us some guidance.

A Narrative Perspective

We propose an approach to the experience of death that is less about following a universal pattern or performing a set of prescribed tasks and more about an artistic exercise of designing our own experience like a work of art. The concept of a narrative (Nelson, 2001) is useful to describe the movement through the time of dying and grieving. A narrative can be thought of as a story that is organized into a plot according to a theme. When death enters our lives, we are inevitably charged with crafting a story in a particular period of time into a narrative of response.

We do this in several senses. In the first sense, the story to be crafted is one that we are performing. We take actions, make decisions, respond to others' actions and move forward along life trajectories as we do so. We live out a plot of events, organized according to themes, and cast ourselves and others as characters in this plot. Grieving is a story that evolves through internal emotional responses, but also through participation in cultural rituals, through the sorting of legal affairs, through relational exchanges, through private moments in which we continue to invoke the presence or voice of the dead person. In the course of their grieving, bereaved persons do not only visit gravesites and have peak experiences of emotion. They also carry a sense of their changed relationship with the dead person through many ordinary moments of life – buying groceries, visiting the bank, paying bills, continuing to work, minding children or grandchildren,

15

and so on. Any or each of these activities have the potential to be woven into the plot of a grief narrative, depending on what is privileged by the thematic motif.

Similarly, dying often evolves as a particular story that traces different contours of the landscape for each individual. It may involve the daily routines of a lengthy illness, the high drama of diagnosis, the disruption of medical tests and interventions, legal and financial plot complications, the experience of emotional uncertainty, and decisions that lead to different denouements with regard to hospice and end-of-life care. Or it may arrive unannounced as a sudden, tragic event that disrupts other activities of life. The thematic elements that give shape to a narrative are themselves given cultural force by legal, medical, and religious discourses that influence the actions and rituals of individuals who are dying and of those around them.

In a second sense, the experience of death or bereavement can be thought of in narrative terms, because we make meaning of it by telling the story of our experience to others. We render experience meaningful by representing it in narrative form. Aristotle termed the raw elements of story as the *fabula*. The task of constructing a narrative, in Aristotle's terms, means taking the *fabula* of a death or grief experience and developing an organized account of it. It is turned thus into a well-formed narrative. Much of the richness of human experience derives from the layering of raw experience with meaning through representation. Our cultural worlds provide us with ready-made representational frameworks (including models of grief stages) into which it is easy to enter plot elements and thus live out thematic influences, which were already implicit within the concepts we were scarcely aware of deciding to adopt. Our desire in this book is to engender conversations that thread the raw elements into a larger agentic theme.

How do we perform this task of constructing a narrative out of experience? The philosopher Gilles Deleuze (1993) offers one answer in his book, *The Fold*. He talks about incorporating plot events of life into subjective experience by making a series of folds. Deleuze describes it as like sewing a hem: folding, twisting, and pinning along a line. The line is the narrative plot. We fold experience back on itself and, each time we do so, add a layer of depth to it by retelling it, in addition to performing it in action. The practice of counseling is one cultural context where such telling and retelling, or folding and refolding, might transpire.

In the process of "telling a story", we also encounter the social world in which we must anticipate and deal with the responses of others (as Bakhtin, 1986, teaches us). We do not only live the plots of our narratives; we also tell the story to others. Telling a story actually requires someone to tell it to, even when we are only "telling" the story to an imagined evaluative audience in our thoughts. This audience includes the deceased too. The experience of grieving or dying is thus entered into the narratives that others are forming about how we are doing. We are positioned (Davies & Harré, 1990) in their narratives by their responses and must either accept such positioning, refuse it, or modify it. In this sense, we never grieve alone but in the company of the deceased and of a community of people who shape our experiences.

In a final sense, the experience of death or bereavement can be thought of in narrative terms, because we do not form stories about our dying or our grieving or live them out in any totally original way. We borrow from existing narratives along the way. If new to death and grief, we have at least observed others and learned how to tread the path. If we have any uncertainty, we are surrounded by texts that guide us: scriptures, self-help books, movies, academic psychological knowledge, hospital pamphlets, sympathy cards, newspaper obituaries, funeral rituals, or the formulas repeated in memorial services.

17

These are the cultural repositories out of which we draw to form our own lived stories. There are distinct patterns to what is regarded as the customary range within which the performance of our personal stories makes sense in our communities. We must craft our own personal stories, but we do so in response to relational influences and in forms governed by cultural notions of genre, discourse, and meaning, which can easily be mistaken for universal aspects of human nature.

Crafting the Experience of Grief

The task of crafting stories of death and grief involves designing pathways through a maze. We make choices about how to respond, about the weight accorded to responses of others, and about which cultural forces to embrace and which to let slide. This selection is precisely what can be crafted in therapeutic conversations. There are always multiple paths from among which to choose. Therefore, to theorize the experience of grief, it is important to develop a flexible enough account to accommodate multiplicity without reducing the story to one true version.

We have chosen the concept of "crafting" intentionally. It signifies something less grand than scientific modeling. It is more ordinary than some artistic endeavors for which one has to go through extensive training before one is allowed to participate. Crafts are accessible to everyone. It involves deliberate action, rather than passive acceptance of suffering. It has an aesthetic quality too, living halfway between an art and a science. The term "crafting" has been used before. Judith Butler uses it in conversation with Athena Athanasiou (Butler & Athanasiou, 2013) and references Foucault's work on the governing of a self, always in the face of social norms, against which it is necessary to struggle. Judith Butler refers to such crafting as a "mode of poiesis" (p. 69) in which a person works simultaneously on the body and on disciplinary norms to create something in relation to others in what Athena Athanasiou refers to as the "interval" (p. 71) between what is crafted onto us and our own efforts to craft our own project.

If this makes crafting sound a little elusive, then that is the intention. In an important sense, it is in an aesthetic project that we are engaged, crafting a work of art that we hope we, and others, will find satisfying. It is a creative process that is shaped by stories, meanings, actions, and rituals. Our choices are governed by a sense, however shaky this sense may be, of what we deem apt. We construct our own narratives out of a knowledge base and comforting sensibility that is almost intuitive, telling us what will fit within the lives we lead as we craft something both very ordinary and simultaneously exalted.

This intuitive sensibility is not just unique to an individual, however. It is informed by the discourses and cultural practices to which we have been exposed. We are like artists adding brushstrokes to a picture we are painting, but we are provided by our cultural world with the canvas, the fine and thick brushes, and sometimes the colors we can apply, not to mention the artistic conventions we are expected to follow. As we apply paint, we shape the finer details, mix different hues, and place them on the canvas in line with our particular preferences of expression.

As with any self-portrait, we are both subject and object. Our project is reflexive, because we are always witnesses to our own process of becoming. We present ourselves simultaneously to ourselves and to others, while we are creating our presentations. Such reflexivity is uniquely human and requires our understandings of grief psychology to include a focus on the role played by our reflexive intelligence, embodied principally in our use of language and, therefore, of discourse. Theoretical accounts that simplify experience to uniform natural sequences will always remain inadequate.

An Ethical Task

The task of designing a pathway through experience is also an ethical one. Our narratives are governed by what we value, hold dear, stand for, and might even on occasion be prepared to die for. If value systems are thus pertinent to our experience of grieving, then we must implicitly be engaged in a process of evaluating how we are doing. William Labov (1997) makes this point about narrative. He argues that any narrative contains within it an evaluative point. Consider, for example, the value of laughter in Waka's family story. It both constructs a response to death and informs them about what they prefer to highlight in their telling of the events.

We thus develop preferences for ways of dying or grieving that are more or less dignified, more or less authentic, more or less respectful of the dead, more or less comforting, more or less socially responsible, more or less functional, or more or less compatible with modern life. Our lived story of grief is thus a story of moral or ethical principle, as well as of aesthetically pleasing form.

All of the above also pertains to the art of conducting helpful conversations with people who are dying or grieving. A good conversation, in the therapy room or in the bedroom of those dying or elsewhere, can help to highlight these value preferences and create an opportunity to live closer to what we cherish, or further from what we abhor. Here, too, we are threading our way through a maze to fold in what gives meaning. We are engaged in the construction of a narrative, this time principally involving the lived experience of another person. Counseling is an art form as much as a science. It is also an ethical project governed by an aesthetic sensibility, as well as by ethical values.

We would propose that avoidance of the imposition of an expert knowledge about how a person *should* conduct their life is an important ethic that should govern this process. We would favor a process governed by a spirit of inquiry, rather than certainty (Anderson, 1997). Curiosity about what is useful in a particular circumstance might be more useful than evidence-based certainty. It is more important to inquire into a person's sensibilities and preferred stories of self and community as they face difficult circumstances than to work for the aesthetic and ethical values sanctioned by research evidence.

For these reasons, we would eschew the imposition of any universal meaning of grief, any idea of compulsory stages of grieving or dying person must traverse, or any requirement to perform necessary tasks to grieve well (Hedtke & Winslade, 2004). We would reject the idea that one must accept one particular reality of death – either one's own death or that of a loved one – to correctly comply with a norm.

On the other hand, we would emphasize practices of grief counseling that are respectful of the relationships between the deceased and the bereaved, that enable bereaved persons to exercise agentic choices in their own lives, and that make sense within the local world of folk knowledge (Bruner, 1990; White, 2001) to which ordinary people have access, rather than requiring them to submit to expert psychological or medical knowledges.

In Bruner's (1990) terms, folk psychology refers to a set of normative descriptions about how "human beings tick" and is a "system by which people organize their experience in, knowledge about, and transactions with the social world" (p. 35). It is the ordinary, everyday knowledge people act upon when they decide what other people are like, how they should act, how their actions and ideas might be interpreted, what possibilities exist for ways of being in the world, and how they can commit to those ways of being.

Concern for the Self

The philosophical foundations for the approach we are outlining lie in the later work of Michel Foucault (1986), in which he advocated the project of "concern for the self". He also spoke of this project as the "care of the self". The care of the self that Foucault was referring to has nothing to do with what is often described in humanistic psychology as "self-care". It is not about pampering oneself or being kind to oneself or individual "empowerment". It is more like intentionally producing one's life as a project or series of projects. For Foucault, this is less a task of realizing or actualizing one's true self than it is about always becoming anew, or a different person than one has been. It is a project of training oneself, as practiced by the ancient Stoics (Hadot, 1995), through immersing oneself in valuable thoughts, reflecting and meditating actively on experience, and deliberately choosing a pathway forward in life.

In the modern world, what the ancients carried out by way of meditative exercises is often embodied in therapeutic conversation. We go to a counselor to engage in reflection on experience and to make sense of it. Good counseling offers us the chance to pause in the flow of activity of life and affords us the space to reflect, to make meaning, and to fold these meanings and reflections into our living with a renewed vigor. We encapsulate private experience (the lived experiences of life) in a relationship (counseling conversations among them) and, therefore, in discourse (the cultural backdrop against which these occur). What discourses the counselor will be informed by matters greatly to the process we are engaged in as they talk to us. If we are not careful, we can unwittingly fold into our meaning-making discursive influences that do not fit into our world or that contrast sharply with the painting we are producing of our lives.

Becoming

What kind of process is it, then, if it is not just a natural process? One answer is that it is a process of *becoming*. Death might be thought of as a project of becoming, and in grief we are making an adjustment to the relational context of our becoming. In the story above, Waka and her family are involved in several different lines of becoming: becoming a patient; becoming a family; becoming Japanese; becoming resilient; and so on.

The concept of becoming has received attention from a number of different writers about human subjectivity. We shall pay particular attention to the "poststructuralist" work of Michel Foucault, Gilles Deleuze, and Jacques Derrida in this regard. Foucault argues that the most important task a person faces in life is that of becoming somebody. This does not mean, for him, becoming what is already imprinted in our DNA, lodged in our personality structure, or pre-existing in our psyche. It is not a project of actualizing a "true" self that is already there (as has often been the focus of humanistic psychology). Nor is it a developmental stage that becomes an achieved goal. It is more like becoming what we have never before been. Living is an ongoing process of becoming, rather than of simple unfolding. Becoming then has no endpoint, but rather is a direction we are always evolving toward.

Deleuze (1994) elaborates further. For him, becoming is about progressive differentiation, of becoming different, of becoming other than who we have been. Becoming implies both being and doing, or existence and action. If we apply this to the concept of grieving, then we can be said to become, in at least a small way, a different person as we grieve. We are affected by the event of the death that has happened in the relationship with a loved one and we are never the same again. This certainly is true for people who find death staring them in the face. How often do we hear from the person who has cancer that the diagnosis, while tragic and horrible, also opened them to life?

Nor need the process of becoming end when someone dies. As someone is dying, they are paradoxically engaging with a new challenge of living; that is, of becoming. After death, the dead are often given new "voices" that continue to inform the life of the living. In this sense, they are still in the process of becoming, even after they die.

What, then, is crucial in therapeutic conversation is a focus on what kind of person our clients are becoming. They are invited by the event of death to remake themselves, to become other than who they were. At least some part of them has been constructed in relationship with the person who is now dying or deceased. This way of being must now change as a result of the change in circumstances that death introduces. The relationship with the deceased is also in a process of becoming and it too starts to become something different when one party to it dies. The line of becoming does not cease with death – for the living or for the dead.

In conventional approaches to grief, the emphasis has often been placed on saying goodbye to the deceased, letting go of the relationship, and sloughing off a sense of oneself in which this person is implicated. It is often assumed that death ends a relationship, both the physical and emotional. The implication has been that the grieving person should return to a state of individual wholeness, akin to how they were before the relationship with the deceased person began. The bereaved are often discouraged from thinking or talking about the dead and encouraged to efficiently "move on" as an indicator of good mental health.

It is our contention that the assumptions behind this approach will not do. It is not respectful enough toward those who have died. It excises them from those they love and diminishes the ways in which their voice and influence might continue. It also rests too much on the assumptions of individualism, even of the so-called "rugged individualism" of the "self-made man", so beloved in neoliberal forms of capitalism, that have been incorporated uncritically into many psychological practices. Letting go of a relationship requires a wrenching effort that people often feel to be painful. When we act as if this is the correct way to grieve, the bereaved are urged to return, as soon as possible, to an individual status and renounce any sense of being defined by the relationship with the deceased. They are forced back into a place of lonely responsibility solely for themselves. We believe there is a better way.

This individualistic assumption is often called realistic and is a common benchmark used to evaluate how well a person is doing.

22

If they are accepting the death of their loved one, they are doing well, but if not, they may be said to be "in denial". Letting go and saying goodbye is, however, only one of many possible ways of becoming. It is our belief that there are other, more attractive pathways of becoming. Narrative grief counseling has been exploring these alternative pathways for some time and we shall explain some of the creative efforts that people have used to become other than who they were, but without forcing themselves back into lonely individualism, with a diminished sense of relationship to others. We would include here the possibility of ongoing relationship with the deceased (if that is desired) as a source of strength and as an affirmation of love.

Agency

To articulate a path of becoming, a person has to maintain, or craft, a sense of agency. They need a say in how the story is told. Think of Waka's mother wanting to have a say in her own medical care and her funeral. To chide her for not doing death according to a preconceived formula would take away her, and her family's, agency to create what was, for them, beautiful and meaningful. There are different ways of conceptualizing agency available in the psychological and philosophical literature. It is, therefore, necessary to outline the approach to agency that will animate this book.

23

For a start, we do not think of agency as an inherent aspect of human nature, available as an automatic starting point for the actualization of a self (the humanistic assumption). In the sense we are using the term, individuals are not born with agency. It is a more refined concept than that.

From a poststructuralist perspective, agency is formed in relations of power, in response to what we are required to become by the forces around us. When we simply go along with these forces in a compliant way, we do not take up a position of agency. We can be said to be constituted, or determined, by the line of force of a power relation. When we refuse a position offered to us in a power relation, or seek to modify it, or attempt to negotiate with it, or to "evade its traps" (Foucault, 2000, p. 162), then we step into a sense of agency. We can see this clearly with Waka's mother, when she continues to be "calm and happy" while knowing she has cancer. She is defining what matters to her, her response to cancer, in a way that fits with her preferred way of living. This is an expression of agency.

Power Relations

Michel Foucault (1982) defined power as "actions upon the actions of others" (p. 220). Power relations then are the sites in which human beings struggle to influence each other, either wittingly or not. We are sometimes acutely aware of these influencing forces when we are engaged in argument with another. At other times, however, we are so familiar with a pattern of forces that governs our responses that we take it for granted that this is how things are. We would only become aware of such circumstances as power relations if we decided to reject the taken-for-granted assumptions and do something different, for example facing death with laughter. Breaking the rules teaches us quickly how power works.

In the modern world, however, power is not always based on the application or threat of physical force. Foucault shows how modernity has developed much more sophisticated methods of producing responses to life situations inside our heads and requiring us to monitor ourselves to fit within defined social norms. The governing of people's lives has thus become much more a process of producing in members of a society the mentality that is established as normal. Foucault (2010) called this the process of governmentality.

So what might we think of as the power relations in which the experience of death and grieving might be cast? How are personal experiences of death and grief governed? An obvious direction to look is toward the medical discourse that governs treatment procedures, assigns the identity of patient, individualizes suffering, designates (in the *Diagnostic and Statistical Manual of Mental Disorders, Fifth Edition*, 2012) grief as a pathology, dispenses medication, and legally pronounces the moment of death. There are also economic discourses that specify how long a bereaved person might be permitted to withdraw from performing their duty as a participant in the world of work, with very specific universalized hierarchies (little time off is afforded when a favored aunt dies, for example). There are legal discourses that govern who can decide about the dispersal of the property of those who have died. This discourse also establishes a hierarchy of power (for example, a new spouse carries more authority than do the adult children of a dying person). And there are religious guidelines that determine rituals and practices for the handling of a body and govern the performance of memorialization after death.

Through all these discourses, responses are patterned, or striated (as Deleuze, 1994, argues). There are also then the "smooth spaces" (Deleuze's term for the opposite of striated spaces) of social exchange, for example within families, where differences of opinion are worked out about who will speak at a funeral, how the smaller personal possessions of the deceased will be reassigned, what will become the acceptable ways to speak of a particular deceased person, and what should never be mentioned. These decisions are also governed by power relations, but they often emerge from more local and immediate concerns. They may be striated by, say, gender politics or religious discourse, but may also be more loosely governed and open to greater free play of influence and interpretation.

Asking Questions

As this book progresses, we shall outline a series of lines of inquiry that we find helpful to assist people to map out their path through these territories – both the smooth and the striated ones. We shall resist the temptation to articulate a model of grieving codified by a set of propositions. Instead, we seek to articulate a model of inquiry that makes room for a range of possible models of response that people might embrace in accord with their cultural preferences.

It is not by chance that we shall feature a range of questions many people have found helpful, rather than propositions about what people are going through. The approach to what might be therapeutic or helpful we are advocating here is governed more by the kind of performative knowledge that Gilbert Ryle (1949) described as "knowing how" than it is by the more usual social science approach of producing knowledge governed by "knowing that".

Questions are linguistic or discursive tools that allow us to interrogate the narratives by which people live, in the search for which narratives might be the most invigorating and sustaining. Such questions may be considered deconstructive in the sense that they pry loose the unquestioned authority of dominant assumptions just enough to allow new and sometimes beautiful possibilities to emerge. This approach affords the greatest opportunity for inviting bereaved persons to take up a position of agency in relation to the design of their own grief, to continue becoming. This is the place from which to explore the aesthetics of grief, to treat it as a project one might enter into, rather than an inevitable process of suffering one must endure.

We shall say more as the book progresses about the kind of questions we suggest as most useful, but for now let us think back to Waka's story of her mother's death. Imagine meeting with her or other family members some months after the death. A useful therapeutic conversation would endeavor to pick up on lines of becoming that were mentioned in the story and invite them to be developed further. There are hundreds of possible questions that could be asked but we might, for example, be interested in asking some like these:

- How has "the rehearsal" been valuable to you and your family in the months since your mother's death? Has doing that made anything easier or more difficult?
- When the nurse asked about how much your mother knew about her cancer and you thought inwardly, "That's my mother, that's our family," what was it that you knew about yourselves and about her at that time and how has that sustained you through this time of grief?
- How have you continued as a family to laugh together and to think about your mother as with you in doing so?
- Have there been times when you have noticed the fireflies or cherry blossoms and have seen them through her eyes? What difference has this made for you?
- If your mother were floating above you, what would she say about how your life is unfolding since she died?

These questions are by no means exhaustive, but they signal the approach to counseling we are advocating. It is based on inquiry into the specific practices people are engaged in in the process of becoming. It assumes the possibility of agency. It is founded on a critical perspective toward the conventional knowledge in grief psychology. It aims to produce local knowledge, rather than to confirm universal truths. It credits people with the ability to craft their own pathway through grief, rather than having to submit to accepted practices. Such crafting may even achieve moments of beauty, even in the face of the harsher aspects of death.

CHAPTER 2

Reality Gains the Day

Unearthing an aesthetic appreciation of responses to death and grief requires an understanding of what has gone before. All journeys into new terrain respond to existing maps, or trace a direction from which new steps might diverge. To understand death and bereavement and to map a fresh topography for counseling conversations, it is useful to start with how the ground beneath our feet has previously been mapped. We ultimately wish to venture into a new language about death and about our responses to it, but we do not start from neutral ground.

27

The purpose of this chapter is to map out where the psychology of grief has been. In keeping with the themes of this book, we shall pose some questions to guide this survey. For each model we describe, we suggest posing the following questions:

- What happens to relationships between the living and the dead?
- What opportunity is there for persons to craft their own responses?
- How much is creativity possible for the dying and bereaved to fashion meaning within this model?
- Who is in charge of the story that is told – the counselor or the bereaved person?
- How much are cultural responses or natural responses valued?

Among the historical themes of grief psychology, it is easy to see the individual's internal experience elevated over any sense of relationship. The overarching pattern consistent (until recently) through all the models surveyed is the valuing of independence and separation over intimacy and relationship (Hagman, 2001; Neimeyer, 2001; Valentine, 2006). Whether the focus is on the dying person (as in Kübler-Ross, 1969) or the bereaved person (as in Worden, 1991; 2009), the tendency is the same. All these models encourage completion (of unfinished business), letting go (of the relationship), and moving forward (without the deceased). The sense of connection between the living and the dying person (before and after their death) has regularly been decathected away (using Freud's 1917 term), along with the emotions of grief. Counseling models have followed suit, suggesting acceptance, and completion, and a final goodbye. Only recently has a different note been sounded that resonates more with a sense of relational continuity.

While the traditional moves may be helpful in some situations, they are not universally helpful and may potentially be harmful in some circumstances. The question we raise is whether there could be more productive, move loving, and more inclusive practices that support the retention of relationship in the face of death. Through all the work in which the finality and inevitability of separation from a sense of relationship has been assumed, this possibility has lain dormant. Similarly, the emphasis has been on privileging the knowledge of the counselor over the creativity and agency of the bereaved person. In these circumstances, it is hard to craft a response to grief when it is already crafted for bereaved persons in advance. Moreover, the modernist scientific assumption of grief as an expression of human nature, rather than as a culturally modulated experience, has tended to privilege a Western model of grief as universally valid and has paid little attention to cultural variation.

It is our intention to offer an approach that attends to these possibilities. We do not accept this as unrealistic. On the contrary: we think it produces considerable benefit, because it enables people to take comfort from the sense of continuity of life that it confers. It allows the bereaved to uplift the stories of those who have gone before and to have ongoing access to new relationship possibilities.

In subsequent chapters, we shall map out how such possibilities might be constructed in conversation. This new map furthers the opportunity for relationships to be celebrated and honored and no longer excluded, simply because death occurred. It is through the crafting of such connections that intricate meanings are invited that can enliven experience, rather than intensify suffering. They can even allow for rituals of beauty to be performed that embody a sense of transcendence over death. It is these moments that this book is about. What has come before is steeped in particular historical contexts and led to practices that were perhaps a snug cultural fit in their day. This chapter will survey some of this history, and tease out the meta-narratives that have created a one-size-fits-all template for grief. Traces of religious doctrine, sociology, and philosophy will be drawn out, as well as influences from economics and law. All of these influences have coalesced to form a dominant discourse of modern grief psychology, which has influenced, and at times dictated, practices. To illustrate, we start with an example.

Sandra was interviewed by the first author in a retirement center where she lived. She specifically came to the conversation wanting to discuss how her husband, Philip, had died seventeen years prior by taking his own life.

```
LORRAINE: Can you tell me a little about your
          husband? What was his name?
SANDRA:   Philip. He was a brilliant man, but a
          man with severe depression. He struggled
          with that his whole life. He tried psy-
          choanalysis when we lived in Vienna with
          some of Freud's disciples for ten years,
          but that made matters worse. He tried
          drinking too to solve his depression, but
          that didn't work either. Ultimately, he
          committed suicide.
LORRAINE: That must have been terrible.
SANDRA:   It was terrible. Obviously with suicide
          there's a question of guilt. I questioned,
          "Should I not have seen these signs?" He
          had always said - from the beginning of
          our relationship, "I am going to kill
          myself one day."
LORRAINE: When he would say those things, you
          must have found them unsettling.
SANDRA:   Yes, we sought counseling. He went
          to my former therapist a few times when
          things got bad. This turned out to be a
          great help later for me that she knew him
          and was fully aware of his depression. She
          was able to help me to get over the pain
          and eventually over the terrible guilt as
          a result.
```

29

LORRAINE: How did she do that?

SANDRA: I don't think I would have made it without her. She helped me to accept that he was dead by looking at it objectively. She helped me face reality that he wanted to die and wasn't coming back. He had told me that practically when we first married, shortly after we were married. I was angry he did not leave a note when he died. My therapist explained he resented me for keeping him alive for such a long time. That helped too.

LORRAINE: And that was a comforting thought for you?

SANDRA: She would tell me, "You were OK. You did nothing wrong." It let me understand that I could move on and not feel guilty. She could honestly say, "We knew he would do it sooner or later." She told me that she discussed his case with the other counselors and this was their consensus; he was terminal.

LORRAINE: What was it like to hear this?

SANDRA: It was a relief. We knew he was terminal. She helped me to find closure and to enjoy the fact that I had an active life. She encouraged me to get back to work and to be social. The grief was terrible. But the guilt was far worse. Seeing a counselor and knowing I didn't have to punish myself for his death anymore made a huge difference.

While we would certainly not begrudge Sandra feelings of relief and to no longer be tormented by guilt, we are left questioning how her counselor directed her in this particular direction to assuage her guilt. It seems that Sandra has been offered personal relief at the cost of whatever might be salvaged in her relationship with her husband. The therapist has given her (or perhaps, colonized her with) interpretations that offered little respect for her husband and encouraged Sandra to let go of the relationship with him. We think this is a heavy price to pay and only amounts to a debatable interpretation of reality, one where the counselor's version of truth seems to be privileged over Sandra's experience. As noted in the previous chapter, the experience of grief has been shaped by various lines of force, which operate in the background of Sandra's experiences and her therapist's training and thinking. These influences often emanate from the medical establishment, although not exclusively, and shape conversations about death and grief in the counseling office.

The Changing Conversation

While grief psychology has remained relatively consistent for the past one hundred years, it has not always been so. Prior to the modern era, death was described in predominantly religious terms and disease was considered evil or even as punishment for wrongdoing (Foucault, 1973). However, death and, as we shall see, grief were gradually brought more and more under the control of the scientific method.

Philippe Ariès (1974; 1981) suggests that the way we think about death has transformed it from a very public, occasionally messy, communal and normal experience to a private, sanitized, and isolated event under the regime of science. The location where death occurs has shifted, with implications for how death is marked and how we grieve. Prior to the twentieth century, people mostly died at home. Community surrounded them and cared for them before death, as well as for the family once the person had died. Visible signs of mourning were evident – whether in the attire of the bereaved family or the shutting of windows in the home as a sign that a family was mourning a loss (Ariès, 1981). Death was marked in public. Rituals defined how one should behave when a loved one was dying in a manner that contextualized the relationship between the deceased and the bereaved.

World wars and the advent of antibiotics ushered in a germ-free promise in modern hospitals as places to treat wounded or ill individuals. Hospitals had previously been places of rest and confinement, often for the poor (Ariès, 1973), until the 1918–19 flu epidemic that killed between twenty and forty million people worldwide gave new purpose to hospitals (Hockey, 1990).

Death in the hospital proved to be antiseptic and hidden away from the general public. By the end of WWII, death was routinely medically managed. This meant people became "patients" and their bodies were reduced to a series of physical symptoms. Patients often were not told their diagnosis to maintain hope for recovery. Death became

31

the invisible enemy for the medical profession. Grief psychology was birthed alongside the medicalized worldview that reduced expertise to a progression along the medical timeline.

The implication of the medicalized death experience is that personal stories are shaped, if not dictated, by the lines of force that constitute the dominating institutions. For example, not speaking of death openly, or the emotions surrounding it, led to a patient being commended for dying without complaint or expression of fear. Stories might be told of the patient's stoicism to the very end.

Anthropologist Geoffrey Gorer (1965) interviewed 1,628 people in England about their experiences with death and bereavement. He captured how medically managed death disconnected, or even actively deceived, people who were dying by refusing to tell people they were dying, distracting them, and ignoring their concerns.

Stories of death and grief are still managed by the use of metaphors of strength. The dying, if they're lucky, may be cast as heroes. Stories about cancer often draw from militaristic jargon. We speak about a person fighting cancer or surviving it (like a military campaign). A person who dies from cancer is often said to have died (often bravely) after a long battle. Stories are created by the system that gives them birth – in this case, a medical machine (Deleuze & Guattari, 1977) that does not value disease, death, or grief (although it does concede that death is a formidable enemy). How we think about death has implications for living with grief. While some might turn to religious comfort, for the past one hundred years, the medical profession has dominated the way in which the bereaved have relieved their suffering. Grief has been closely aligned with the physical body. This alignment is understandable, since many early contributors to the topic were themselves medical doctors.

In particular, the writings of Sigmund Freud, Melanie Klein, John Bowlby, Erich Lindemann, Colin Murray Parkes, and Elisabeth Kübler-Ross were significant in constructing the meaning of grief as an individual, symptomatized, private, inner experience. This position made sense in the medical world and it can be found in our example. Sandra is guided to adopt this view of reality by a well-meaning counselor. Early theorists set the therapeutic stage and grief counseling continues to support a pathologized and individualized focus. The first generation of theoreticians were also, as Gergen would describe, "the translators of deficit" (1994, p. 155). A deficit orientation became taken for granted. As Gergen writes, "As intelligibilities of deficit are disseminated to the culture, they become absorbed into the common language. They become part of 'what everybody knows' about human behavior" (1994, p. 158).

Let us select a few common denominators at work among these early writers to showcase how grief counseling has developed.

Freud and Grief as an Illness

Much has been written about how Freud's work has influenced modern psychology. Only a small body of Freud's writing pertained to grief and only one article, published in 1917, entitled "Mourning and Melancholia", in which he was concerned to distinguish between the two. Freud wrote this paper within an eleven-day period, along with three other papers, that, according to his biographer Ernest Jones (1955), were "among the most profound and important of all of Freud's work" (p. 185).

The fact that mourning appears in the article is almost peripheral. It is as if those who mourn were the control group for those suffering from abnormal melancholia. Even in his title, Freud links these two experiences of mourning and melancholia and in doing so, set in motion a century of practice for intervening with grief.

Freud establishes mourning as a reaction to the loss of the person or a connection to an idea. In grief, as opposed to melancholia, he believed there would be an endpoint and that people are capable of victory over this condition, recapitulating the well-worn adage, "Time heals all wounds." Freud himself (1917) wrote, "We rest assured that after a lapse of time it will be overcome" (p. 153).

It is important to look at the phrases in Freud's work that gave rise to such practices. In the following quotation Freud is delineating the work of mourning.

Now in what consists of the work which mourning performs? The testing of reality, having shown that the loved object no longer exists, requires forthwith that the libido shall be withdrawn from its attachment to the object. Against this demand a struggle of course arises – it may be universally observed that man (sic) never willingly abandons a libido-position, not even when a substitute is beckoning to him. . . . The normal outcome is that deference for reality gains the day. Nevertheless its behest cannot at once be obeyed. The task is carried through bit by bit, under great expense of time and cathectic energy, while all the time the existence of the lost object is continued in the mind. Each single one of the memories and hopes which bound the libido to the object is brought up and hyper-cathected, and the detachment of the libido from it is accomplished . . . when the work of mourning is completed, the ego becomes free and uninhibited again.

(1917, p. 154)

In the expression "it can be universally observed" lies an assumption of universal human nature that allows the extrapolation of one person's experience to the next person. It removes in one stroke the vast array of cultural responses to a person's death and of grief. Universality limits the crafting of creative responses and decreases agency for the bereaved. The grief endured by a European patient is thought to be the same as the grief endured by patients in every other cultural context and historical time.

Noteworthy too is that when mourning is completed the "ego becomes free and uninhibited again". Thus the road is paved for future interventions to free the bridled ego, often encouraging the separation between the deceased and bereaved persons. It is this removal of energy that discourages connections between the living and dead.

The unbridling cure is provided through the process of decathexis; that is, through the emotional release of the libido's attachment to the "object". Such examination and release of memories (hyper-cathected) allow the libido to let go or return to wholeness. Otherwise mourning becomes intertwined with melancholia and yields to a foreboding future.

The imprint of this paragraph continues to this day in the psychological discourse of grief. Although many no longer speak in the actual terms that Freud used, the assumptions that Freud makes have been reiterated many times by those who came after him. They have bestowed power onto the counselor or physician to make meaning of the circumstances and insist on their own knowledge at the expense of the bereaved.

Sandra is offered these assumptions through the designation of pathology in her dead husband which limits her creativity and ability to speak otherwise of him. Freud argued that mourning must include the acceptance of the person as actually medically dead, verified through objective medical pronouncement, as in a death certificate or visual confirmation. It is the acceptance of this reality that allows for the libido to remove its energy, even when the task is unpleasant. The behest of reality is to be obeyed. We see this reasoning in a personal letter Freud wrote to his mother, informing her of the death of his daughter, Sophie, from influenza. The letter, dated January 26, 1920, was later published by his son, Ernst.

Dear Mother,

I have some sad news for you today. Yesterday morning our dear lovely Sophie died from galloping influenza and pneumonia . . . I hope you will take it calmly; tragedy after all has to be accepted. But to mourn this splendid, vital girl who was so happy with her husband and children is of course permissible. I greet you fondly.

Yours, Sigm.

(1960, pp. 185–6)

Thus, Freud held to his 1917 treatise as an acceptable way to mourn his daughter. Three years later, when Freud grappled with the death of his favored grandson, Heinele, he gives a more nuanced description.

He was indeed an enchanting little fellow, and I myself was aware of never having a loved human being, certainly never a child, so much . . . I find this loss very hard to bear. I don't think I have ever experienced such grief.

(Freud, 1960, p. 344)

These examples give us a glimpse into the complicated experiences of grief. It is easy to speculate that Freud's writings about grief and mourning are a product of his professional orientation as a physician, as well as a product of the contextual stories of his era. His ideas about death and grief, as with his general theories of personality, are invested in the autonomous individual and processes of introspection. They also restrict the role of interpretation to the expert who pronounces on the psychological meaning of experience.

Freud's construction of grief is an individual model that assumes people are separate in life from one another and this continues into, and especially after, death. The separation of relationship is intended to encourage the diminishing of feeling toward the deceased and does not promote any active engagement in memories of, or conversations with, the deceased. These same themes of letting go and laying to rest the relationship run throughout the brief recounting of the conversation with Sandra and her therapist.

While Freud's work remains a benchmark in grief psychology, it stands in contradiction to an aesthetic approach to death and grief,

35

grounded in relationship and culture. An aesthetic approach supports the intentional remembering of the deceased, and the fostering of relational connections, both in life and in death. It seeks to assuage guilt through honoring and enhancing a relational understanding.

Missing from Freud's psychological theories is a sense of the possibility of re-inclusion of the dead loved one. Instead, he uses the concept of decathexis to let the relationship slide into obscurity. Let us turn our attention briefly to a few other first-generation theorists, before we address these implications further.

Melanie Klein and Object Relations Theory

Klein was a major contributor to object relations theory and extended its implications to include the psychology of grief. She provided an important link between Freud and other related writers, like John Bowlby, although her writing is often omitted from modern grief psychology. Klein (1940) connected adult experiences of mourning with the first year of life. After studying under Freud's colleagues, Karl Abraham and Salvador Ferenczi, Klein contended that the child goes through states of mind comparable to those of the adult, and early mourning is revived whenever grief is experienced in later life. She argued that the infant struggles when it is weaned from its mother and that mourning for the mother's breast becomes the basis for grief in later life. The loss of the mother's milk is the child's first experience of loss and it is recapitulated each time further losses are experienced. This idea removes agency from clients as one can never be completely free from this initial loss. Klein's research contributed to the notion in modern grief psychology that each subsequent loss becomes another occasion for reevaluation and readjustment. This idea has been incorporated by grief counselors in the attribution of secondary loss to earlier losses.

Klein also contributed to grief psychology "defenses" that allow the person to accept unconscious losses. She placed special emphasis on denial, as a result of a comparison between the external and the internal representation of the deceased. Death of a loved one shakes both the external reality and the internal image, according to Klein.

A few brief comments are needed. Klein's theory relies upon the interpretation of the therapist, since it is doubtful that any client would make such a meaning link. The power to make someone feel better is located only in the therapist's interpretation, which leaves the client with little or no agency. It is a pessimistic theory, too, because there does not seem to be any way out for the bereaved person. One is condemned to inevitable suffering, because one was weaned and is doomed to a life with little opportunity to craft one's own response to the particular circumstances. The relationship between the bereaved person and the deceased is not treated as equally important as the relationship with the mother who weaned the child. Moreover, the assumption of weaning before the age of one represents a cultural custom that is scarcely as universal as the assumptions of the psychology of loss.

The Trauma of Grief

Erich Lindemann often goes unnoticed in grief counseling books, but his ideas actually deserve a place in the story of grief psychology. Lindemann (1944) defined grief as an abnormality. He is credited with two terms that have had a major impact on how grief is currently spoken of. One was the concept of "anticipatory grief" and the other was his reference to "grief work" (Rando, 1988). Although Freud also made mention of grief as work, it was Lindemann who brought this into the common lexicon and his work expanded Freud's ideas of the pathology of grief (Worden, 2015).

Deriving from economic metaphors, "grief work" describes an emotional experience in terms of an economy of labor. Action and movement are engaged to achieve the desired goal of severing ties to the deceased person, but without questioning whether such movement is helpful, or whether grief might at times not be about work, or even whether viewing emotions through an economic metaphor is apt. It certainly limits a creative response to grief. According to Lindemann (1944):

> The duration of a grief reaction seems to depend on the success with which a person does the *grief work*, namely emancipation from the bondage to the deceased, readjustment to the environment in which the deceased is missing and the formation of new relationships.

> **(p. 156)**

Lindemann's bias toward relational emancipation shares the Freudian notion that the bereaved need to relinquish connections with the deceased. Emancipation suggests a process of liberation, in which freedom from the relationship is valued, as if being in a relationship with the deceased were a form of pathology. The deceased loved one is referred to as like an albatross to be cut loose. Lindemann references relational bonds with a deceased person with the term "bondage". He is not referring to bondage to the emotional experience of grief, but bondage to the deceased person. The bereaved are given little opportunity other than to sever the connection.

This view is related to the context of Lindemann's research. He interviewed people grieving as a result of tragic circumstances. Their loved ones had died in a terrible fire at the Coconut Grove restaurant; a horrible 1942 incident, killing four hundred and ninety-two people in a Boston nightclub. Lindemann does not characterize the pre-morbid relationships as problematic. These connections between the living and the deceased were described in positive terms, including victims who are family members and young people out celebrating recent marriages or anniversaries. Regardless of the context of the relationship, Lindemann proposes that the bereaved need respite from the emotional pain and must work through it.

Lindemann's interviews set the stage for his taxonomy of identified sets of grief symptoms and categories of responses. His descriptions derived, perhaps, from his professional perspective as a physician by highlighting the somatic symptoms of sighing, universal exhaustion, and absence of interest in food. His symptomatology can be broadly found in the lay literature of the current day that speaks of the symptoms of grief and anticipatory grief and emphasizes grief as an individual, physical ailment.

Lindemann's work opened the door for later elaborations of anticipatory grief and the effects of traumatic grief. While there may be a need for specialized attention to those suffering following traumatic circumstances, his model suggests an overwhelming and exhaustive sense of laboring through painful events. The metaphor of "grief work" overlays harshness on top of what is already potentially hard. Those who counsel the bereaved speak of grief in terms of work. Work assumes a certain duration, a task orientation, perhaps an alienated activity, and, for many people, a clock-in and clock-out performance. We must question what job is at hand and whether there is an endpoint when the job has been completed.

Grief and Attachment

Another architect of modern grief psychology was John Bowlby. Like Freud and Lindemann, Bowlby was a physician and psychoanalyst widely credited for his work on separation anxiety immediately after

WWII in Britain at the Tavistock Institute. He spoke of the attachment of children and parents during the first years of a child's life, specifically the bond between a child and the "mother figure", the term used to cover the biological mother, nannies, and healthcare workers involved in caring for children. Bowlby has since been criticized for extrapolating his research findings to the general population (Burman, 2008, p. 131).

Bowlby wrote four articles on mourning (1960; 1961a; 1961b; 1963), three of which were focused on pathological mourning (that is, maladaptive, prolonged mourning or pining for the deceased person). He viewed attachments and mourning as organic, instinctual processes that occur naturally, and internally, unless interfered with. He compares human mourning behaviors to patterns found in animals and, by analogy, argued for the human experience of mourning as a natural, biological process. He referred to mourning, both normal and pathological, in terms like "stemming from primitive roots" and an "instinctual response system" (1961, p. 320).

Bowlby's theory was heavily influenced by the physical sciences and he often referenced Darwin to support his ideas. He made little distinction between a physical wound and an emotional wound, suggesting that loss is like a physical illness and can be studied objectively, and understood in much the same way. The bereaved were considered to be in a state of "biological disequilibrium" due to "a sudden change in the environment" (1961, p. 322). He suggested this condition could be studied and treated as if they were "wounds, burns and infections" (1961, p. 323).

39

This emphasis on a natural biological process, or an instinctual illness (which linked human response to animal knowledge), could be used to describe the suffering of people of all ages and from all kinds of loss, according to Bowlby. Mourning was thus like suffering a viral infection and became an automatic biological reaction traced to the loss of the mother figure. If not properly handled, the bereaved would digress into pathology. Like the aforementioned theorists, Bowlby's model is focused on the individual and is steeped in pathology. He suggested three phases that the bereaved must navigate. Simply stated, these would be: disequilibrium, disorganization, and reorganization (1961). These ideas are similar to what Freud spoke of as the testing of reality and, finding that the love object is no longer there, acquiescing to reality. According to Bowlby, the bereaved person continues to search for the deceased, but does not find them. This disappointment mounts and, as the hopes of reunion fade, the searching behavior usually ceases to refocus on the "lost object" (1961, p. 334).

Bowlby set himself apart from both Freud and Klein by suggesting that their work was flawed. In Bowlby's estimation, Freud misunderstood a bereaved person's hatred for the lost object. Bowlby suggested anger and disdain is normal and adaptive, whereas Freud assumed it to be a form of pathology. In both circumstances, culture and local knowledge were omitted from consideration. Bowlby also suggested Klein's focus on the first year of life limited her theories about adult psychology.

In spite of his desire to draw distinctions, Bowlby's work was influenced by, and still supported, a psychodynamic, essentialized view of psychological functioning. His explanation of grief was focused on individual reactions and supported an intra-psychic understanding. He added the idea that grief is akin to physical illness, from which we can recover. He viewed the human experience of grief as an evolutionary, Darwinian response. As we will see, Bowlby's ideas have been heavily used in grief counseling to distance the bereaved from the stories and memories of those who have died.

The Pathology of Normal

Colin Murray Parkes, the British psychiatrist, researched and wrote about treatment, in part as he felt it had been neglected in the literature of psychiatric illness. He noted in 1972, "this condition has been so neglected by psychiatrists that it is not even mentioned in the indexes of most of the best-known general textbooks of psychiatry" (p. 6). Parkes did, in fact, conduct research and used metaphors from Freud, Lindemann, and Bowlby, among others (Parkes also worked at the Tavistock Institute in London) to support his notion that grief is characteristically an abnormality. He referenced grief with an air of scientific expertise, suggesting an abnormality about which the client would not surprise the knowledgeable physician. This perspective strips a person of the agency to speak on their own behalf.

Parkes (1972) interviewed small groups of widows and continued this research at Harvard to develop a taxonomy of risk factors for bereavement. While Parkes predominantly interviewed women, he used male pronouns and descriptors, except when referring to specific stories. As he described the "phases" of grief, like Freud, he assumed a universal human subject without accounting for cultural diversity of response. "The old environment must be given up, the new accepted. . . . Resistance to change, the reluctance to give up possessions, people, status, expectations – This, I believe, is the basis of grief" (1972, p. 11).

Like other theoreticians, Parkes felt the dead had no part to play in the intra-psychic experience of grief. According to Silverman and Klass (1996), "He [Parkes] sees no useful place for interaction with the dead after the grief is resolved" (p. 11). His ideas were, nonetheless, distinctive. Parkes often referenced attachment theory to grief and saw grief as interwoven with experiences of love (Blythe, 2010; Parkes, 2002) when the joy of loving in life becomes pain when death occurs. This idea has become popularized in grief psychology in expressions like, "We grieve in response to how much we have loved" that position bereaved people in precarious places. Parkes suggested phases that were resolved through the letting go of connection. Like most early grief theorists, he distinguished what was real from what was imagined.

During the initial phase, the bereaved must hold an internalized image of the deceased to compare them to those they see in their daily lives. This image allowed newly bereaved persons to correct their vision, when they falsely saw their deceased loved ones. Without a clear visual memory of the deceased, the bereaved could apparently be fooled into believing their loved one was still alive. With each possible sighting that was proven incorrect, the mind, according to Parkes, adjusted to the reality of the loss. Searching behavior was a biological drive (like animal behavior in search of food) and was experienced as restless pining soon after the death. Like Freud, Parkes considered this a normal, short-lived, and efficient aspect of bereavement. He stated, "Pangs of grief begin within a few hours or days of bereavement and usually reach a peak of severity within five to fourteen days" (1972, p. 39).

Like his theoretical predecessors, Parkes condemned the desire to stay connected to those who have died as pathologically refusing to accept reality. Parkes suggested that a desire for connection is problematic, and may be attributed to personality disorder. Moreover, through the derogatory use of the term "hysteroid" he suggested that this response is more prevalent in women. Parkes's ideas contained assumptions that devalue women's knowledges and led to gendered models of grief. He presented deficit-oriented accounts of women as weak and dependent wives who were described through their connection to their husbands, and their experience of grief was regarded as symptomatic of their social position.

Despite these patriarchal assumptions, Parkes did offer an account of bereavement that included some aspects relevant to our work. In particular, he suggested there could be some "mitigation" of grief, when the relationship story and the connection with the deceased

41

were reported as comforting and helpful. Without the pathologizing and patriarchal lens, the idea of mitigation might contribute to a therapeutic possibility beyond what Parkes imagined, one that could include a creative place for the dead to live on. One of the aims of an aesthetic sense is to build upon the usefulness of what is mitigating for therapeutic practice.

The next seminal theorist who deserves mention for her contributions to grief psychology is Elisabeth Kübler-Ross. Her work represented a bridge between the aforementioned theorists and modern-day practitioners of grief counseling. Her model of death, dying, and grief established a benchmark within grief psychology.

The Five Stages

Elisabeth Kübler-Ross is perhaps the best-known name in grief psychology today. Her groundbreaking ideas catapulted a congealed theory of grief into mainstream conversation. Her work was, in part, a response to the medical profession not speaking openly with patients about death. By contrast, she spoke boldly and challenged the silencing of conversations about death. She renewed an interest in death and grief in professional and public discourse. Her work also contained assumptions that have sadly been used to diminish those who are grieving.

Kübler-Ross was keenly dissatisfied with the social influences that suppressed conversations about death and grief. Growing up in a small farming area in Switzerland, she contrasted her experiences of death with those she encountered as a physician in the large American city of Chicago. The stark contrast left her believing that medical practices actually created greater fear of death for both patients and medical personnel. "The more we are making advancements in science, the more we seem to fear and deny the reality of death . . . dying nowadays is more gruesome in many ways, namely, more lonely, mechanical, and dehumanizing" (1969, p. 21).

The dying person had been left out of medical and psychological conversations and her (1969) book burst into the world to change this. She felt not telling the terminally ill about their inevitable death was disrespectful and hoped to combat the fear and avoidance she saw among medical professionals. It was her hope to use the dying person's knowledge and to include the dying in the conversation. Her respect for candor could have set the stage for greater agency and voice for the dying and, in some instances, did just that. Interestingly, she did not write extensively about those who were bereaved, but focused her attention on people with terminal illnesses.

Kübler-Ross proposed a possible trajectory for what a person might experience emotionally before dying. She believed the process of coming to terms with dying was not easily done in a medically dominated, death-denying culture. Against an illusion of immortality, she claimed, we struggle to conceive of the time in which we might not exist. From this assumption, she argued, emerges the widespread belief that death is bad. This belief, she argued, is based on the activation of the psyche's defense mechanisms, leading to a model that is intra-psychic and residing within the individual, rather than the relationship. As a physician, she also adopted the common view of psychoanalysis and was heavily influenced by Freud.

Each of her five stages is a reaction to the news of approaching death, which sets up a collision between the individual's reaction and the common perception of immortality. The mind requires time to adjust to this newly conceived mortal status. The overall structure of Kübler-Ross's stages was of a movement through sequential stages – denial, anger, bargaining, depression, and acceptance. In spite of her own cautions (Valentine, 2006), her work has been translated into other uses that are different from her original writing, particularly with bereaved families.

The first stage in her model was denial, defined as a "temporary state of shock from which he [the patient] recuperates gradually" (p. 54). She described it as an understandable reaction that affords patients time to adjust to the news. She urged professionals to act in forgiving ways with people who were angry, sharp, ignoring, and sullen. She spoke of denial as a normal way of receiving bad news and, in fact, leveled some responsibility at those doing the telling. This is very different from how "denial" is used in practice today. Her suggestions for professionals encourage respect.

On the heels of denial, the dying person began to understand what they were about to lose. It was then the anger emerged. It was anger at having to change one's plans and at the loss of control over one's life. As with denial, she did not write in pathologizing terms, but saw anger as a normal response. She encouraged professionals to be compassionate, because anger was simply a response to a growing understanding of what was about to be lost by the dying person; the works left undone and pleasurable activities halted. For some, she explained, anger is temporary, but for others, it might remain for longer, and she was without expectation that this be resolved prior to death. While these responses are individually located and have a psychodynamic etiology, a respect toward the dying is notable.

Bargaining was the middle child of the five stages. It involved the negotiation of a possible trade, either with the medical personnel or with God in hope of gaining more time to live. This stage assumed some degree of acquiescence to the disease. Without an inkling of death, there would be no need to strike a deal or seek the favor of a delay. It might be expressed as willingness to die, once the patient had lived past a certain occasion, like a child's birth. To be granted the favor, one had to offer something as well, perhaps some special and private promise made to God. One can almost hear the opening to a relational exchange in which the dying person is asked about the desire to witness a relational event. Like Parkes's mitigation, this could have offered a line of flight (Deleuze, 1988) into new territory, but it was interpreted only as a step toward the ultimate goal of acceptance.

The fourth reaction to the news of impending death was the onset of depression. Depression may result from repeated surgeries, debilitating lethargy, overwhelming losses, financial cost, or disfigurement. It was depression in the face of the inevitable, inescapable demise. In keeping with a psychodynamic orientation, Kübler-Ross defined this depression as necessary for the dying person to pull away emotionally, to go within themselves, and to take their leave. The modernist cultural assumption of centrality of individual autonomy, rather than of relational connection or of belonging to a cultural community, remained noticeably intact here.

Acceptance was the successful completion of all that had come before. It was about arriving at a detached resignation about death. For the dying person to arrive at this destination, it was pivotal, according to Kübler-Ross, that they be allowed the perfect combination of supportive medical professionals, space for being alone, and an understanding family. She distinguished acceptance from giving up or avoidance and described it as a genuine peace with death, achieved after a great journey. It was to be revered as the achievement of a monumental task. Acceptance was couched in Freudian terms as a separation and withdrawal of attention to relationships.

Kübler-Ross speculated that the trajectory of a bereaved family would be similar to that of the patient in their emotional processing, but her description was very brief. She offered a sketchy outline of the family experience as a form of denial, which would give way to anger, at the illness, the prognosis, and the hospital personnel, followed by guilt, and eventual acceptance. Family members did not apparently

44

share the bargaining phase, or the depression stage. These three sug-gested stages – denial, anger, and acceptance – were what prepared a family to allow a person who was dying to separate from the family emotionally, so they might die with peaceful resolve. On both ends of the dying relation, the patient's end and the family members' end, the goals were the same – separate, detach, and find peace.

In more recent years, there have been some challenges to these ideas, but those included above have been the major voices in the development of grief theory over the last one hundred years. Overall, counseling practices have embraced assumptions of the need to let go, accept, separate, and emotionally move forward.

Modern Grief Practice

Let us turn to how these theories became counseling practices. This will not be an exhaustive account, but a sample of those counseling practices developed from the aforementioned theorists. We will draw from the work of William Worden and Therese Rando and again look at how the assumptions of individual models of grief psychology impacted on Sandra's experiences and virtually cut her husband's contributions to her life out of the picture.

The Tasks of Grieving

William Worden's book on grief counseling was first published in 1982. There have been three subsequent editions, the latest published in 2009. The popularity of his text has been unrivaled, partly because it was the first, and for years the only, book that suggested how to have a therapeutic conversation with a bereaved person. Worden drew heavily from Bowlby, Parkes, and Lindemann to create a work-ing template of "tasks" for the bereaved to accomplish and a recipe for counselors. While he slightly altered the wording of the four specific tasks over the years, Worden commented that he defined the tasks in the hope of setting himself apart from models that used terms like phases or stages. While he specifically did not disagree with the iden-tification of phases, or with Bowlby or Parkes, he did state their terms are too passive and wanted to suggest a more active bereavement process (2009, p. 38).

Worden did not, however, envision a more agentic griever who had choice within the process. He encouraged grief counselors to alle-viate suffering by encouraging an insistence on reality and supported the completion of unfinished business. Worden's tasks required of the mourner, with the assistance of counseling:

Task I: To accept the reality of the loss
Task II: To process the pain of grief
Task III: To adjust to a world without the deceased
Task IV: To find an enduring connection with the deceased in the midst of embarking on a new life.

(2009, pp. 38–50)

In 1982, Worden's terminology was much harsher than in later editions. The previous third task was about adjustment to the environment without the deceased and the fourth was about moving on in life without the deceased. In later versions, he explained an appreciation for the "continuing-bonds" idea and made more accommodation for this idea. While we wholeheartedly support a shift in this direction, we remain curious about the trajectory of the tasks. Tasks I, II, and III seem to be directing the bereaved to let go, separate, and move on, while Task IV suggests the relationship is continuing. We question the built-in contradiction, which might lead to confused counseling conversations. Worden also retained in his counseling methods an emphasis on the severing of ties and on thinking of grief as an individual malady. He provided a list of ten "principles" of effective grief counseling (2009):

Help the survivor actualize the loss (p. 90);
Help the survivor to identify and experience feelings (p. 91);
Assist the survivor to live without the deceased (p. 97);
Help find meaning in the loss (p. 98);
Facilitate emotional relocation of the deceased to provide time to grieve (p. 99);
Interpret "normal behaviors" (p. 101);
Allow for individual differences (p. 102);
Examine defenses and coping styles (p. 102); and,
Identify pathology and refer (p. 104).

Thus, while there was an expressed interest in meaning and in continuing bonds, the principles were overwhelmingly focused on the individual's inner process of loss. Counselors were still guided in the 2009 text to talk about the deceased in past-tense language and invite the bereaved to write farewell letters (p. 105). Since such acts leave the deceased behind, we are left wondering about the value of the relationship between the living and the dead.

There also continued to be echoes of Freud's assumptions among the goals, principles, and suggested activities. The bereaved were required to face the "reality" that the person was dead and gone and would not return and the counselor was to reinforce this with "real" language like dead or died (2009, p. 90). This task was intended to confront what Worden referred to as denial and Freud spoke of as "the testing of reality". We see this in the conversation between Sandra and her counselor. Sandra's counselor supported her to not fall prey to denial by reinforcing the dividing line between the living and the dead. "She helped me to accept that he was dead by looking at it objectively. She helped me face reality and he wanted to die and wasn't coming back."

Worden left us with a mixed bag of recollection and reminiscing, the retention of the eventual goal of letting go of the relationship and moving back into a different life. Success was not conceived as entertaining a connection with the deceased person, for fear of failing to complete the first task. Worden's system for grief counseling did not allow for holding on to a sense of relationship after death, even with the slight modification made in recent additions. It was about the divestiture of connection with implicit rules about how and when and why it was to be performed. We are left with questions about how helpful or comforting this model is to the bereaved. It appears in all versions to embrace the discourses of modern grief psychology, where the bereaved are not in charge of their stories, but are told how to face someone else's preferred reality in the interest of tidy completions.

47

The Work of Grief

Therese Rando mined the same vein as Worden, because their theories shared ideological origins. Rando drew on Bowlby's attachment theory and also saw grief as an experience of severing connection. Like Worden, she understood grief as "work" or tasks to complete. Rando (1988) stated, "As a griever, you need to appreciate the fact that grief is *work*" (p. 16). It was not supposed to be fun. Rando's conceptualization of grief was focused on loss and difficulty. Not only do we grieve the death of persons; we could also grieve the loss of things, as in Freud's description of the loss of the "Fatherland" or of an idea (Freud, 1917/1959). Loss was a form of deprivation and grief was a response to change (Rando, 1988), whether from death, from an age-related deterioration of sight, from accepting a new job, or from relocation.

With this understanding of loss as a category of psychological experience, Rando expanded the meaning of grief by reviving Melanie Klein's concept of secondary losses. According to Rando, secondary losses were the nonphysical losses that resulted from the primary loss, which was physical. For example, a person whose spouse had died responded to the loss of the person and missed their presence and voice. This was considered a primary loss. That same bereaved spouse also lost income and was forced to move to a more affordable location. Loss of income and of the home would be described as secondary losses.

Rando assumed that we are hard-wired to grieve. Grief is a biological and almost cyclical response to an event that is shaped by the context and developmental age of the griever, but the mechanism of creating the grief is the same. She explained:

> Over and over you encounter loss in your life. To a greater or lesser extent, the same process of grief occurs in reactions to each of these losses . . . the very same process of grief that initiates the temporary despondency of the nine-year-old boy whose best friend refuses to play with him, also initiated the full-blown grief response of the man whose wife is killed by drunk driver.
>
> **(1988, p. 16)**

Regardless of the type of loss, she suggested a linear, curative process of adjustment to the loss. Rando collapsed other models into three phases, but her model also resolves with separation. The phases she specified were: 1. avoidance, 2. confrontation, and 3. accommodation. She suggested that, because loss was the common denominator for each of these phases, everyone had to express three things to adapt to or to accommodate the loss. We question the formulaic nature of this model and how it positioned bereaved people within a narrow range of agentic actions. Rando's model required the griever to address:

1. Their feelings about the loss
2. Their protest at the loss and the wish to undo it and have it not be true
3. The effects of the assault on the person caused by the loss.

(1988, p. 18)

48

Rando's model offered the griever grace for "denial", noting that this was a normal response to shocking news. Sandra would have fared well in this model to the extent that she was willing to accommodate and adjust to the news of her husband's disappearance and subsequent suicide. Rando did insist, however, that progression occurred, where the bereaved was able to acknowledge the loss, before reaching "the accommodation phase". If the bereaved had worked appropriately through the previous phases, the accommodation phase was when the bereaved person could begin to have a new life. This was not, however, an absolute state in which the pain was never again present. She described it as a realistic moving forward. As with most modern grief psychology models, she admitted the relationship between the living and the dead, and gave a minor nod to the deceased, when she spoke of accommodation.

In spite of suggesting a new relationship, Rando held tightly to the old, psychodynamic view of the divestiture of the connection with the deceased. There were other places where Rando made slight references to a possible relational model, but fell short of embracing it. In her guidelines for what the actual "work" of grief entailed, we see this dichotomy as well. Rando listed four things that "must" occur:

1. Change your relationship with your loved one.
2. Develop a new sense of yourself to reflect the many changes that occurred when you lost your loved one.
3. Take up healthy new ways of being in the world without the loved one.
4. Find people, objects, or pursuits in which to put the emotional investment you once had placed in your relationship with the deceased.

(p. 19)

Rando's heavy emphasis on the individual as the locus of the story excluded many relational opportunities for the deceased person's stories. Proximity of place was given to finding a new life, one in which the deceased did not feature much and in which "health" was measured by how well the bereaved adapted to this new world. To attain admittance to this world, the bereaved performs the requisite amount of grief work that is considered "active work" (Rando, 1995, p. 219) that required the appropriate expressions of emotion. If one "had to" do this work, by implication there "must" exist a deficit condition waiting to be ascribed to those who failed in this task. The work was a pathway to decathexis, as Freud might have said, and a method of constructing a new individual (and less relational) identity where the bereaved engage in the "undoing of the psychosocial ties that bind" (ibid.) between the living and the dead.

Through models like Rando's and Worden's, we see the strong connection between conventional psychodynamic thinking and grief psychology. While the same assumptions were dressed up in the current terminology, they were still based on the same underlying principle of removing energy from the relationship between the deceased and the living. Less than this was still seen as aberrant.

The end results were advice for counseling conversations that adopted the letting go of relationships as to be expected when a person died. While this may be useful for some, as was claimed by Sandra, it is also possible to see her as compliant with the model. What might happen, we would wonder, if she were invited to identify the aspects of the relationship with her husband that she could hold close to her, despite his death? What if her counselor had been more interested in inquiring into what gave her comfort, rather than pronouncing truths to her? What if she were invited to work out her own pathway through grief with her own creativity to guide her, rather than a pre-existing model?

Our concern is that modern grief psychology models may be helpful for some but may also be disadvantageous for too many others, who struggle to let go of an ongoing connection with a deceased loved one. The models have embraced practices that devoice the living but have not fostered agency in response to the experience of grief. The models also devoice the dead by not reincorporating their teachings, words, stories, and presence into the ongoing lives of the living. The models that support severing of ties have been rooted in long-standing preferences for rugged individuality that does not value relational creativity or inclusion. It is this relational model that we will continue developing in this text: one that weaves in stories of the dead alongside the living to provide meaning and richness that are not possible when we overlook all that the dead continue to offer us.

A Shifting Tide

The last two decades have witnessed a sea-change in the discourse of grief (Hagman, 2001). In the last twenty years many have levied claims against the modern grief practices and have developed new ideas in the field of thanatology. Our voice is not alone in this quest. This "new wave" of grief theories is marked by the following shifts (adapted from Neimeyer, 2001):

- Skepticism regarding the universality of emotional paths mapped out by grief theorists
- Questioning of the assumption of the need to withdraw psychic energy from the deceased
- Inclusion of more aspects of cognitive functioning
- An emphasis on more local practices for processing particular types of loss
- Greater interest in the impact of loss on identity
- A less pathologizing approach to grief
- A focus that widens out from the individual to relationships within families and communities.

These are all themes that we can support. Later in this book, we shall pick out many of them in particular ways. These emerging models have used different language to open up new thinking about bereavement and what might be acceptable, or even normal. Speaking of "continuing bonds", for example, is no longer seen as anathema, even though other models continue to dominate.

The text, *Continuing Bonds* (1996), was a revolutionary step toward an alternative, and multi-cultural, account that diverged from the models that cut ties between the living and dead. There are in this text numerous beautiful explanations of the lives of bereaved children, young adults, siblings, parents, adoptees, and spouses who have an ongoing connection to the person who has died. Each chapter chronicles sociological and anthropological research (mostly qualitative) that attests to the presence of the continued bond and annotates the limits of conventional models of grief psychology, Freudian ideas about mourning, and attachment theory. However, no chapter suggests how to foster such a conversation that might lead to this preferred outcome. There are one and a half pages at the very end of the text that suggest "implications for therapeutic intervention", which explains that therapeutic interventions for continuing bonds are outside of the book's purview.

Since the emergence of the continuing-bonds idea, there have been several studies that have suggested contradictory results, noting that continuing bonds in and of itself may, or may not, add to the risk of complicated grief (Currier, Irish, Neimeyer, & Foster, 2015; Root & Exline, 2014; Stroebe, Abakoumkin, Stroebe, & Schut, 2012). Included in the studies are questions about a bereaved person's perception about whether they should be attached to the deceased person. These doubts perhaps testify to the extent to which the dominant model has discursively influenced the meaning they make of

51

their experiences. The studies are not conclusive but raise questions about when the theoretical model may fall short of therapeutic benefit. It is possible that these dramatically differing results are in part due to the absence of a therapeutic practice to differentiate between effective and ineffective, or damaging, practices to reincorporate the stories in useful ways.

One development has been a shift from an emphasis on the processing of emotional psychic energy to what Neimeyer (2001) refers to as "meaning reconstruction". The "two-track model" (Rubin, 1999) or the "dual process model" (Stroebe & Schut, 1999) attempt to fill the dearth of practice models that address the continuation of a relationship. Both create openings for a new way to consider a connection with the deceased. Both offer techniques for measuring simultaneous processes for acknowledging and confronting the physicality of death and subsequent changes in lifestyle, while seeking meaning and connection to the deceased. The dual process model has undertones of critique of grief psychology (Stroebe & Schut, 1999), and the two-track model holds many points of similarity, but has been influenced by Jewish tradition (Rubin, 2015).

However, in both cases, it seems to us that the continuing-bonds track is the second track and the first track still contains throwbacks to the previous models that have influenced grief psychology. We do not think this is necessary. As this book develops, we shall attempt to outline some alternative views. The next chapter expands on these views.

52

CHAPTER 3

Re-membering

The focus of this chapter turns to the value of re-membering[1] for counseling conversations with bereaved persons. It is based on a social constructionist account of the process of remembering and on a relational emphasis on identity, rather than a strictly individualistic one. It takes account of the continuing bonds idea and extends it into a distinctive counseling practice. First, however, we present an example of a counseling conversation with a man whose mother has recently died. There is no attempt in this conversation to finalize his relationship with his mother, nor to interpret the meaning of what he is experiencing. Instead, the counseling is animated by questions that invite him to do the meaning-making and these questions assume the value of reincorporating the interests, concerns, hopes, and values of the deceased in the life of the living. That, we would argue, produces greater comfort and ameliorates psychological pain more than an emphasis on accepting reality. Before explaining this further, however, let us tell David's story.

In the middle of David doing his master's degree, his mother died unexpectedly. David was deeply affected by her death. In an email, he wrote, "These past few days have been really painful. There is a sense of sadness and sorrow and this emptiness that cannot be filled . . . I still think I am living a nightmare and I want to wake up to hear and see my mother once more."

What follows is a conversation with Lorraine about re-membering his mother. It is included here as an example of what a re-membering

53

---

1 The use of the hyphen to separate the term is intentional and will be explained in this chapter.

conversation can look like. In pursuit of a process that will help people craft their own pathway though grief, re-membering has an important role to play. It is not the only concern of counseling conversations about grief, and subsequent chapters will pick up other themes, but here the focus will be on the practice of re-membering conversations and the thinking behind them. Lorraine begins by asking David to introduce her to his mother.

LORRAINE: Tell me a little bit about her. First off, what is her name?

DAVID: Dalia.

LORRAINE: Dalia...Would you be willing to tell me a little bit about your mom, Dalia, and who she has been in your life?

DAVID: Yeah. As far back as I can remember, if I go back to when I was one or two years old, she's been a woman who has suffered a lot. My father was very abusive with her and I remember those things. He did terrible things to her. I am the oldest of four children. He left when I was about five years old and I thought, "Thank God!" From then on, she had to go to work. She worked about fourteen hours a day from Sunday to Sunday. She would tell me to look after my brothers, because I was the oldest. From when I was five, there was for me no childhood. I had to take the role of a father. Luckily for me, her mom was kind enough to give us a hand and she helped us with the little one — the newborn. So I only had to worry about the other two. She would leave the food cooked and I would just have to warm and serve it, but I still had to watch them. My mom was very responsible. I admire that she never gave up, even though I saw her crying and crying after my father left. Just three months ago, I was saying to her that it was a good thing my dad left her, because he was so abusive. She was surprised, because I had been so young

54

at the time. I explained things I remember step-by-step and she said, "That was
exactly how it happened." I said, "It was
good that he left, because otherwise you'd
be dead by now from so many hittings." She
agreed with me and said I was right.

Notice that the focus so far is mainly on the past. David tells
Lorraine about some painful and difficult memories, but they will
also serve as background to an understanding of Dalia's strength and
fortitude. The focus on the past shifts in the next segment. Lorraine
asks David the question that takes him out of talking in real time
about what occurred in history and invites him into a timeless
space of reflection on what his words mean.

LORRAINE: What do you think it meant for her to
have that conversation with you?
DAVID: I think it meant a lot for her. She
cried and then I told her how much I loved
her and admired her, because she did an
excellent job raising us. She was always
working. Not one of us have what we call
"bad habits". Not one of us is a smoker
or drinker or a drug addict. We're all
responsible males. We work and pay our
taxes like everybody else and we try not
to get ourselves in trouble. My brothers
always look at me like a big brother and
father figure. And I always say to my mom
that I appreciate that you relied on me to
help you raise them.
LORRAINE: Even when you were five and just a
young boy, what do you think she saw in
you that she knew she could count on you?
DAVID: She saw in me a leader who was very
responsible and very mature. One of the
things she told me is that my dad loved me
and he would pay attention to me. And I
have some flashbacks, but they get erased,
when I remember that he was really mean
to my mom.

55

As outlined in the previous chapter, modern grief psychology, through the themes it has emphasized, has attempted to sever the relationship between the living and the dead. This emphasis has had consequences for bereaved people, who are expected to capitulate to the expectation that they should say "goodbye", "move on", and complete "unfinished business". For many, however, this model does not reflect the reality that those living with grief prefer, which is to include the deceased for days, months, and even years following the death. Rather than inviting David to sever his relationship with his mother, Lorraine asks him to engage with it.

In recent decades, there has been a slight shift toward the inclusion of reminiscing about the deceased in the professional literature (as outlined below). Hybrid models continue to encourage completion of the relationship, recommending that reality be accepted (that is, acknowledging the death), and only then to have pleasant, wistful recollections, but these recollections are often to be nursed by the bereaved individual alone.

These models of grief have focused on the relationship between the deceased and the bereaved in the past, and the time of death serves as the demarcation between then and now. The encouragement has been for the living to resume their individual status; that is, to individuate and separate in just the right amount to again become "a self". In Lorraine's conversation with David, the focus begins on things that he remembers from the past, but quickly moves to incorporating aspects of the past into a present, and even future, focus.

LORRAINE: Your mom, she worked very, very hard. Was that for her whole life that she worked very hard?

DAVID: Yes.

LORRAINE: What do you think she hoped for in working so diligently for so many hours?

DAVID: All she cared about was for us to have a house and food. To provide for us. She worked in the hotel, fixing beds, like a maid. She would depend on whatever little salary she would get and tips.

LORRAINE: Where was this?

DAVID: In Mexico.

LORRAINE: And how old were you when you came to California?

DAVID: She came first and got herself together
         and a couple of years later, she went back
         to Mexico for us and brought us. I was the
         first one and four years later my brothers
         came. Once again, she started this new
         journey — to a country where she didn't
         know English and had no documentation. She
         was really brave to go over the border,
         risking her life so she could provide food,
         because she wasn't making enough money in
         Mexico. She wouldn't spend anything when
         she was working here in California, but
         would send everything to my grandmother,
         so we could have clothing and food. I
         always admired that.

LORRAINE: Why do you think it was that she
         was willing to come here and sacrifice
         everything?

DAVID: In a way, she never felt like she gave us
         enough. She wanted to get us a better edu-
         cation, a better life. When I was 12, one
         of my aunts, who lives in California, said,
         "Why don't you come here?" My mother said,
         "But I am closer to my kids in Mexico." My
         aunt explained, "You will never give them
         what they need, if you stay there." So she
         was really brave to come here — to gen-
         erate the determination to come. It took
         about thirty days to get to California.

The conversation starts to feature an inquiry into what kind of
person David remembers his mother as, and then into the values he
incorporates in himself as a result of being her son. In other words,
the facts of history denoted by events give way to the connotations of
those events for the sense of the self. The self in modern psychology is
often internally focused. It satisfies the image of a person who is sufficient in his or her own resources and drives toward self-reliance and
high self-esteem. He or she emerges through a series of developmental tasks in a blend of autonomy, drive, thinking, internal locus of
control, and emotional balance. The modern self may be influenced
by a person's biological family, but ideally the family of origin offers

only a starting blueprint, from which people take their leave, as they become adults.

This definition of a modern self has, in part, been shaped by the modern predilection for science as the truest form of knowledge (Seidman, 1994). Individual identity has been strongly connected to essentialized ideas, among which intelligence, genetic inheritance, and personality feature prominently. This self can also lack self-esteem or fulfill defeating prophecies – both of which are concep-tualized in essentialist terms. Within the modernist perspective, the self has been successfully externalized, objectified, and subsequently reified in an internalized form (Berger & Luckman, 1966).

Belief in this ideal has been established firmly in Western practice, particularly in the United States. It is often romanticized in the image of the "rugged individual". As Gergen (1989) suggests, the dominance of such thought has established the "conventions of warrant" (p. 74) that justify the superiority of individuality. This warrant influences and directs conversation for general psychological discourse, as well as for bereaved people.

Contrast all this with the still emergent postmodern version of the self, which is largely defined by what is internalized from significant relationships. It echoes what is assumed in many cultures around the world (Geertz, 1973). The postmodern self is constructed through lan-guage and discourse. Each self is made up of multiple selves, which are nuanced through subtle differences and linguistic content. Our present and our future determine which stories from our past are told (Cottor & Cottor, 1999; Gergen, 1994), each having the possibility of highlighting particular nuances of "self". In this form, our stories and identities are not fixed in one linear reality, but exist in a vibrant dia-logical form (Bakhtin, 1981; 1986). The term "dialogical" here refers to the ongoing energy generated from people's utterances to each other in an endless stream of dialogue that is never finalized (Bakhtin, 1981; 1986). It is in dialogue or conversation that our identities are shaped and reshaped, countless times, through story. As Gergen (1999) notes, there are no independent selves. "We are each constituted by others (who are themselves similarly constituted). We are always related by virtue of shared constitutions of the self" (pp. 11–12).

Such postmodern views of the self have important implications for grief psychology and for conversations with the bereaved. Rather than encouraging settling for the resumption of individual life after the death of a loved one, a counselor might encourage someone to re-conceptualize the relationship. Rather than eliciting a singular story of loss and the construction of farewell letters, a counselor might seek out multiple stories of relational change. Rather than supporting the restoration of a self-sufficient version of the self, a counselor might seek restoration of the relational context. In other words, we might pursue an understanding of the process of grieving that is not constructed at the expense of the relationship.

Not surprisingly, then, as postmodern psychology grew, ideas appeared to open up a more relational dimension of grief. For example, this relational way of thinking led to the (1996) book, *Continuing Bonds* (Klass, Silverman, & Nickman). Like Michael White's (1989) *"Saying Hullo Again"*, the title spoke to the emerging social constructionist difference in how grief is thought of. It was a portent of what would follow. By implication, this book required a revision of conventional notions of grief counseling. While *Continuing Bonds* did not venture far into the field of clinical practice, it did open the space for others to do so.

What the continuing bonds idea achieved was a conceptual account of a more relational version of grief. It has been supported by a series of studies that verify that people do retain a sense of relationship with their loved ones after their loved ones die (Costello & Kendrick, 2000). It meshed with the more relational idea of the self that was the subject of much postmodern writing. If, in fact, people exist within an interconnected, complex fabric of life that includes the living and the dead, then we must accommodate grief psychology differently. It is no longer ideal to disassociate from the deceased, any more than it would be ideal not to allow space in a given community for a living person. The dead continue to hold a relational position with the living. The idea of what it means to be an individual needs re-visioning in a postmodern context, but this, in turn, shifts the position of the deceased. Such re-visioning re-establishes more relational selves and a model in which the living and the dead can remain connected in story form.

Let us return to Lorraine's conversation with David, in which the version of the self that emerges is a relational self. It is constructed from exchanges between David and his mother and brothers and there is a blurring of the boundaries between them.

> DAVID: I was talking to my brothers the day she died. My other brother drove here from another state and we were having a group conversation. My brother also shared how our mother was really brave to come here, leaving us in Mexico, then going back to

59

get us and coming back to California. She did that again and went back again for the remaining kids. She risked her life three times crossing the border. The first time, when she brought me, we came through the tunnels at the border and she twisted her ankle. We were running to the tunnels and I didn't feel her presence, so I told the guy who was guiding us, "I don't see my mom." He said, "Don't worry about her. I'm going to come back and pick her up later." I said, "Heck no!" I went back to my mom about a quarter mile behind. When I found her, she was like a hurt animal rolling on the floor inside the tunnels. So I grabbed her and I said, "Mom we are together on this." She kept saying, "Keep going. If I don't make it, remember your brothers." She would always say that, "Think of your brothers, think of your brothers." I said, "I'm not going to leave you." I grabbed her and put her arm around me. I was 15 and physically not very strong, but I was determined. We walked together and we made it to the end.

The second time my mother crossed the border was with my younger brother. The guide was going to leave her in the desert and my brother had to help her. She risked her life three times just to get us. I have to feel so proud of her.

LORRAINE: So your mother was a woman of phenomenal determination. Is that right?

DAVID: Yes. Another characteristic of hers was that she wouldn't speak much. She wouldn't say, "I love you," but she was always there.

LORRAINE: So how do you know in your heart your mother loves you?

DAVID: It is like this telepathic connection. We didn't have to say it. We just knew there was love. She remained single for fifty-five years devoted to her kids. She was committed to us. Even right now, I am 37 and my younger brother 31 and he is single. She would say, "Now I have to care for the youngest."

LORRAINE: What did she want to instill in you? What kind of values would she hope you would have and what were her hopes about what kind of man you would be?

DAVID: I remember she would say, "Never be like your dad." She didn't have to say anything more. That is all she said.

LORRAINE: What did that mean in terms of how she wanted you to be?

DAVID: She wanted to see in me what she didn't see in my father. She didn't want me to get abusive or be mean. She wanted me to fear God, respect my family, my wife and children, and to be a person who is actually successful.

LORRAINE: You said something else about her that caught my fancy. You said that, if she were to walk in, I would instantly like her. I would notice her warmth.

DAVID: She was very welcoming.

LORRAINE: Do you think other people noticed that about your mom too?

DAVID: From what I know, yes. Most people know this is true. Like the people at church. I saw this at her funeral. They were saying they could not believe that she was gone.

LORRAINE: What did you take from that? That there were other people at your mom's service who were heartbroken?

DAVID: That means she was the lady that I always thought she was.

LORRAINE: Which was?

DAVID: That she was a woman who made herself likable to people. She was very attentive to people. She liked to do things for others.

61

Membership

The work of anthropologist Barbara Myerhoff (1978; 1982; 1986) contributed significantly to this new way of thinking about self and identity. Myerhoff coined the term "membership" when speaking about identity, which opens a new kind of conversation about death and grief. A person's membership club serves as a major reference point for the construction of identity that complements the continuing-bonds philosophy.

In the relationship between the person and the other members of their club, identity positions are offered and taken up, and identifications are authenticated. From this perspective, a membership club is constituted by the aggregation of the reciprocal exchanges of such processes of authentication. The club forms a significant discursive community, from which we draw resources to make sense of the events of life. Meanings are also exchanged within this club. Hence, the claim can be made that the meanings, stories, and performative acts of a person's life exist substantially within such clubs.

A person's membership is held, in life as in death, through the shared stories that live within the membership group. These identities and stories are not the sole property of an individual, as assumed in the modernist definition of the self, but live within networks or communities. They are a collective remembrance of times, experiences, and shared histories.

> A life, then, as not envisioned as belonging to the individual who lived it, but is regarded as belonging to the world, to progeny who are heirs to the embodied traditions, or to God. Such re-membered lives are moral documents and their function is salvific, inevitably implying, "All this has not been for nothing".
>
> **(Myerhoff, 1982, p. 111)**

Also of interest in the discussion of identity is the work of Edwin Shneidman. As director of the National Institute for Mental Health and a professor at the University of California Los Angeles, he was known for his interest in suicidology. Shneidman (1973) documented his research into suicide notes in a forensic study of suicide. He introduced a concept of identity as outliving a person's life in his idea of the "post-self", commenting on how the writer of the note does so with both a sense of the audience in mind, as well as of how they will continue to feature after death in the lives of the living.

Shneidman indicated that, even when contemplating death, people planning suicide speak to this imagined audience and draw comfort from it. He noted that this sense of legacy, even at a person's darkest moments, stood in contrast to an identity thought of as an individual construct. He suggested that it was this post-self that opened the prospect of a surplus legacy that exceeded the manner in which a person died:

we can examine our fears and hopes about our reputations and influence after death – about what we may call our "post-selves". . . . Few of us utterly abandon thoughts of survival in some form or other. They are our fragile hopes of escape from total annihilation.

(p. 43)

In effect, people who entertain ideas about dying imagine themselves to continue to feature in the stories of those who are still alive. They insert themselves into the stories of the people who outlive them. This is how the person who is about to die can make sense of a future in which they are not alive. Shneidman stated that these thoughts were of comfort to people facing death, in that there was a legacy of sorts. Abraham Maslow (1970), shortly before he died, illustrated Shneidman's view that we desire our stories, and indeed our selves, to continue after we die. In a piece he wrote for *Psychology Today*, he talked about all that he had written as a series of coded messages to his great-great-grandchildren. Although they had not yet been born, he hoped that they might one day learn about his words as expressions of his love for them. We are used to thinking of legacy mainly in terms of money or property but Maslow was conscious of leaving behind him expressions of affection, bits of advice, and lessons he had learned about life that might be helpful for his descendants.

In White's terms, we might say that the self and the post-self are held together within an association of membership. The dying person wants to know that they will continue to feature in the lives of their membership club, and that their lives have mattered. In contrast to a modernist view of identity as individually constructed and owned, the concepts of the post-self and the membership club provide access to an identity that outlives one's corporeal life. Both counter the possibility that our lives are inconsequential. As Shneidman stated:

To cease as though one had never been, to exit life with no hope of living on in the memory of another, to be obliterated, to be expunged from history's record – that is a fate that is literally far worse than death.

(p. 52)

It is time to return to the story of David and Dalia. In this segment, the membership club to which they belong is invoked. The club has been extended, however, to include new members, especially David's wife and children.

LORRAINE: So what has it been like for you to be witness to this very warm relationship between your mother and your wife? If your wife were here, what would she say about her relationship with your mother?

DAVID: At her funeral, my wife said, "She was my second mother." She lived with us for ten years. They had a really nice relationship for ten years. It was more about support than anything else. There was this connection between them, as my mother saw her as a daughter. In fifteen years, there was only one argument between them.

LORRAINE: How do you explain there were not more arguments in all these years?

DAVID: My wife is very welcoming and friendly also. Jovial. And they had this relationship where they would do things with each other.

LORRAINE: They were very warm and jovial women together.

DAVID: For me it was a blessing. I never had to decide between my wife and my mom.

LORRAINE: What would your mom say she appreciated about how you had a hand in that?

DAVID: She would say, "You're a good husband." And my wife would say to my mother, "You raised a good man."

64

LORRAINE: What would your mom say, when she saw you and your wife together for those ten years? What was it like for her, that you paid attention to her advice?

DAVID: She was very happy. My mom would see me being attentive to my wife, I would hug her and tell her I loved her. My mom would witness this and start crying from happiness.

LORRAINE: When your mom would see you paying attention to your wife and being affectionate, what did that mean to her?

DAVID: It meant a lot to her. She would tell my wife she was really proud of me. She didn't tell me, but would tell my wife, who then told me. She would tell my wife how much she appreciated it. She wouldn't tell me but I could see it and see her tears.

LORRAINE: When you would see her tears, did you know what that was about?

DAVID: Yes, it was for happiness.

LORRAINE: And was it happiness that all of her efforts had gone some place?

DAVID: I perceive it as, "It was worth working all these years to see my children."

LORRAINE: Is this right, David? It is almost like she gets to see the fruits of her labor.

DAVID: Exactly. She was able to see the end result. I was able to raise my children too and give them an education and so I have been able to follow her legacy in how I raise my children. This is the kind of person I would like to see in them. I am not imposing, but I am suggesting to my kids — follow this path and you will be a lovable person.

LORRAINE: When you say those non-imposing things to your kids, how do you hear your mother's voice in there?

65

DAVID: It's saying, "You did well. Now it's your job to teach them to do well."

LORRAINE: Are you conscious of that? When you say to your kids, here's a possible path or here's who I hope you become, are you aware of her voice in your head?

DAVID: Making the connections, I believe that is what I am doing. Following her legacy, but now in my own words.

LORRAINE: When you imagine saying to your kids, I want you to do well in life, if you were to imagine your mother's legacy in there, would you add anything to or subtract anything from that message?

DAVID: No, there's nothing to add or subtract. I am just doing as much as I can to make her legacy alive...She was so happy to see me be successful. She was there when I was in high school, and community college, and with my bachelors, and now. And she would say she was so proud of me. And just kept saying, "Keep going. Keep going." And now with my kids, I am telling them to keep going. I am bringing my mom's legacy alive in them. It's like hearing her voice again when I tell my kids to keep going. Keep going. Keep going.

LORRAINE: When she was in the tunnel with you, those were her words. Is that right, that she was saying, "Keep going. Keep going. We go there together."

DAVID: Yes [nodding]. To keep going and keep going together. She wanted me to go alone, but I said no. We go together. Same when she was crossing the desert with my three brothers. It was, "Keep going," and "Keep going together."

LORRAINE: So how will you keep carrying her now to keep going?

DAVID: I was thinking of quitting school recently and I told her two weeks before

she died. "No, you have to keep going."
My wife said, "Keep going." My kids said,
"Dad, keep going." So the keep going words
are alive in my wife and in my kids. So
here I am now to keep going. To honor my
wife and children and mother.

LORRAINE: Let's imagine when you graduate, and
you are walking across the stage to get
your diploma, tell me your mother's words
when you do?

DAVID: "Son, I am proud of you." She wouldn't
say much, but she would cry and I would
hug her and kiss her, because I would know
they are the tears of pride. I would say,
"This is your legacy. The fruits of your
labor."

LORRAINE: Where would you like those fruits to
go? She will walk with you across that
stage, just like she walked with you across
the desert. And then, where would you like
the walk to go?

DAVID: I would like her to go to my children. I
think I am going to see the fruits of her
labor in my kids.

The Construction of Meaning

When a person dies, the bereaved are called upon to make sense
out of what has happened and what the death means for their lives.
Death creates a pause into which explanations must flow, whether
or not the death was expected, and whether or not the relationship
was a positive one. We must pause to reevaluate and find new trib-
utaries along which the currents of connection to those who have
died might flow.

Attig (1996; 2001) insists that the bereaved must "relearn their
world". "We reweave the fabric of our lives and come to a new wholeness" (p. 38). Something resembling this approach has also been
developed by MacKinnon et al. (2014) for groups of bereaved persons with what they refer to as uncomplicated grief. The challenge,
of course, is finding a way to relate to someone who was alive and is
now dead (Rubin, Malkinson, & Witztum, 2012).

In recent years, a growing emphasis has developed on grief as featuring a variety of ways of making meaning of death. For example, Neimeyer (1998; 2001) refers to the process of relearning the world as meaning reconstruction. He stresses that bereavement forces us "to renegotiate our identity" to the extent that it is entwined in relationship with the deceased person. He describes this as generating a reconstructed personal narrative to replace the one that featured the deceased as a significant figure in the previous life of the bereaved person. The value of thinking in terms of a narrative, as Hibberd (2013) notes, is that it "intertwines" (p. 682) thoughts, emotions, and actions. The emphasis in such an expression moves away from a more passive process of suffering into a more active process of constructing meaning. When a person dies, what the living previously knew has irrevocably changed. According to Neimeyer (2001), meaning reconstruction allows the bereaved to re-author a life-story or specific events to fit within a more purposeful narrative (Neimeyer, Prigerson, & Davies, 2002).

Hibberd (2013) specifies some particular aspects of meaning-making as "sense-making, benefit finding, identity change, and purpose in life" (p. 670). Sense-making refers to making sense of the loss itself. Benefit-finding locates silver linings in the context of grief. Identity change is a shift in one's life narrative produced by, say, role changes ("I used to rely on my spouse for things I now have to do myself"). And purpose in life is about finding a new purpose for living through grief ("I am now dedicated to preventing drunk driving among young people"). Neimeyer and Gillies (2006) concur about the first three of Hibberd's categories of meaning-making, but leave off the fourth category, purpose in life, presumably because it is similar to identity change. However, Neimeyer and Sands (2011) cite research in which thirty-two distinct approaches to meaning-making were found among parents whose child had died (p. 12), although sense-making and benefit-finding were still prevalent. The sense-making effort included many themes that featured religious beliefs or a divine plan. Meanwhile, compassion for others suffering in similar ways featured highly among the benefit-finding efforts at meaning reconstruction.

In conventional grief psychology, by contrast, meaning is reconstructed in relation to the twin concepts of attachment and detachment. Meaning has been constructed, and evaluated, on the basis of how well a person is performing the culturally endorsed practices of "letting go" and "moving on". The bereaved could potentially carry out these tasks, without forming meaning about death and about afterlife, whether these meanings were expressed or remained internalized, or even were held in secret.

The relationship, however, cannot remain the same as it was during the life of the deceased. The responsibility for maintaining the relationship, for example, is much more one-sided and the voice of the deceased has to be imagined and ventriloquized by the living, rather than being spoken by the deceased. There are relational transitions that need to be acknowledged. Bereavement thus requires some degree of a shift in the meanings that we make about a relationship, simply because the responsibility for maintaining the relationship changes.

Meaning reconstruction can also incorporate the ways in which the deceased loved one might continue to be a part of the lives of the bereaved. From a postmodern perspective, the meaning to be constructed is less fixed in a single reality, and more open to the making of deliberate choices. The meanings people develop might allay emotional distress or create more suffering.

For example, when a young soldier dies, meaning given to the war by the soldier's community influences the experience of grief for their loved ones. On the one hand, a parent's sadness or anger might be palliated by believing their child died for a just cause. On the other hand, the meaning of the same child's death changes for a parent who believed the war was unjust or pointless. The meaning of the event of death might thus be weighted by the context that pertains before, during, and after the actual event. In both circumstances, the parents want the soldier's death to count for something (Klass, 2001).

Meaning construction is not, however, a singular, one-off event, but a continuous process that takes place in relation to others. The bereaved are called upon to find their way toward a new relationship with the deceased, one that is not the same as what they once had, and to construct sustained meaning in this posthumous shift. When they are guided to reconnect and rebuild a new relationship, the pain of grief is diminished. As Shapiro (1996) suggested, "Grief is resolved through the creation of a loving, growing relationship with the dead that recognizes the new psychological or spiritual (rather than corporeal) dimensions of the relationship" (p. 552).

Memory

How we conceptualize memory makes a difference to how we think of grief. The very word "remembering" is informed by drawing upon memory. How the meaning of the concept of memory has been constructed impacts not only upon what may be recalled after a person has died, but also on who has access to the vantage point of recollection. In recent history, memory has most commonly been conceptualized in terms of the individual's cognitive system for recalling stored data and as an accumulation of reinforced habits (Middleton & Edwards, 1990). Such a construction of memory as living within the individual has been founded on container metaphors. Small fragments of experience are housed within such containers to form a whole (Middleton & Brown, 2005).

In the modern scientific paradigm, memory has also been connected to the neurological function of the brain. Accordingly, aspects of memory have been classified, studied, and named. There is an interest in the distinction between short-term memory and long-term memory, for example, particularly in discussions of the effects of Alzheimer's disease. Memory can be seen as representational or dispositional (Bernecker, 2008), which contrasts the veracity of recalled images with the process of constructing them. Memory has usually been constructed in the modern view as an internal, subjective experience that can be compared with an external world of objective truth (Shotter, 1990). Psychology has, for the most part, not conceptualized memory in terms of a relational dimension, or considered group or collective memory. These emphases would require the incorporation of social psychology and anthropology to socialize memory (Middleton & Brown, 2005).

To understand re-membering practices for those living with grief, we need to look critically at how the concept of memory is constructed. We must account for the participants in a memory, emphasizing the social as well as the individual implications of what is being remembered. In citing Misztalci's work on memory, Middleton and Brown (2005) addressed the shift in perspective and the implied issues of power in the construction of a memory:

> who is remembering what version of the past and to which end? The importance of sociological concerns is its emphasis on the social organization and mediation of individual memory. Although it is the individual who is seen as the agent of remembering, the nature of what is remembered is profoundly shaped by "what has been shared with others".

(p. 14)

The more relational account of memory has dramatic implications for grief psychology. We only need to look at the psychological diagnosis of mental illness, and at subsequent intervention techniques, to note the impact of conceiving memory in modernist terms. For instance, in the 1980s, much was written about "recovered memories" for clients who suspected they had been abused in childhood (Geraerts, McNally, & Jelicic, 2008; McNally, 2005). The theory assumed that, in situations of trauma, the psyche buried the horrific memory and the defense mechanism of repression was employed to cope with trauma. The unattended memory had the ability to haunt the client with a host of symptoms, including eating disorders, disturbed sleep, dissociative experiences, and unsuccessful relationships. Therapeutic practice "retrieved" memories to free clients from these ghosts. Practices that promoted memory recovery were built upon a particular modern definition of memory, in which memory operated like a camera, recording the events of one's life. Such recordings were stored, as if they were files on a computer. Memories were assumed to be individual commodities and remembering was a solitary practice of discovering what was stored on the hard drive of one's mind.

Memories were, thus, accessible through proper access to the hard drive of stored data. Much of modern counseling practice was built on these assumptions that both employ rigid cognitive models and treat the brain with an exalted status. Through insight and introspection, one could free oneself from whatever the painful memory of childhood might be, whether traumatic or not. Memory has been considered solely as an individual, neurological, and biological product that can be trained to benefit its owner. The *who*, as noted in the preceding Middleton and Brown excerpt, becomes the individual client; the *what* has been the freedom from a troubling event, and the *to which end* has been to fit the self within a cultural construction of happiness.

The postmodern alternative is to view memory as embedded in social networks, relationships, and cultural processes (Bartlett, 1932; Middleton & Brown, 2005; Middleton & Edwards, 1986; 1990). "Social memory" is the collection of stories, processes, and relationships that shape the context and meaning of personal memory (Middleton & Brown, 2005; Middleton & Edwards, 1990). Remembered stories are not owned by one person, but are a creation and construction of a shared language that is not only relevant to the past, but is also reflective of current concerns and constitutive of future stories. Middleton and Brown (1990) posit that memory of events, whether happy marriages or traumatic deaths, are recounted via collective and shared experience. Future recollections are stoked by the stories of the larger whole, rather than solely by an individual perspective. In fact, it may be impossible to have any memory that is not contextualized with another person or a family or a group.

Stories can also be told in a communal environment and handed down through generations. In the process, stories can expand and contract. The fabric of a story is woven into what it will become in the future, when the memory is recounted. Each retelling connects to various other times, when the memory will again be shared, and with each person who was, at one point or another, a fellow teller of the story.

Fredric Bartlett was one of the first psychologists to highlight the social and cultural process of memory. In his research during the 1920s, participants were told a simple story and then asked to repeat what they had heard. As they repeated the story, they retold it with slight variations that reflected the participants' cultural background and emphasized knowledge of particular interest to them. According to Bartlett (1932), participants supported their recollection of the event as they were informed by similar situations. Memory, in his view, is attentive to the event and resonates with the person's historical and contextual experiences.

Bartlett explained that personal interests would be underscored and would fill gaps in the story-tellings. He also argued that what was considered of interest had a direct social origin and was influenced by context. Memories, according to Bartlett, are thus not "fixed and lifeless", but coordinated with other people in a way that responds to the shape and hue of what is being recalled.

Memories are conveyed, exchanged, and constructed largely in language (Bartlett, 1932; Middleton & Brown, 2005; Middleton & Edwards, 1990; Shotter, 1990) and we cannot make sense of them outside our linguistic traditions (Shotter, 1990). Specific memories are always part of a larger collective memory, shaped by the cultural transmission of rituals, events, and images, which are then used to negotiate shared meanings that transcend time. Remembering involves stepping into a stream of meanings (Bakhtin, 1986) and, according to Middleton and Brown (2005), "Collective remembering is a continuous dialogue between present and past, where what is recalled is used as a 'framework for meaning' for understanding the present without determining the direction of the future" (p. 22).

Postmodern Grief Psychology

From a postmodern perspective, memories are not owned by the individual who has died. They do not necessarily die with the person's brain, or end at the limit of the individual's experience. Instead, memories have a home in "prevailing approved general interest, the persistent social custom" (Bartlett, 1932, p. 244). Memories of people thus remain available for "determining the direction of the future". Shared memories do not have to be "fixed and lifeless" (Bartlett, 1932, p. 311), but may remain vitally alive. They are not, as was once thought, an individual's internal recollection, but an event and a process that occurs in time and in relationship. Middleton and Brown (2005) support Bartlett's conclusion that memory is produced not within the individual, but in the context of social groups that "can continuously remake the past" (p. 21). Memory thus becomes a construction that is performed.

It follows that memory can be understood as transcending death. It continues to live in the collective processes of shared meaning-making within communities. The deceased's stories, rituals, and images can, therefore, be revitalized and interwoven into the lives of the living in the present. Historical memories that contain threads of recollection and meanings are all part of the larger tapestry contained in a cultural context.

The implication for counseling is that therapeutic conversation might facilitate all of this to happen. It is a strikingly different purpose than what has often been described in accounts of grief therapy. The reality to be accepted here is not one of individual isolation, but one in which stories continue to be exchanged and in which the reverberations of the life of the deceased continue to echo, long after death. In these reverberations, new tones might even be heard as new developments are folded into the mix.

Narrative Therapy and Grief

The emerging field of narrative therapy has its philosophical roots in the theories of social constructionism. As a postmodern theory, much of its practice has been guided by new ideas about the self, relationships, identity, memory, power, knowledge, language, and story. Originally introduced to the family therapy field by Michael White and David Epston (1990), narrative therapy has been widely developed throughout the world and applied to a variety of personal, social, and political problems. Narrative therapy provides counselors with a means to use the premises of social constructionism in conversations that construct changes in people's lives. According to White (1991), "the narrative metaphor proposes that persons live their lives by stories – that these stories are shaping of life, and that they have real, not imagined, effects – and that these stories provide the structure of life" (p. 28).

As narrative therapy has become known worldwide, the focus on story and meaning in a therapeutic model has been found useful in many settings and with many types of problems. Narrative therapy has been successfully used in various settings, such as family therapy (Madsen, 2007; White, 2007), community work (Freedman, 2014), prisons (Denborough, 1996; Ikonomopoulos, Smith, & Schmidt, 2015), school counseling (Winslade & Monk, 2007), group work (Hedtke, 2012b), and mediation (Winslade & Monk, 2000), to name a few. Equally varied have been the topics and problem areas to which narrative practices have been applied. For example, narrative practices have been successfully used with disordered eating (Gremillion, 2003; Maisel, Epston, & Borden, 2004), childhood abuse (Mann, 2006), addictions (Clark, 2014; Monk, Winslade, Crocket, & Epston, 1997), working with children (Smith & Nylund, 1997; Nylund, 2000), addressing homelessness (Baumgartner & Williams, 2014), understanding learning disabilities (Olsen, 2015), dealing with HIV/ AIDS (Ncube, 2006), and trauma (Denborough, 2006).

The Dulwich Centre in Adelaide, Australia has been at the hub of narrative information since 1983. It has not only been instrumental in the development of narrative ideas and practices, but has also offered extensive worldwide training in the theoretical and practice elements of narrative therapy. Its publishing house has been a mainstay of narrative books and professional journals. There are thousands of therapists and community organizers around the world associated with narrative practices, many of whom have read or studied materials from the Dulwich Centre.

For the purposes of this text, we have focused on a singular element of narrative re-membering conversations and practices. This focus was specifically introduced to the field by Michael White (1989). While re-membering conversations can be used in relation to a host of varying concerns in counseling, the focus here is specific to the use of re-membering conversations for the dying and bereaved. Let us briefly explain the history and meaning of "re-membering".

Michael White's article, "Saying Hullo Again", introduced a new approach to conversations with bereaved people. White had been influenced by Barbara Myerhoff, specifically the ideas of membership and re-membering. While White did not expressly use this metaphor in 1989, he did reference Myerhoff's work and referred to "reincorporation" of the person who has died, in speaking with a client whose partner had died six years previously. We see further traces of Myerhoff in his later work (Epston & White, 1992; White, 1997; 2007) and he specifically used the term "re-membering" in 1997. The concept was later developed for use in many contexts besides death and grief (Russell & Carey, 2002).

In the title of his 1989 article, White confronted the assumption in modern grief counseling that the bereaved must say goodbye to those who have died. He believed that such an approach created distress for clients:

Without prompting they [the clients] put therapists in touch with their loss and its subsequent effect on their life, freely relating the details of their sense of emptiness, worthlessness, and feelings of depression. Such is their despair that I have often felt quite overwhelmed at the outset of therapy.

(p. 29)

Rather than pursuing further conversations of completion, White explained how he endeavored through the "saying hullo" metaphor to pursue a new line of inquiry. He hoped to open up possibilities for the relationship between the deceased and the living to be reclaimed. He proposed a series of questions to his client, Mary, about her partner, Ron, which challenged the cultural assumptions prescribing emotional distance between the living and the deceased. By remembering and reaffirming Ron's belief in Mary, and his stories about their relationship strength, Ron became linguistically accessible to her. This line of inquiry gave Mary respite from the pain she had encountered in her attempts to say goodbye to Ron. She stated, "When I discovered that Ron didn't have to die for me, that I didn't have to separate from him, I became less preoccupied with him and life was richer" (p. 31).

White concluded that the careful reincorporation of the lost relationship resolved what has been thought of as "pathological mourning" or "delayed grief". The bereaved person gains the opportunity for a new relationship with her own self and engages in a re-authoring of her life to include the hopes and dreams and stories of the deceased. This line of inquiry gave Mary respite from the pain.

White's (1997) book expanded on re-membering ideas and practices. The membership metaphor moved a therapeutic conversation gracefully around the fixation on identity as defined by biological connection to a family. Incorporating the new idea of membership afforded clients the possibility of actively engaging in the reconstruction of identity conclusions through re-membering stories. The preferred membership constellations resulted from agentic choice by the client, rather than being formed exclusively on the basis of birthright. White borrowed from Myerhoff (1982) to name these conversations "re-membering practices".

To signify this special type of recollection, the term re-membering may be used, calling attention to the reaggregation of members, the figures who belong to one's life story, one's own prior selves, as well as significant others who are a part of the story. Re-membering then, is a purposive, significant unification, quite different from the passive continuous fragmentary flickering of images and feelings that accompany other activities in the normal flow of consciousness.

(p. 111)

Myerhoff, and then White, employed the use of the hyphen for "re-membering" to set this word apart from reminiscence. It is intended to connect the story and the person and embed the connection in the membered status. According to Russell and Carey (2002), "The hyphen is all-important in thinking about the distinctions between re-membering and remembering, as it draws attention to this notice of membership rather than to a simple recalling of history" (p. 24).

Re-membering with the hyphen has therapeutic value in many contexts but the thinking remains consistent. Re-authoring the membership status of key figures in one's life increases agency for the person at the center. For example, a client who was abused by a biological parent can create intentional distance by reconfiguring the membered status of those in their life. The process of re-aggregation affords clients the opportunity to have a greater say about the status of particular relationships. White (1997) referred to the aggregated groups of one's membership using the metaphor of a club.

The image of membered lives brings into play the metaphor of a "club" – a club of life is evoked. This metaphor opens up options for the exploration of how a person's club of life . . . is constituted through its membership, and of how the membership of this club is arranged in terms of rank or status.

(p. 22)

We are all born into such a club and along the way we add to, and sometimes subtract from, its membership list. Immediate family members usually have a place of significance in the membership club, and we then add friends, colleagues, partners, children, and even pets. In a sense, membership and narrative have the ability to transcend death. If the stories exist within a group of people, when one member dies, the stories can remain alive in the membership club. This idea frees grief psychology to think differently about a relationship after a loved one has died. Those facing death can charge the membership club with the task of maintaining their stories among the shared stories of the club. They can bestow their legacy through stories that will live on in others' tellings.

The bereaved can take comfort in knowing their loved one continues on in a storied form, in the shared membership club. The need for a tidy ending before death is thus removed. Myerhoff (1992) notes that completeness is "sacrificed for moral and aesthetic purposes" (p. 240). There is no need for a dying person to be finished with their stories before they are ready to reach the end of life. David's mother's admonition to "keep going", for example, continues her voice and the fruits of her labor indefinitely.

Another example of a context in which this process can be observed lies in the deliberate construction of a social identity for a stillborn child. Godel (2007) cites many instances in which parents use photographs, poetry, websites, funerals, and memorials to document the imagined life of a stillborn child. Often a narrative is constructed of the meaning of the child's life. The continued telling of stories crafts an ongoing relationship, and in fact may encourage a new appreciation of the relationship. Often, in death, a relationship can be reborn. The task for the living is to find a place for the voice and stories of the dead to reverberate around the club in ways that remain contextually fluid. Others have suggested that maintaining a connection with the deceased is comforting and helpful (Attig, 1996; 2000; Klass, Silverman, & Nickman, 1996; Neimeyer, 2001), but the concept of ongoing membership invigorates this connection with much stronger purpose. Moreover, bereaved people who look for avenues to continue the bond and affirm the relationship can create an ongoing relationship, rather than simply preserving what was in the past.

Re-membering Practices

To craft a conversation where the deceased person's stories continue to feature, we must start from the presupposition that a relationship does not die when a body dies. The self that dies continues to be distributed through many who shared their stories and were impacted by their life. The same self may still continue to "meet" people, in a storied form, long after their death and that introduction may enliven the experience of those to whom they are introduced. In this sense, the telling of stories can be said to bring the dead to life. Let us outline a few of the keys that unlock such a conversation and include questions from our example.

The first aspect a re-membering conversation must include is an introduction of sorts (Hedtke, 2012a). The living need to know who the deceased person was and who they continue to be. Without such an introduction, it would be hard to know how to inquire or respond to the bereaved. Therefore, grief counseling should feature an invitation early on to the bereaved person to introduce the deceased person to the counselor, as was done in the first questions asked of David about his mother. Asking some introductory questions stands in contrast to telling about how the person died and is intended to bring the life of the deceased into the counseling conversation by painting a picture of who the deceased person was.

We intentionally use present-tense verbs when speaking about where the conversation currently lives and the past tense when referencing the deceased person's former activities. Future tense or subjunctive verbs are useful when speaking about a future where the stories and the relationships might continue to feature.

Introduction often renders visible what the discourse of grief psychology erases. It sets the stage for weaving the legacies of the deceased into the practices of the living. Introductory questions paint a picture of the deceased. It would not be uncommon to ask, "Could you tell me about the person who died?" or "Who was he? What did he look like? Sound like?" The intent is to invite the deceased into the conversation in such a way that counselors will be able to craft future questions that can be specific to the relationship, rather than following a boilerplate model. We would also seek an introduction to a deceased person's interests, hobbies, professions, passions, and things they enjoyed. These questions build the foundation of a re-membering conversation. They are the portal through which aspects of relationship might be reinstated between the living and the dead. They treat the dead as silent partners, who nevertheless exert an influence in a conversation. Re-membering assumes that grief is about at least two people, the living and the deceased, and counselors need to learn about both of them.

Beyond the initial introduction, the counseling process can focus on who else mattered to the deceased person and a counselor can seek to gather a sense of the community in which the relationship belongs. Again, in the conversation with David, we hear of his mother's connection to him, his brothers, his children, and a larger sense of community. All of these contexts serve as entry points into a conversation where his mother continues to be made visible.

Making a deceased person's stories accessible through a variety of pathways starts to construct bridges between what was and what now is. This, of course, is only appropriate when the relationship itself is of the quality that can serve as a resource for the bereaved person. On these bridges the storied legacy of the deceased can be affirmed, refreshed, continued, developed, or even enhanced in the years following their deaths. Stories become precious gifts that can be bequeathed through generations and called up in times of challenge or celebration. When David is asked, "Having her as your mom, did this open some important life lessons about how to treat others?", he is invited to reflect on the bridges between her and his values. The opportunity is thus afforded for him to reflect, whenever he treats another person kindly, on the importance of his mother in his life. When he teaches his children about kindness, the bridges transcend generations. He might talk to his children about how their grandmother's kindness continues to be expressed in their actions. Myerhoff (2007) puts it like this:

79

That means we have to reincorporate them; it means we have to pay attention to what it is they tell us about who we are. We have to find out how to feed them back to ourselves, and how to be nourished by them, and how to tell the people who give them to us that we are nourished by them.

(p. 25)

Subjunctive Mood

When speaking of the dead, it is customary in Western culture to speak in the past tense. This cultural habit linguistically seals off the dead from participation in the present and renders them more distant and less accessible. It is a point of tenderness with which persons who are bereaved often struggle. They are used to the availability of the present tense for talking about their relationships with those they are close to. Death makes it awkward to do so and risks approbation or disapproval, because speaking about the deceased in the present tense might be interpreted as not accepting reality, or worse.

The English language leaves few choices in this situation. Modernist thinking has favored sharp distinctions between the past and the present and perhaps makes grief harder to know how to handle. Our language is lacking in how to speak of the dead. We, therefore, need some new linguistic tools to use in therapeutic conversations. The intentional use of the subjunctive mood offers this possibility. Even though commentators like H.L. Menken (1956) and Somerset Maugham (1949) have written obituaries for the subjunctive in English, it nevertheless stubbornly refuses to die. We would suggest that the subjunctive mood might actually be a dear friend of the dead and of re-membering conversation.

The subjunctive is the voice of the "as if". It enables a speaker to make speculative references without committing to the actuality of a situation. It is thus the grammatical mood of the virtual and it opens up a space between the past and the present. Its importance for the re-membering conversation is that it enables us to ask about what someone *might* say, *would* do, *may* have to contribute, if they *were* able to speak. The use of the auxiliary verbs (might, would, may, and were) is the most common way that, in English, the subjunctive mood hangs on. The subjunctive allows for an inquiry into the deceased person's preferences through ventriloquizing their voice. This is achieved by asking the living to speak as the imagined voice of the dead and to weigh in on preferences, to comment on possible outcomes, and to editorialize on events in the present.

For example, a counselor may ask a question like, "What might your loved one notice about how you are handling these challenges?" The "might" steps through the veil of indicative reality and opens up the virtual, subjunctive mood. It is this stepping through that places the deceased in a speaking position again and often boosts a sense of them as still having agency. Such questions as, "If your loved one were here now speaking to us, could you imagine what she might say?" open up relational inclusion that can shift indicative realities. It is thus possible to bring the imaginal world into actuality by inquiring how the living person is impacted by the imagined voice. To this end, the counselor might ask the living person, "What do you think of this idea?" or "How does knowing this make the pain easier to bear?" Notice here that these verbs are indicative. The subjunctive has thus allowed a conversation to move from the virtual to the actual as the living person begins to follow the advice of the deceased person's subjunctive "voice".

Jerome Bruner (1982), the American psychologist, spoke of the subjunctive as making it easier to entertain the possible. According to him, personal development is not only achieved by speaking about what is "real", but by entering the playful world of the subjunctive. Since the dead do not "really" speak, the subjunctive language supports an effective alternative to the linguistically binary choice of speaking in either the past or the present tense through the use of indicative verbs. The subjunctive can provide a place where the dead person's voice and influence can live on.

It may also be thought of as a liminal space in which it is temporarily useful to pause in the midst of a rite of passage, as Van Gennep (1961) and Turner (1986) have conceptualized it. The advantage for grief counseling is that the voice of the deceased can be invoked in a way that can be incorporated into the consciousness of the living. Crafting a future can intentionally include the products of this consciousness and an interplay between the living and the dead can be instigated. In the process, a counseling conversation can intentionally seek out moments of beauty, which may be expressed, for example, as a cherished value or a life lesson worth holding on to. Layering reflections of what the deceased might say into the daily tasks of the living has the potential to make the pain of the grief more bearable.

A central purpose of a re-membering conversation may be encapsulated in a subjunctive inquiry, such as, "Who might you become when you see yourself through your loved one's eyes?" This is an inquiry into the process of becoming, but it is not the becoming of an individual, like decathecting the energy from a relationship and purging oneself of any sense of relationship to the deceased. Rather, it invokes a process of becoming that does not dispatch the memory, legacy, and stories of the dead to the grave but seeks to maximize the possibility of the deceased person being woven into the lives of the living.

In this chapter, we have traversed the revisionist territory of grief psychology. Themes that have emerged have emphasized the continuing-bonds idea and the practice of saying hullo again, rather than goodbye. The importance of memory for the ongoing life of the deceased is obvious, but less appreciated is the account of memory as a social process, rather than as a primarily individual, cognitive process. When this perspective is adopted, the idea of re-membering as located within a community of identity – a membership club – becomes salient. However, the focus of the chapter is not just on these concepts as empirical descriptions of what people who are grieving do. Our interest lies in the implications for practice of these ideas. Narrative therapy offers an important avenue for the development of such practice. This chapter has illustrated how this might be achieved. It ends with an account of the use to which the subjunctive might be put for this purpose. In the next chapter, we shall take up some of the identity shifts that emerge from these practices.

82

CHAPTER 4

Becoming Bereaved

Through the defining events of life, all of us seek to "become some-body". Smyth and Hattam (2004) used this expression to talk about young people who were "dropping out, drifting off or being excluded" from school but who nevertheless sought out pathways of becoming. We think this idea applies also to bereavement and is a useful way to talk about identity issues and grief. If pursuing learning, or develop-ing an identity as "a teenager", is always a process of becoming, then bereavement might also be a site of becoming different from the per-son one was before the death of a significant other. It is the process of defining oneself as different in response to events that shifts our ever-changing sense of self.

The approach to identity we shall take in this chapter emphasizes becoming rather than just being. Many developmental psychologies focus on achieving states of being; that is, completing milestones as points of arrival. The focus is often about the mastery of such a state or accomplishing intellectual and emotional permanency rather than on the fluidity of the journey. To illustrate the difference, think of how the question, "Who are you?" leads toward different answers than the question, "Who are you becoming?" The latter question treats identity as always fluid and in process, rather than as static and given, and rec-ognizes the identity migrations that people are always making. It also breaks away from the "slice and dice" compartmentalized approach to identity that assigns identity as a fixed feature of belonging to larger social groups, say to ethnic groups or genders or social classes. Becoming, rather than being, emphasizes mobility and change ahead of stability and orients toward a future. It references the past as well, rather than trying to isolate an image of identity in the present moment as timeless.

Conceptualizing identity as becoming impacts on how a bereaved person might think about themselves and how those in the counseling professions might be helpful to those who are living with grief. A person would not just be assigned membership of the category of bereaved persons. Likewise, the dead would not be relegated only to a past identity but are also in the process of becoming other than who they were.

It might sound slightly odd to think of a dead person as continuing to become more than who they once were, but thinking of identity as produced in stories frees us to do just this. Bakhtin (1986) points out, for example, that the Shakespeare that his contemporaries knew was not the same person that we know now. Martin Luther King, too, has continued to take on new qualities and added significance since his death. If this happens for widely exalted public figures, it can also happen for ordinary people too, if we pay close enough attention. For example, for someone whose body dies, identity may continue to evolve through the discursive positions (Davies & Harré, 1990) accorded to this person by others who participate in the process of identifying him or her, in tiny or in more substantial ways.

Hence it makes more sense to speak of identity in terms of a migration than a destination. We are always moving somewhere. Gilles Deleuze (1987) spoke of people in the modern world as nomads, rather than as settlers in this sense. The implication is that counselors should help people trace the identity journey and map out its trajectory, rather than fix its coordinates.

As Deleuze (1990) also argues, the event is logically prior to identity. That is, a counselor might understand someone better by inquiring into the events that are implicated in who the person is becoming than by starting from an identity category and inquiring into how the person might resemble (be identical to, or identify with) others in the same category. Another way of saying this is that identity is contingent and contextual, rather than foundational.

This approach necessitates a relational approach to identity, rather than an individualistic one. Identity shifts in a dialogical relation to others (Bakhtin, 1986). It can be said to be contingent upon the lines of force (Deleuze, 1988) that give shape to a relation. As identity is never completely under a person's control, it cannot be considered the personal property of an individual, but belongs to the production of shared narratives through which meaning and power are exchanged. From this perspective, a singular identity is never completely stable but is subject to the winds that blow across the face of a relationship. The identity story that a person develops might be thought of as the most common positions that are taken up or given in associations with others across a range of relationships. This includes, of course, relationships between the bereaved and the deceased and the way in which the stories of the deceased are told.

The implications for grief counseling are that a counseling conversation might become a site for the development of an account of becoming and could itself constitute an event. The old concept of the need to "accept reality" when a person dies does not allow much room for becoming, and limits the range of stories that can be recognized. This approach appears to treat identity as a cloak that must be worn. More useful is Todd May's (2005) question that derives from the philosophy of Deleuze: "Who might one be?" It is a question that has a forward-looking aspect and also recognizes a spirit of experimentation, rather than resignation to simple facts. We are reaching, therefore, for an approach to counseling people affected by grief that is more open-ended than any stage model can offer.

The point is that the identity a person becomes is narrowed by the forces of subjectivation, but they remain indeterminate. In what follows, we shall illustrate this point with reference to some challenging situations, in which the identities of the bereaved and the deceased are constrained by cultural expectations. Good counseling, however, can help people become other than such expectations.

Suicide, Homicide, and Stories of Identity

The identity of a deceased person can be narrowed depending on the mode of death. When a person dies an unexpected death at their own hand or at the hand of another person, the stories surrounding the death itself can eclipse the stories of the life of the deceased. Families and loved ones are left with a residue of questions about their loved one's final moments that can haunt them for years. While counselors are often called upon to help make meaning out of such challenging events, the identity stories fixed by the moment of death can become stumbling blocks to the deceased person becoming anything else.

Some situations present people with particular challenges in making meaning of death. Violent or abrupt death is clearly an example of this. Hence, making meaning of suicide, murder, plane crashes, car accidents, and other accidental deaths is especially challenging. What often occupies people in these circumstances is what is referred to as "sense-making" (Hibberd, 2013; Neimeyer & Gillies, 2006; Neimeyer et al., 2008; Neimeyer, Klass, & Dennis, 2014) – especially making sense of the death itself. Such deaths are often the most difficult to make sense of and hence meaning-making is at its most acute in these circumstances (Neimeyer & Gillies, 2006; Neimeyer & Sands, 2011). Jordan and McIntosh (2011) agree, specifically with regard to suicide, and add that making meaning of suicide requires more time and effort to reclaim the parts of the relationship that have not been obscured by the violent death (Rynearson, 2001).

One of the first concerns bereaved persons in these circumstances have is to explain the death to themselves and to each other. They are often left ruminating over questions that bother them. "Why did he take his own life?" "What was so painful that she resorted to such an extreme decision?" "Did he suffer pain before he died?" These are pragmatic questions that are hard to get past unless they are addressed. They deserve to be faced squarely. Counseling bereaved persons, when someone has taken their own life, makes these questions especially poignant. It might often be best done in company with others who cared about the deceased person, such as family members or friends.

Neimeyer et al. (2008) suggest asking several related questions of bereaved college students who are seeking to make sense of sudden deaths:

- How did you make sense of the death or loss at the time?
- How do you interpret the loss now?
- What philosophical or spiritual beliefs contributed to your adjustment to this loss?
- How were they affected by it?
- Are there ways in which this loss disrupted the continuity of your life story?
- How, over time, have you dealt with this?

(p. 32)

However, the awful nature of the death itself can easily overshadow any other sense of the person's life before they died. If we are not careful, we can give more power to the death than it deserves. This, in turn, creates a situation in which the loss occasioned by a person's death overshadows other aspects of the person's life that might be embraced as narrative themes and help make sense of the death (Murphy et al., 1999). A re-membering conversation can help get past this dilemma.

After listening to clients' thoughts about the reasons for the suicide, it is possible to ask questions about the person's life, rather than only about the death. Neimeyer, Klass, and Dennis (2014) refer to this as the "back story". This is a useful description that signals where to look for it, but it is important that the back story not remain in the background. There is enough to be gained from inquiring into it sufficiently for it to become much more central. As Neimeyer, Klass, and Dennis also emphasize, there is considerable therapeutic value in constructing a narrative of connection between the deceased and the bereaved "in lieu of a final goodbye" (p. 489). At first, asking questions about the life of the deceased might focus on links between the person's cherished values and the reason for the suicide. However, it can expand from there into an inquiry into the links between the lives (despite the death) of the deceased person and the bereaved person.

It is certainly understandable to try and piece together shattered puzzle pieces when death does not square with stories of life. However, we want to question how identities produced by suicide or homicide, for example, tend to overshadow other possible identity stories. They leave out much of what can be helpful in the aftermath of suicide, homicide, and other tragic deaths. To counter this possibility, it is necessary to re-include identity narratives that derive from the life of the deceased before the tragedy of death.

Let us illustrate this with an interview with Krystal, who is speaking about her paternal grandfather who died by his own hand.

LORRAINE: Krystal, I know – from talking to you before – that you have had somebody who died as a result of suicide.

KRYSTAL: Uh hum.

LORRAINE: Can we talk about him for a little while? Just kind of get a sense of who he was in your life, who he continues to be in your life, and maybe a little exploration of the impact of the way in which he died. Can you introduce us to him?

KRYSTAL: Yeah, my grandpa's name is Ken. I called him, sometimes mostly, Grandpa Ken, and then other times G-Pa. Which a way he used to sign his letters in e-mails to me. He was a really hard worker throughout his life, and he did mostly construction.

LORRAINE: OK.

KRYSTAL: He was like the "man's man", but so kind and gentle. I don't know that he had always been that way, but with me he was that way, and with some of my younger cousins.

LORRAINE: OK. While you were growing up, he was an important person in your life? Did you see him very often? Was he around in your life?

KRYSTAL: Yes, he lived in the general area, and every time there was a family event or even when he just wanted to see me, he would make sure that he would pick me up, because transportation was an issue for my mom. So he always went way out of his way to include me, so I saw him really frequently.

LORRAINE: So what was it like when you were a little girl? What kinds of things would you do with him?

KRYSTAL: He had a quad [a four wheel motorbike], and so he would take me in the hills on the quad and I'd sit on the front. He'd strap me in with a bungee cord — not the safest of things. But we would go riding through the hills. I would go and stay over at his house for the weekend, or even for, like, weeks. And we went to Denny's a lot. Denny's was like our spot. He would pick me up from school, so I could ditch school a little bit, which was always really cool and special when I was little.

LORRAINE: I can imagine riding on this quad, being bungee-corded in, going to Denny's, like this really must have been a wonderful experience for a little girl.

KRYSTAL: Yeah. Probably one of the best experiences of my childhood, since it wasn't that way with my mom and my home situation. So when I was with my grandpa, that was like a total escape.

In the start of this conversation, we see how close Krystal's grandfather is to her. The introduction of him quickly paints a picture of a man whose life matters and whose stories are vibrantly alive for

Krystal to recount at any time she chooses. Her relationship with him is woven into the story of her own becoming. The questions asked intentionally privilege stories of his life, not his death, and call forth the specialness between the two of them. From this starting point, Krystal is free to invest in the valuing of his life and legacy. It is this valuing that counters the sometimes dismissive attitude and devaluing of persons' lives who die by their own hand. We hear a strong story of how Krystal's grandfather matters to her, not only in her childhood, but also as an adult. How he matters is undoubtedly different as an adult from what it was when she was young. It will also continue to accrue meaning for her after his death.

While the cause of a person's death might feature in the stories of legacy or purpose that the bereaved have access to, the way a person died may also potentially limit the opportunity to connect to stories of living. The stigma of suicide casts a shadow over these stories, in part because suicide is seen as a preventable death (Burks, 2005). This shadow is often laid at the feet of the bereaved. The bereaved, as a result, often experience greater emotional distress than with a non-suicidal death. Such distress is assumed to implicate a response similar to a form of post-traumatic stress (Wood, Byram, Gosling, & Stokes, 2012). Stories might circulate of the bereaved party failing the person who died. Feelings of guilt can result and compound the experience, potentially truncating any positive experience of an ongoing continuing bond, particularly in the case of a child's response to a parent's suicide. In this context, the re-membering conversation shifts to one in which the construction of identity is linked to a renewed connection with the stories of the person's life. We see this in what Krystal highlights about her grandfather.

89

LORRAINE: What did you think, when you were young, and he would bust you out of school, or take you to Denny's, or do all these things? What was it that he liked about Krystal?

KRYSTAL: It wasn't until high school that I kind of really knew what he thought of me, and he told me, and he told my mom, that he thought that I was so smart and so kind and spirited and he liked that I had opinions about things, and that I stuck to my guns about them.

LORRAINE: He was able to value this and see it in you.

KRYSTAL: Uhm hum.

LORRAINE: What's your sense, Krystal, about how that's impacted on you as an adult woman?

KRYSTAL: I think about him all the time. And I think about the fact that what I'm doing right now, he would be proud of. I'm always thinking about him when I know that I have accomplished something. I know that he would be like my biggest cheerleader. So even though he's passed, I still very much think about him and he's still very much part of my process.

LORRAINE: I'm wondering about what that was like for you, five years ago, that he died from his own hand. How did you make sense out of that?

KRYSTAL: I feel really different, I felt different than I think most people might have. At the time, when I first found out, I was so distraught. But then later when I was calm, I felt okay with his decision, in a way. Because the circumstances around the death led some people to believe that it was accidental, and that just made me furious. I just could not accept that it was an accident. It made me absolutely furious to know that somebody so amazing and so special could accidentally pass. And so a lot of people might be more outraged by purposeful passing, but I felt a little more comforted at that thought, that he chose it.

LORRAINE: Because why?

KRYSTAL: Because I know so much about him, and his values and how he intended to take care of his family, and I know that, when the economy crashed, it really impacted him and his idea of what a man ought to be. He was struggling financially and identity-wise. I just think that, if he had chosen it, then maybe it was like his final act to take care of his family.

LORRAINE: So is this right, that it's almost as if his intentional death makes us view that he stood for something, that was congruent or consistent with G-Pa's life?

KRYSTAL: Yes, his life yes. Mine? I wish, no, I wish it hadn't. But consistent with his life and his values, I think so.

LORRAINE: And if it had been an accidental death, then would that diminish the opportunity for him to have agency?

KRYSTAL: Yes, yes. In a weird way, yeah, it does, that would feel worse. That would feel way more tragic to me, because that agency piece is very important to me.

LORRAINE: And would that agency piece also be something that, knowing your grandpa the way you do, would also be something important for G-Pa?

KRYSTAL: Yes.

LORRAINE: To say that he has control over his destiny.

Finding Agency in Suicide and Sudden Death

Krystal is able to hold more than one story as meaningful about her grandfather's death. She is able to incorporate multiple access points into how she constructs the meaning of his life, his death, and his ongoing importance in her life. His identity, in her hands, begins with her sense of shock at his death, travels through her responses to others' stories about him, and reaches a place where she can appreciate his agency in taking his own life as an act of caring for his family. He can thus become different things for her at different moments. Achieving these possibilities, however, may require an intentional process by the bereaved person, often with the assistance of a skilled counselor who can inquire into intricate knowledges about the deceased person and the various points of connection between the living and the dead. Lorraine continues to trace the trajectory of Krystal's understanding.

LORRAINE: When you initially found out that
         he had died, you said that it was quite
         upsetting, but then, as you took on more
         understanding about him and his life, this
         shift came for you. Do you know what it
         was, Krystal, that helped you see those
         things differently?

KRYSTAL: I just really started thinking about
         him and who he was, rather than what every-
         body else was talking about, which was,
         "How could he do this to us?" But it wasn't
         about us. I don't think that he did any-
         thing to us. So I started to really think
         about his own person and what was impor-
         tant to him. I feel like I really knew him
         better than his kids and his other grand-
         kids. I feel like I was better equipped
         to understand maybe what he was thinking
         the moments before, and maybe the planning
         process, if there was any planning ...

92

When we affirm such relational intricacies, we do not need to think
in absolute terms about a person's death. Doing so could narrow the
story of a person's life. This could also be true when a person's death
is not the result of suicide, but perhaps at the hands of another person, or in an unexpected or sudden death, such as in a plane crash
or motor vehicle accident. For example, Robin Thompson, mother
to Ashley, founded The Art of Driving Outreach Program, following
Ashley's death in 2003 (http://theartofdriving.org). Robin felt com-
pelled to do so, both to honor her daughter, and also to make sense
of her own loss in the hope of sparing another parent the pain she
had experienced. Not only does this foundation provide education,
training, and advocacy for parents and teens about safe driving, it also
creates a living memorial that affirms the importance of Ashley's life,
and gives new meaning to the way in which she died, through making
important contributions to others' lives. Robin's grief thus becomes
not only about Ashley's death as tragic. It grows a new meaning as the
launching point for others to benefit.

Krystal, too, tells how she fashioned a new place where her grandfather would have meaning to her, long after his death. Like Robin
Thompson's reconstruction of the meaning of her daughter's life,

and death, as standing for something important, this effort brings Krystal's grandfather posthumously into a new set of possibilities with her. Lorraine's next question inquires further into this process of becoming.

LORRAINE: From those few weeks after his death onward, tell me a little bit about how have you had a sense of your grandfather in your life?

KRYSTAL: Well, he comes up, and I'm using the present tense, because he does, mostly randomly. When I'm driving the car, I'll just think of him, or I'll read something that reminds me of him, or something that he would have sent me, because part of our relationship was he would send me lots of funny things in e-mail. Also, because I've taken steps to purposefully have him in my life, I have notes that he wrote me. I have quotes that he sent me written on my school binder that I see on most days. I got my tattoo for him.

LORRAINE: Tell me about your tattoo.

KRYSTAL: Yeah, it's right here on my shoulder, it's a big heart. One half of the heart is a suicide awareness ribbon, and the other half of the heart is just the rest of the heart, and it's in his favorite color, which is orange. So the tattoo itself is the yellow suicide awareness, and then the orange, which was his favorite, and then the middle of the heart says G-Pa.

LORRAINE: And what's it like when you see a piece of your grandfather there? To see that there, to look back and go, ah!

KRYSTAL: It's so nice, because I did specifically design it with his person in mind. Because, what tattoos meant to him, he didn't like them at all. He hated tattoos and piercings on my other cousins, but on

93

me he said they were great, and cute, and pretty. And piercings were great, and that I should just rock it all. It's sort of a testament to my being his favorite and him making special exceptions for me. And also a testament to wanting to have it permanently in my life.

LORRAINE: There's something about that tattoo that I'm curious about too. It's not just him and his favorite color, it's also acknowledging how he chose his death. Can you speak to me about that?

KRYSTAL: I chose to highlight his choice and his agency, because it means something to me about how I'm going to continue to live my life.

LORRAINE: Which is how?

KRYSTAL: With him in mind, and his agency in mind, and how it matters, people's choices matter.

LORRAINE: When you live with his belief in you close by, what is your life like? How is it different? How is moving into your future different, when you hold that confidence that he held in you?

KRYSTAL: Well, if I don't, I don't move through life the same way. Because I don't feel like I would have naturally had the same level of confidence unless I see him, unless I see myself through his eyes.

LORRAINE: So your life is dramatically different because of his vision, is that right?

KRYSTAL: Yes.

Shifting Verbs

We have to take into account the construction of space, as well as of time, when we create such a conversation. We will address in more detail the implications and fluid practices that shift our linear concept of time in Chapter 7, but let us also mention here the shifts in verb tense that are required in re-membering conversations as they are of particular import when the death, or the relationship with the deceased, was challenging.

It is common in conventional grief conversations to speak about a person who has died through the use of past-tense verbs. As has been previously noted, many even advocate for counselors to use terms that represent "reality" (Worden, 2009) to support clients' acceptance and to not dwell in a state of denial. However, this relegation of a deceased person to the past draws an imaginary line in memory that assigns stories and the possible reinvigoration of a life to a distant and far-away land that was once there, but is no more. The way in which we speak matters for where we might "find" or introduce or invite the influences of a deceased person's stories to accompany us in life.

Since the dead do not actually speak, we need to use particular forms of language to erode the emotional and linguistic distance between the dead and the living. This bridging of two worlds makes accessible a territory for the continuation of the relationship, when so desired, and a place for the deceased person's "voice" to live by being ventriloquized by the bereaved:

the relationship of the dead with the living is invoked grammatically in a way that can continue and not be marked by a harsh distinction between the indicative past and present. The moment of death thus takes on linguistically a less definitional significance for the relationship . . . the subjunctive possibilities for how a relationship might be continued in a new form are opened up and membership can be re-introduced.

(Hedtke & Winslade, 2004–5, p. 203)

Shifting Krystal's grandfather from a person in her past to a man whose influence continues to inform her life now is an objective of such a conversation. When she speaks of having him with her in her daily conversations, in a tattoo, in the notes in her school binders, all are points that connect with who he is still becoming for her, rather than who he was in the past. They involve her in migrating his influences across time from memories of the past to present experience. In the process, the imaginary lines that separate the "then" and "now" are blurred, if not dissolved. Maintaining imagined interactions with the deceased, Rosenblatt and Meyer (1986) suggest, continues the connections between the living and the dead. Vickio (1999) notes the importance of actively incorporating the deceased person's life into the meaning of the living, through tangible objects and ceremonial opportunities.

Returning to the concept of membership (Myerhoff, 1986) that was discussed in Chapter 3, we can easily imagine how this idea sets the stage for relational exchanges. In membership, there is a sense of belonging that is found within membership clubs (Myerhoff, 1986; White, 1997; 2007). This serves not only to make the deceased visible, but also to enable people to stand against the dominant discourses that dismiss the deceased. It can also become a life-saving force, because the deceased person's stories are re-claimed literally from the dead. In a counseling conversation built on these assumptions, it is possible to breathe life into identity stories that might otherwise remain dry and shriveled.

This understanding of a membered club can house many people, both living and dead, as well as people whom one has never met, but may be inspired by (for example, a religious figure, a favored thinker, a sporting hero, or a historical idol). For many, the idea of a club includes animals who have featured prominently in their lives. The stories, both good and not-so-good, live in this metaphorical place and continue to be accessible across boundaries of time and space. When working with the bereaved, this concept of membership opens to a new form of inquiry – one that can create great comfort for those who want to continue a sense of close relationship with the dead, but also for those who want to find respite from the chains of challenging relationships as well.

The notion of a membered club is critical to the crafting of an ongoing connection with a baby that dies at birth, or perhaps even when a baby died during a miscarried pregnancy. The child and the child's life have a home within the membered club. The dreams and hopes of their parents, grandparents, siblings, and friends all hold a space, marking this child's life in the membership club. It becomes possible to continue to access a relationship with this child and have many people carry, and create, a "voice" that they would have perhaps spoken. This child can continue to grow alongside others in the club as well, where their meaning can take on new definitions over the years for those who continue to love this child.

As counselors, we are free to inquire about this child's presence in the club where they will continue to live and hold membership. We could even be very direct in asking subjunctive questions to make space for this child's life with questions like:

- What did they feel like when growing inside their mother?
- What kind of things did they feel when their father or siblings were nearby?
- What would they appreciate about how their family was planning to welcome them into this club?
- What meaning would they hope others would come to know about their life?
- Over the years, how might they imagine their parents'/family's love for them might grow?

Questions such as these make visible the deceased child's presence and construct a place where the child can always live in a storied form. They build the platform for a sense of relationship as ongoing and open to possible changes as others come into the membered club and as people age. They also provide a platform on which meaning can be made, and rituals that define our relationships with the deceased can be folded into our clubs.

When a person dies by their own hand, we need to find a way to assist clients to affirm a place in the club where a new story can be anchored about who the person was and who they continue to be. We can clearly hear this possibility in Krystal's ongoing relationship with her grandfather. Let us now return to the conversation between Krystal and Lorraine.

LORRAINE: I don't know if I have asked this yet . . . But I was just thinking about . . . How is love present in his act of dying by his own hand? How is his love present, for other people, do you think?

KRYSTAL: [pause] I think that is a big part of it. There's two things. I think one is the financial aspect, because he was able to have a policy that helped his family afterwards. I think that the other piece was that he was starting to get up in age and he was not somebody that ever wanted to be a burden, on his children or his loved ones at all. So I think that he was showing his love in a way to alleviate us from anything that might happen in the future. I think he knew something that

we didn't know. I have a hopeful feeling
that, whatever it was that he knew that
impacted his decision, was from a place of
love, and not from selfishness.

LORRAINE: Is there anything else that I didn't
ask you about who he is or about your
relationship, that would be useful for the
world to know about your connection to him?

KRYSTAL: I'm not sure how you would have asked
this as a question, but something that
would be important to know is just that
he is not replaceable, he cannot be
substituted.

LORRAINE: What difference does that make for
you?

KRYSTAL: That makes me feel a lot more peaceful.

LORRAINE: It's nice to have someone who travels
with you who believes in you.

KRYSTAL: And believes great things about me.

LORRAINE: And believes great things, yeah. It's
a beautiful thought to have.

Here Krystal speaks about her grandfather's intentions and knowledges. She cannot be certain about these, but she does surmise and Lorraine's questions facilitate a movement from her surmising about him to Krystal's story of herself. She goes forward in her journey of becoming with a peaceful sense, which she attributes to her grandfather's love. His belief in her, too, is not just something that lived in the past. It continues to have currency and to affect her. It is noteworthy that both Lorraine and Krystal find it appropriate to talk about his ongoing influence in the present tense. It is worth noticing too that this segment ends on a note of aesthetic appreciation. The thought that Krystal's grandfather "believes great things" about her is acknowledged by Lorraine as a "beautiful thought".

Identity and Troubled Relationships

When we reincorporate the dead, we are also free to edit into our own identity the stories that are the most important to us. The dead can always be moved closer or further away. An implication of this freedom is that we can also edit out stories that are not so important.

Re-membering is a deliberate process of construction, rather than a matter of simple recall. The stories that become woven into identity may be either examples of what not to do in life or restorations of a loving relationship that developed over many years prior to an unexpected or dramatic death. As we shift the spatial positions in the posthumous relationship, the bereaved are able to edit in the stories that affirm connections and edit out the stories that create challenges.

It need not be a question of denying reality, but rather a process that supports agency in the face of the hardship and challenges brought by grief. It is this construction that opens the door to re-visioning, or creating careful distance in relationships too when abuse has occurred.

When a relationship has crossed into abuse, whether physical, emotional, or sexual, the benefits and privileges of membership need to be reassessed. It would be grossly inappropriate for a counselor to work to give more voice to the deceased, if that person has abused the privileges of membership. In these circumstances, a counselor would never, for example, ask of a bereaved person, "What might this person (the dead person who abused you) say about X, Y, or Z?" Such a question positions the voice of the abuser as still having privileged access to the membership club of the bereaved, where they might perpetuate a destructive relationship.

It is often more sensible to speak to how the bereaved person might wish to edit the deceased person's voice and to actually quiet its influence in their life. Since membership is a fluid process that requires care and tending, membership that has been broken or taken advantage of can be quieted, downgraded, and placed in a position of limited access to speak on behalf of the living. Pursuing a line of inquiry based on these premises can restore for the bereaved an experience of being in charge and help them to take back their lives from the abuse. In this way, the line of becoming need not feature so strongly the identity story that was associated with the abusive relationship.

This emphasis in counseling is delicate and involves linguistically rearranging a person's "membership club" to increase distance between the identity story and the abusive relationship, and to decrease distance between the person and more helpful connections. By way of example, a brief story might help.

When Maggie came to counseling, her father had died about two weeks previously. She expressed surprise at feeling knocked off-kilter by his death and described how she had all but stopped speaking to him twenty years prior. She described a challenging relationship with him that included many painful infractions where he hit her when she was a child and would berate her appearance. She felt powerless and humiliated by him. She had hoped her mother would rescue her from the regular reprimands that he had dished out to her and her sister, but her mother too had been at his tyrannical mercy. When Maggie left home for college, at 17, she vowed to never talk to her father again. She stayed in contact with her mother and sister and found creative ways to see them over the years, but she kept her promise and ex-communicated her father from her life. She had wondered what it would be like when he died and had suspected she would not notice his absence, since he had been cut out of her life. When her mother phoned her to say her father had had a massive stroke and died, Maggie felt a deep pang of grief. She could not explain why this was. She had opted not to go to his funeral and had felt her mother and sister understood this. She nevertheless had found herself crying and distraught and sought help to make sense of this.

Death brings a momentary pause even in the most challenging of relationships, as Maggie was noticing. It affords the opportunity to reconsider how, or whether, a deceased person's membership status should be rearranged in the life of the bereaved. It might be, as in the case of enjoyable relationships, that the membership is upgraded and celebrated. But in Maggie's situation, this would have been offensive and damaging to her. Neither was it the trajectory of becoming that she wanted. Instead, it was important to inquire about how she found the strength to do what she had done in creating a life for herself apart from her father's influence. A skilled counselor would ask about how she had been able to stay connected to her mother and sister and in what creative ways she had been able to accomplish this. There might be an opportunity to be curious about the values and skills she had been able to call upon that spoke to her ability to manage and support beneficial relationships, while decreasing destructive relationships. A line of questions could include:

- How did you learn these particular skills and develop them?
- What might you wish this experience to stand for in your future life?
- Who else might you want to inspire and influence with this particular knowledge you have developed?

These questions would not privilege or reactivate her father's membership in her life, but instead would center her voice and responses as primary. It would include bringing others into the conversation to further this strength, like her mother, sister, and a future audience of people to learn from her. Such inquiries offer her the chance to realign key memberships in her life and open up the possibility of holding a definitional ceremony (Myerhoff, 1982; 1992; White, 1997; 2007) to recognize the developments. In the process she might strengthen her own resolve, while also strengthening her connections with beneficial others in her "club of life". This process makes public preferred aspects of identity, especially the identity that is becoming aligned with Maggie's stories of herself. As Barbara Myerhoff states (1986):

One of the most persistent but elusive ways that people make sense of themselves is to show themselves to themselves, through multiple forms: by telling themselves stories; by dramatizing claims in rituals and other collective enactments; by rendering visible actual and desired truths about themselves and the significance of their existence in imaginative and performative productions.

(p. 261)

This chapter has spotlighted identity formation in grieving, but has done so from a particular perspective. One concentration has been on processes of becoming, not just on being. From this perspective, events matter more than categories of personhood. Another concentration has been on identity as a relational construction as well. It is formed in the intervals between people rather than just inside the individual. Identity thus expresses who we are becoming in relation to others who matter to us and this does not end when someone dies. Good counseling takes advantage of this fact by asking the kinds of questions that continue to enliven connections with those who are deceased. Sometimes, complex nuances of meaning need to be teased out in the process. In the next chapter we shall explore further a particular way of accounting for such different nuances of meaning.

CHAPTER 5

Rescuing Implicit Meanings

To craft a response to the loss of a loved one, you need some tools and you need raw materials to work with. In grief psychology, it was long thought, as we have seen, that the most important aspects of psychic energy were raw emotions and that the key task was to let these wash over a person, do their damage, and retrieve the debris in their wake. The bereaved person could only be passive in response and allow the stages of grief to take place. The etymological roots of "passive" lie suitably in the concept of suffering.

The Turn to Meaning

The social sciences have in recent decades witnessed a turn to meaning, particularly social and linguistic aspects of meaning (Frankl, 1963), that has been successful in some quarters in dislodging the tidy arrangement in psychology of the study of discrete emotions, cognitions, and behaviors (O'Connor, 2002–3). As a result, it has become much more acceptable to talk about the meanings people make of death (Hibberd, 2013; Neimeyer & Gillies, 2006; Neimeyer et al., 2008), not just the emotions they feel. This, however, becomes complex when the way in which the person died is sudden or tragic or the relationship has experienced particular challenges. Creating meaning then can involve delicate conversation to address stories of shame, stigma, and guilt that can be piled on top of grief (Gall, Henneberry, & Eyre, 2014; Neimeyer, 2015).

The complicating issue is that these meanings are not only the raw materials we are seeking. They are also the tools we have to think with. Deconstructing the meaning of death and grief is thus both something that researchers do to analyze people's experience and a focus for the kind of counseling that invites people to become (co)authors of the narratives that are shaping their experience. The main focus of this chapter, however, will be upon the meanings that clients make about their experience of grieving and how counselors can facilitate the process of meaning-making for them in productive ways.

When someone dies, people make meaning of the event in a way that governs their sorting of the significance of the event, and the relationship, in their lives (O'Connor, 2002–3). Sometimes the meaning can be represented in a statement, such as, "It's a relief to see the end of her suffering", or "He was the victim of a medical mistake and should not have died", or "It is tragic when a child dies before her parents", or "She had a long life and her time had come", or "He died for his country".

Meaning and Discourse

The source of these meanings is more than just cognitive, however. They are drawn from the background discourses that provide us with resources for living. Neimeyer, Klass, and Dennis (2014) show how grief narratives can be informed by and even policed by eulogies, published accounts, and literary texts. We agree and would add, following Foucault (1969), that scientific and academic accounts are themselves far from free of discursive influences. They too are influenced by the radical individualism that is produced by modern capitalism and this shows up in much that is written about death and grief.

Foucault (1989) used a vivid image to refer to this discursive background. He spoke of the "great anonymous murmur of discourse" (p. 27) from which a speaker might draw as appropriate. In this sense, the meanings people make are formed out of the linguistic resource bank built up by a community through a thousand or a million conversations. The role of families in the narration of grief is often a key site for these conversations and thus for the shaping of personal meanings (Nadeau, 2001). Without this resource bank of shared meanings, we could not understand each other in a given cultural context, or within a family. In another sense, however, each discourse user is able to draw from this resource bank in their own way. This is the aspect of discourse use that is the basis of agency.

As Bakhtin (1986) asserts, it is only possible to do this in dialogue with others. Agency, therefore, begins in a response, rather than in an original utterance. Meaning-making is, therefore, partly a function of being a member of a discourse community and partly a function of personal creativity. By emphasizing the first function, we can recognize cultural patterns and social conventions that become lines of force running through experience. It is by emphasizing the latter function that a counselor can assist people to craft their own responses to grief into a coherent narrative, leading sometimes to shifts in the cultural patterns as well. Such an emphasis is achieved in counseling primarily by asking questions of a client. It is not so important what the counselor's answers to these questions might be. It is the client's answers that are more important. The counselor's job is to provide the scaffolding so that a narrative edifice can be built to house a person's grief responses.

As Neimeyer (2001) says, such an approach makes grief counseling very much a "rhetorical process" (p. 264) in which language is being used artfully toward the end of knowing how to go on in life (Wittgenstein, 1953). This contrasts with a psychodynamic view in which meaning lies not so much *in* what people say as *beneath* what they say (Neimeyer, 2001, p. 265), and only available to the trained analyst's interpretation. We are much more interested in taking what people say seriously to mean what it says on the surface, rather than assuming that meaning is hidden away in unseen depths often only visible to the expert, trained professional.

104

Meaning Reconstruction

We have been emphasizing in this book a sense of continuity in relationship after death. As was noted in Chapter 3, the deceased person does not stop mattering to those to whom they mattered while alive, and there is a sense in which those who live on are still answerable to them. In this sense, the deceased continues to feature as a significant other for the bereaved and counselors need to find effective ways to create meaning that is supportive and life-affirming. Many others have also addressed how meaning is made (for example see Frankl, 1963; Hibberd, 2013; Neimeyer & Gillies, 2006; Neimeyer et al., 2008; O'Connor, 2002–3), but our focus is slightly different. We are focused on the ways in which counselors can craft a conversation to elicit meaning-making.

Neimeyer and Gillies (2006) argue that bereaved persons engage in a search for meaning that produces a shift from pre-loss meaning structures to post-loss meaning structures. However, this idea assumes that what structures the experience of bereavement lies in the individual psyche and leaves aside the poststructuralist account of a distributed mind, shaped by discourse. We do not assume either that meaning-making must begin from a deficit condition, such as "a bewildering sense of meaninglessness" (Hibberd, 2013, p. 671) that besets bereaved persons, or a "dissonance" (Neimeyer & Gillies, 2006).

While there is no doubt value in these concepts, we think it is possible to reach for a different conception of the process of meaning-making. We shall seek to explain this approach and to explore its implications for therapeutic practice. To speak about this, we need to introduce the concept of the absent but implicit.

The Absent but Implicit

A key concept to work with in the construction of meaning is what Michael White (2000) described as the "absent but implicit". Drawing from Derrida's deconstruction of presence and Bateson's notion of double description, White described this concept in the following way: "A singular description can be considered to be the visible side of a double description." Citing Derrida, he suggests that a "deconstructive method of reading texts" brings forth

the absent signs or descriptions that are relied upon for a text to establish its meanings.... It is that which is on the other side of singular descriptions of experiences of living – that which is on the other side of what is discerned – that I am here referring to as the absent but implicit.

(p. 37)

Thus many of the descriptions of problem issues that people present to therapists are dependent on "the unstated"; that is, the binary opposite of what is stated. For example, hope and despair might be such binary opposites, or depression and happiness, or problem and solution. To think of them in this way is to understand that concepts, and their descriptions, only exist in relation with each other, rather than as isolated elements. Despair relies upon the concept of hope. We cannot understand hot without cold. Or, depression can only be discerned by someone who knows, however fleetingly, the experience of happiness.

The therapeutic value of this insight into language is that when people make singular statements that are totalizing and appear to lead to a dead end, it is useful to inquire into the social and linguistic context of their development. As White suggests, this might involve their socioeconomic context, their power relations context, or their cultural context. And he also avows an interest in their linguistic context; that is, into their relationship with other concepts. If someone describes their experience with a term like "despair", for example, White suggests inquiry into what the despair "speaks to", "what it is a testimony to", "what circumstances or conditions...made it possible to discern despair" (p. 37).

Where might we search, therefore, to find the absent but implicit element of grief? A singular description of grief might be about the experience of loss only and the resulting sadness. When someone dies, this is the easily visible side. As George Bonanno (2009) suggests, however, there is often something on "the other side of sadness". The value of the concept of the absent but implicit lies in the recognition that two apparent opposites can be realized as intimately related. They both mutually rely on each other for their meaning. They are two sides of the same coin. Hence the experience of loss is also a statement of valuing. You do not miss and yearn for someone that you do not value and care about, or at least have been profoundly affected by. Grieving the loss of someone is in essence a statement about the importance to the speaker of the life of the person who has been lost. It is a small shift, therefore, for a therapist to move from asking questions about the loss to a curiosity about the value and importance of the deceased to the bereaved person. Questions can be asked about the relationship between the deceased and the bereaved (among other relationships in which the two participate). Here are some examples:

- What has your relationship with the deceased contributed to your life?
- What has the deceased person meant to you?
- What are some of the ways in which you have been close to each other?
- What would the deceased person say about you?
- What values might you both be said to share? How were these expressed in the past and how might they still be expressed?

Double Listening

To hear the complexity in what people tell us, it is necessary for counselors to engage in what White calls "double listening" (p. 41). This is a variation, and an advance, on active listening that concentrates on the simple act of paying attention and hearing multiplicity in what people speak about (Guilfoyle, 2015). Double listening, in particular, is used in narrative therapy to refer to listening not just for the dominating narrative or discourse, but also for the response that people make to what dominates their experience. For instance, if a traumatic experience amounts to the dominant story, how a woman protects herself, acts to prevent others from being damaged by the trauma, holds onto values that contradict the logic of exploitation that she has been made subject to, and affirms her own existence in terms other than what the trauma would dictate – these are expressions of resistance, or response, to the trauma (White, 2006). Hearing both the effects of the trauma and the acts of resistance is what double listening aims to do. Often these responses are scarcely noticed or given significance in the shadow cast by the dominant story. In these circumstances, it can be even more valuable for a counselor to draw attention to and inquire further into the subjugated narrative. The concept of the absent but implicit helps make visible such narratives, because they are often implicit in their expression, rather than explicit.

Distinguishing the Absent but Implicit

This concept of the absent but implicit is so important that it deserves some further distinctions to be made. First, we are not talking here about reframing. This is not a matter of the counselor re-interpreting the client's words in a positive way. The shift that takes place is merely an existing implication of what the client is already saying when talking about a loss. As it is already an implication, it is more like the thickening of half a picture so that the listener gets a fuller appreciation of what is being said. Michael White (2000) makes a comment that distinguishes reframing from inquiring into the absent but implicit. He suggests that reframing usually involves replacing a "bad totalization" with a "good totalization", but it is still about a totalization. It still leads to a narrow, single-storied account of life and identity.

Neither are we talking here about being positive or replacing negative emotions with positive ones. It is true that the emphasis on what someone has meant to a bereaved person is often more upbeat than an emphasis on the pain of loss. However, we are not advocating overlooking or minimizing the pain – merely that we inquire into what is already being expressed in a slightly different way. We are not interested either in "compartmentalizing" the pain (Jordan & McIntosh, 2011, p. 230) and locating the making of meaning in some other compartment.

Nor are we advocating anything that would idealize the dead. The emphasis in the kinds of questions we are advocating is on a realistic relationship. Like any relationship, it will have its ups and downs, its positive and negative elements, its beauty spots and its warts. We would stress again that it is the failure to pick up on the vibrancy of a relationship in addition to the sense of loss that leads to a stilted picture. Given the fact that there has been for most of the last hundred years such a strong emphasis on letting go of the relationship, we believe that it has been the overwhelming emphasis on loss in grief therapy that amounts to a greater distortion of reality. The result has been not so much an idealization of the dead as a magnification of the pain of loss.

Neither would we advocate the performance of a "personal psychological autopsy" of the deceased (Jordan & McIntosh, 2011, p. 229) to find meaning. Such a description potentially loads up the task of making meaning of a death with a heaviness that we do not believe is helpful or necessary.

In the interests of clarity it is also necessary to point out that we are not talking about anything like a process of oscillation between what is "loss-oriented" and what is "restoration-oriented", as advocated by Stroebe and Schut (2001, p. 59). Neither do we see it as necessary to formulate two tracks (Rubin, Malkinson, & Witztum, 2011) into some kind of "double helix" (p. 47) in which response to the loss represents one track and desire to maintain a relationship with the deceased represents a second track. We are not convinced that this model of two distinct orientations to loss, or two different tracks, even when they are supported by research, represents accurately what people experience. It is quite different, we believe, to emphasize that what they see as an oscillation between two ideas is better described as two sides of the same coin. In this way of thinking, the restoration of posthumous relationships is far less complicated than it has been made to seem. The separation of these two ideas into two states of being that we oscillate between is, in our opinion, more an accommodation to where grief psychology has been, and the dominant need to formularize events, than it is a function of the complexity of what people actually experience.

To make inquiries into the absent but implicit, several assumptions need to be in place. A counselor needs to assume the value of the continuing-bonds idea and of what Michael White (1989) called

108

"saying hullo again". This is a reference to the kind of inquiry that does not so much privilege "saying goodbye" to dead loved ones as reclaiming the relationship with those who have died. If death neither ends a relationship nor requires the forfeiting and relinquishing of that relationship, then these questions can be asked in a way that feels fluid and not forced.

Second, the assumption that there will be multiple stories of any relationship also needs to be held. If it is, then it does not feel strange to make the shift from inquiring about a sense of loss to inquiring about *what* feels lost – namely the vitality of the relationship. If we are to invite people to hold onto their bonds with those that are deceased, and perhaps discover new nodes in that relationship, then it will not feel strange to be curious about what continues to give life to that relationship, even after the death of one of the parties. To illustrate these ideas, it is now useful to provide an example of a therapeutic conversation. The following conversation took place between Emma and Lorraine during the course of a workshop.

An Example of a Counseling Conversation

```
LORRAINE: Thank you for your willingness to
          talk to me.
EMMA: I am terrified, but that's OK.
LORRAINE: Are you?
EMMA: Yeah. The conversations I'd like to have
      are complex and hard.
LORRAINE: They are complex when we are talking
          about people we love. You mentioned that
          your daughter died. Would it be OK if we
          spoke about her?
EMMA: Uhm, yes, I think so.
```

It is worth noting at the start that there are competing stories operating for Emma. One is expressed in her desire to talk and the other in the word "terrified". Complexity requires double listening. To characterize Emma as reluctant would only hear part of what she says. Lorraine invites her to proceed through a simple invitation to introduce her daughter.

```
LORRAINE: I would love to meet her for start-
          ers. Being the mother of a girl, I would
```

love to meet your daughter. Can you tell me her name?

EMMA: Her name was...is Sophie.

LORRAINE: And can you tell me about Sophie. Can you tell me what she looks like?

EMMA: Gorgeous. She was about five foot six. She had...she has the most amazing olive skin. She had very dark hair and eyes that were sometimes the deepest brown that often looked quite black. She was petite and very exotic. She would turn everybody's heads when you walked in a room with her. She loved shoes. She had more shoes than other people have clothes. Boots especially and the higher the better. And she could just walk amazingly in them, so eloquently. She liked bling, all that glitters.

LORRAINE: Tell me about the kind of things she liked to do. Did she work? Did she go to school?

EMMA: She did. When she passed, she was working, of all places, in an animal refuge. She had not long moved to far north and she was working with animals. Prior to that she was an exotic dancer for many years, she was a stripper and was very good at that. I am not sure that was the best thing for her, but she was very good at it. She had a tragic existence – some really rotten things happened to her and set her life on a very different course from what she thought it was going to be when she was a teenager. She had planned to become a lawyer and then stuff happened and it went on a very different path. Friends were really important to her. She had an amazing sense of loyalty. It really didn't matter what the friend was like. If they needed her, she was there. She would help anybody. You'd be walking along the

110

street and there might be somebody that
most people wouldn't want to acknowledge
and she would ask them if they were OK,
offer them a cigarette. She was very caring and very loyal. She liked animals.
Animals didn't hurt you the way people
did, she said once. She loved spending
time with them. It didn't matter if it
was the cat or the dog. She loved horses
especially. She did some course with race
horses and at the zoo. So spending time
with animals was very important to her.
She would go into so much detail about
how she'd work with the new animals that
had been brought to the refuge. She talked
about it with such passion.

It should be noted too that Sophie died by suicide. However, Lorraine avoids focusing on her death and instead concentrates on what Emma might say about her daughter's vitality. This is not a denial of her death, but an inquiry into what is absent but implicit in death – that is, life and vitality. Lorraine selects out for further inquiry the things that Emma speaks about that convey the strongest sense of vitality and asks about meaning in relation to these.

111

LORRAINE: When she was with animals, what did
you think that offered her?
EMMA: I think a connection to things that didn't
cause you pain, but just brought you joy.
Where she was living most recently, there
were cassowaries [large birds] that con-
stantly walked past her kitchen window.
There was only a little fence and the cassowaries had a track and when we spoke on
the phone, she would tell me their antics.
She must have been absolutely fascinated
by them. She'd give them a voice. There
was a big monitor lizard that would come
visit her garden and she'd put the scraps
outside for the cassowaries and the monitor lizard and she would give the lizard a

voice when she was telling me about him. All his actions had a particular voice. She would tell stories of their life. It was amusing.

LORRAINE: Her comfort with animals, did that speak to something she held as important?

EMMA: Yes, very much so.

LORRAINE: And what is that, do you suspect?

EMMA: Unconditional love.

LORRAINE: How did she learn that unconditional love is important?

EMMA: From me.

LORRAINE: What story would she tell me about what her mom taught her about unconditional love?

EMMA: This is where it gets hard. No matter what she did or said to us, my husband and I would always be there for her. No matter what turn her life took, we would love her. It didn't matter that she was an exotic dancer and not the lawyer, she was our child and we loved her just as much. All we wanted was for her to be happy. When she was using drugs, it was the same. The trauma that she put us through, when she had psychotic breaks. It was all OK, because we loved her.

LORRAINE: What would Sophie say about how that sustained her during that time? When she was in places that were dark, how did her mom and dad's unconditional love sustain her?

EMMA: I don't know...I guess at times, she could blame us. She could get angry with us, because of what was happening to her. So she didn't have to take responsibility. And I guess when you come down on the other side, we were going to be there. There was always somebody that was going to be there.

Collecting Treasures

Here, Lorraine inquires into Sophie's love of animals and hears some stories that illustrate her values. Then she inquires further into what this speaks to. That is when the concept of unconditional love appears. It is a concept that is relevant to the relationship between Sophie and her mother, Emma. It is referenced to a series of events in Sophie's life that are barely alluded to as "dark" places. Out of these events, the shining jewel that Emma selects out, however, is the relational value of unconditional love. In the face of these events, the unconditional love may seem absent but its implicit value is extracted and made visible. The conversation continues with curiosity about how her friends knew Sophie. The concept of "Sophie's treasures" emerges and Lorraine seizes upon it as a further opening to things that might be re-membered about Sophie and held close.

LORRAINE: And you also said she had a lot of friends.

EMMA: Yeah, she did.

LORRAINE: Would they describe her with anything different than what you did?

EMMA: A sense of fun. Her going out and probably getting drunk, things I would avoid. So her partying skills. I know her very best friend misses her fashion advice...When she really misses Sophie, she gets on her bed and she has all these treasures related to Sophie and she surrounds herself with these Sophie treasures.

LORRAINE: I'm wondering what kind of Sophie treasures you have?

EMMA: Many of them are in my heart. Many of them are stories that I don't get to talk about or share anymore, which is very distressing. For thirty-two years she was my whole life, and I thought about her every day and I worried myself sick about her. And, of course, she dies and I am not supposed to think about her or talk about her or do anything with her anymore. That's very hard. What do I treasure?...I have jewelry that she gave me . . . one photograph. A poem that she wrote about "my mom". The way she spoke at my dad's memorial service.

LORRAINE: How did she speak?

EMMA: While family was very important, when family was a big group, she found family very hard, because she was always worried about being judged. And of course, they didn't like the choices she had made and at times that was made quite clear to her. Standing up in front of one hundred and fifty people wasn't her thing, but she did it and she spoke about her relationship with my dad, and my nephew and my niece stood with her. It was just a beautiful thing to see the love that she displayed at that moment, doing something that pushed her way beyond her comfort zone.

LORRAINE: Why do you think she did that?

EMMA: Because family's important. Because, my dad is important to her. Her biological father and I split up when she was just an infant. She and I lived with my dad until she was six. So he was like the first male role model.

Crafting Vitality

Now we have another contrast between family "judgment" that is silencing and courageous speaking up about the importance of relationships with people. In the face of judgment, speaking up seems likely to be absent, but its implicit value is made visible by the actions of Sophie and of her cousins who stand with her. Lorraine is curious about further meaning that might be made of this moment – again a moment of the crafting of vitality. Lorraine uses Emma's response in speaking of Sophie to invite her to incorporate what she treasures by re-membering Sophie into Emma's own living.

LORRAINE: Is that something that is typical of Sophie? When something was important that

she could hold off that sense of judgment
to honor relationships?

EMMA: Yes, yes, honoring relationships was very
important.

LORRAINE: How have you honored your relationship with her?

EMMA: By continuing to live. Especially because,
for us, for a long time, dying would have
been a very good thing, because it meant
we would have been with Sophie. We only
had the one child. Life has become more
challenging for us. By stepping outside
of my comfort zone by doing this [the
interview]. By trying small ways to not fit
society's norms about how I should grieve.
When I went back to work, six weeks after
she died, we had this conversation and
I said something about how it is really
important that we continue to speak her
name. And it is really important that you
ask me about her, because this is how I
can honor her.

LORRAINE: So has something shifted in you from
when Sophie first died, when you were saying that it was almost better to not live
anymore to now saying, "I can speak her
name"?

EMMA: I think it has.

115

This time, Sophie's transgressive act in the face of judgment is
echoed by Emma's transgression of the rules about not speaking of
her dead daughter. Emma takes a stand on behalf of speaking her
daughter's name, which becomes an act of resistance, and she invites
others to join her. Lorraine flips it back to Sophie's voice and inquires
about what Sophie has contributed to this act of cultural transgression.

LORRAINE: How has she helped you create that
change?

EMMA: By letting me remember. By helping me. By
letting me talk about her. I guess in a
sense by dying. Without that, I wouldn't

be here, you see. My life was going in this direction and now it's not and I have to find meaning. I have no plans to take my life, so I have to find out my path.

LORRAINE: So how has Sophie helped you?

EMMA: She walks with me. She's in here always [pointing to her heart].

LORRAINE: So having her talk with you and having her in your heart always, does that change the direction of the steps you take?

EMMA: Yes, because, she is not here. So I have to find ways to honor her life. Otherwise I do not know what the point of my life is.

This last statement is worth pausing over for a moment. Notice the difference between the two statements. Emma is aware of the sense of loss – "She is not here." Then she immediately speaks of her desire to honor her daughter's life. This sounds like an ongoing commitment to her daughter. It suggests a sense of relationship that continues, despite the loss that she is simultaneously recognizing. It is the double-sided coin. Emma continues speaking about how honoring Sophie gives meaning to her own life. We do not think it makes sense to separate these statements into dual tracks or dual processes. They are part of the same experience and are mentioned in the same breath in a very resonant utterance. For this reason the concept of the absent but implicit seems more accurate. In other words, the sense of loss carries within it a consciousness of the implicit desire to treasure the life of a deceased loved one, and vice versa. Lorraine seeks to expand on this moment.

LORRAINE: Have you found some other ways where you honor her life?

EMMA: Not yet, but I think I am working towards that.

LORRAINE: Do you have a sense, if we were to ask her, about where she would hope you might take that honoring, do you have a sense about what she might say about that?

EMMA: I don't know... She would tell you... how proud she is of me for not giving up. She would tell me, when she was alive, how much of a role model I was for her. I used to worry a lot that I had let her down, because of the tragedies of her life, and I didn't fulfill my role as a parent as I saw it or that society tells me. I didn't protect her. I was most fortunate, I guess, because I had this conversation with her, right before she died. She said to me that I didn't get to decide whether I was a good parent. She got to decide. It wasn't my place to decide whether I was good at being a parent. It was her place to decide that and she thought I was. I couldn't use that as a crutch anymore. I had to stand up. I think this pride and honoring that she had of me would continue.

LORRAINE: How will you continue to parent her now?

Emma's story is about a past conversation. Lorraine's question invites her to expand it further through time. It flows from the past into the present and then can be carried to a future. It also assumes an ongoing relationship. The job of parenting is not over. Emma still has to think about how to be Sophie's parent, to craft her relationship with Sophie in the context of her death, and she can be guided by her daughter's words about how best to do this. As if blowing air into a balloon, Lorraine continues to enlarge the meaning that has been spoken of.

EMMA: Same way as before - with unconditional love. That is all I have. I cannot live her life. As much as I would like to make choices and decisions, I can't - so all I can give her is love.

LORRAINE: If you were to do this for the next thirty-two years, what difference would it make to you?

EMMA: I guess it means that I won't want to die so much. I guess it means that I will keep plodding along and living, because, if I give up, somehow I am not honoring her existence and her story would die with me. This way, her story doesn't die, it keeps going.

LORRAINE: Your life becomes her life-line, is that right?

EMMA: Maybe. I haven't thought of it that way.

LORRAINE: I am not sure if that fits or not.

EMMA: No, I will think about it. That might be a nice thing.

LORRAINE: If that were to be the case, then what would you want her story to stand for?

EMMA: I think for the things she stood for. For friendship. For loyalty. For helping people that need help...even if that were a street person or an alcoholic who might just need a cigarette, an offer of kindness. Friendship and family.

LORRAINE: If you knew that her story and your telling her story invoked that in other people – to be kind, what difference would that make for you?

EMMA: I have no idea...A sense of community, of accepting people for who they are. And that is a sense of unconditional love, of unconditional friendship. This is what was really, really important for Sophie. Perhaps that is what kept her going for so long.

LORRAINE: How much she loved other people and animals?

EMMA: Yeah, yeah. I remember, just before she turned 18, sitting with my husband and talking about what we would buy her for eighteenth birthday. And we decided a funeral plot, because that was the path she was on and we thought we wouldn't have her for very long...because it was so scary and destructive. And yet she made it to 32.

LORRAINE: Now when you start looking at that retrospectively, part of how you explain this to yourself, that she made it from 18 to 32, was that it has to do with unconditional love?

EMMA: It was always unconditional love, but maybe even more so. Because she was no longer there in our house where we could have much of a say or influence. It was about saying, "We are still here. The door is really open still."

LORRAINE: So now you do have a say in how her story of unconditional love is shared with the world. I am wondering what that's like for you?

EMMA: I guess that is to be found out...I think it is eye-opening. The story I am now going to share is that I have been stumbling around about why am I here and I am now wondering if that is my purpose and direction.

LORRAINE: Which direction would that be?

EMMA: That unconditional love. Sharing that with everyone. And sharing her story of unconditional love. It's a good thought.

LORRAINE: So, if that were the case, what would you hope that would mean to someone who needed unconditional love?

EMMA: That they find it. And accept it.

LORRAINE: If that was Sophie's inspiration for you or somebody else to give that unconditional love, what difference would that make for you?

EMMA: I don't know at the moment. I would have to think about that. This is all very new now.

LORRAINE: Is that OK, then, to let it sit in this place, as we are putting something new into the stew to think about?

EMMA: Yes, something new to think about. Something that is really positive and that has a direction. It is something to ponder and sit with. Maybe, see, the pain and

119

emptiness isn't going anywhere, but there
may be something else there as well.

New Meanings

What Emma has crafted in response to Lorraine's questions is a story
that contains a rich new vein of meaning. It is not only an uplifting
story of vitality, but it also clearly contains the sense of loss. Emma's
last statement captures this and that the pain can be accompanied
by a now more visible story of unconditional love as well. We see
this again in the next segment where the pain that Emma has experienced is acknowledged and Emma is invited to mold the pain into
a new meaning. In this sense, the pain has not been ignored but the
story of meaning that is constructed has grown into a new line of
flight. Once again, though, this new line of flight is possible through
noticing the absent but implicit that could be missed, if we were to
only focus on the pain.

LORRAINE: Are there times, when that pain is
present, that you find yourself doing something or saying something at times that is
soothing?

EMMA: Sometimes it is just about breathing and
acknowledging that it is there. I work
with teenagers. And things come up when
they ask questions about suicide or it
comes up in conversation. I have to remind
myself that this is not Sophie, it is just
history.

LORRAINE: Do you ever tell the kids about her?

EMMA: I don't think it is acceptable in this
society to talk about suicide. A lot of
them know she is no longer here, but not
that she died by suicide. I did speak
about her at work the other day though. It
was really nice. I was talking with this
girl and we were talking about vegetarian-
ism. And I was saying that, yes, that is
what I am. And I have a beautiful memory
of going to the beach with Sophie and her
convincing me to eat fish and chips. It was

the most beautiful fish she had ever eaten.
We went to this amazing beach and we sat
there and ate fish and chips. So I said
to the girl that this was very special,
because she had died. And it felt really
lovely to share that.

This segment opens with a question that is built on double listening. Lorraine assumes that, where there is pain, there will also be something that soothes it. Emma tells a story about her transgression of the general discourse of suicide. It should not be mentioned and, in particular, suicide should disqualify the telling of heartening stories about the life of the deceased. Emma is now determined to do what the discourse denies. This further development of resistance is also a story of agency that the silence has tried to rob Emma of. In this sense, she is crafting her own path through the pain, in spite of the discourse. Lorraine, of course, is curious about this line of flight from the path of pain.

LORRAINE: Would Sophie hope that you would
    do that more? [Emma nods.] Would Sophie
    want her life and her death to stand for
    something?

EMMA: Yes, very much so.

LORRAINE: If her life and her death could stand
    for something with the kids that you work
    with, would she like that?

EMMA: Yes, yes.

LORRAINE: And would that mean that once in a
    while, and I am not sure how, but would
    conventions need to be broken?

EMMA: Yes, very much. And I think that's what
    I would like to do. That's my hope and
    that's unconditional love. Because so many
    people take their lives this way.

LORRAINE: If she knew that you were going to
    tell that story of her life mattering and
    her death mattering, and if she knew that
    those stories could potentially save the
    life of a teenager, what would Sophie say
    about that?

EMMA: She would be very honored. She would say, "Do it, do it." She had run away from home and from school, and the wheels had totally gone off her life but I didn't know it. I got a call from the hospital. I thought something terrible had happened. But she was good, except that she hadn't been going to school, but that is another story. One of the girls had gone to her parents' medicine cabinet and had taken some drugs and experimented with the drugs. She had gone to the teacher and then the hospital and they were trying to figure it out to help her. She would say, "Go ahead and do that," if it were to save somebody else. But also, it would be about respecting people. She would want that too – to honor people.

LORRAINE: In the future, if you were to follow this invitation she has offered you, to save a young person's life, what difference would that make to you and to your relationship with Sophie?

EMMA: It would honor it. It would be a constant connection. It would be a way for me to demonstrate my unconditional love, even though she physically isn't here anymore. It would be a very good thing. Anything that remembers and honors her is a very good thing. She is a special person.

There is no disavowal of the pain again here. Its power is acknowledged and there is no emphasis on only thinking positively. However, the conversation mitigates the pain by exploring the meaning of Sophie's death, and, importantly, her life, in relation to Emma's ongoing living as a bereaved person who still has to go to work. Between Lorraine and Emma, a story is scaffolded and crafted in which Sophie has an ongoing voice urging her mother on in the contravention of unhelpful discourse and urging her too to use Sophie's story to benefit, and even to save the lives of, other young people. Hibberd (2013) might refer to this kind of meaning-making as "benefit-finding", although what Emma is speaking of is much more than a "silver lining" (p. 677) when she is talking about claiming her daughter's life to potentially save another person's life.

Notice, too, how time is stretched here in an elastic way (more about this in Chapter 8). The story flows effortlessly between the past, the present, and the future and Lorraine eases this flow through the use of the subjunctive mood (Hedtke & Winslade, 2005), the mood of "as if".

Inviting Audience Participation in Narrative Construction

Since this conversation has taken place in a workshop in front of an audience, Lorraine seeks to return in the end to this fact, and invites Emma to locate her stories about Sophie in the context of this workshop. This is done in recognition of the social construction of grief narratives (Neimeyer, Klass, & Dennis, 2014). The implication for counseling practice is that if grief is constructed in social settings, then counselors should take advantage of whatever social exchanges are available to anchor counter-stories that help people make new meanings of bereavement.

LORRAINE: Can I ask you a couple more questions, please? What would Sophie want for people listening to take away that is important about meeting her?

EMMA: That her life had meaning despite the tragedies and despite the hardships she had to face. It's like, we're very hard on ourselves. She had all this crap happen to her and yet she managed to get up every day. She had a really rotten life. In some ways, she put herself in constant danger and these things that, of course, happened, but despite that, she lived. She made plans and got on with it. And she had fun. So despite all the tragedies in her life, she actually did live her life. She had good times and laughed and cried.

123

> She cared very passionately about people.
> Even though she did many wrong things, she
> still loved very much.

The enriched meaning can, however, be strengthened further still through the responses of those who have been listening. Lorraine, therefore, turns to the audience and invites them to make meaning of what they have heard Emma say.

> LORRAINE: (to the audience) I am wondering about how you have been moved by meeting Emma's daughter?
>
> AUDIENCE MEMBER 1: I'd like to comment on what it was like to listen, as I have a daughter that is very, very young. This idea of unconditional love and hearing your story actually allays some of my fears. Sometimes, as a parent, I think about what if things turn out in a way that I didn't hope for. It's very easy to have unconditional love for a baby. And we have this overwhelming sense of involvement and adoration. So hearing your story, no matter what happens, it gives me that sense that I can go on with the turns and twists, including the things that can go wrong. Hearing this, I felt a sense of relief. Thank you.
>
> AUDIENCE MEMBER 2: You work with teenagers. I'm just in awe of that. And the other thing that I wanted to say is how you brought your daughter to life - this incredibly complex human being, so beautifully and bodily radiant, and I don't know the ins and outs of her going into that line of work. I imagined how hard that must have been for you as a parent, watching and loving each other through that. I will take away from this the radiance of her liveliness and her beauty, even though I have never seen a photo of her. That's an image of hope. Despite everything, there's

a light that shines out of that woman's life that cannot be quenched by whatever happens. To me, that's an inspiration. And thank you.

AUDIENCE MEMBER 3: Thank you for your beautiful description of your daughter. We got to know her as a person. I felt there were three people here, two of whom I could see and one I couldn't. I am going to take away the one I couldn't see. The messages were so strong about her values, of what was important to her. I am going to take away both you and Sophie.

AUDIENCE MEMBER 4: I really appreciate your story. I lost a brother in a very public arena, where there was a lot of judgment and he was seen one way. Where I resonate with you is the love I felt for him and how I see him and this is what I cherish.

These are rich reflections that are likely to strengthen Emma in the story she has crafted. They are not opinions, or discussion points, or objective responses. They are expressions of how listeners are subjectively affected by what they have heard. They are solicited by a question that invites people to bear witness to the impact of Emma's story. Following Myerhoff, White (2007) refers to those who bear witness as "outsider witnesses" and adapts the reflecting team process (Andersen, 1991) to the purpose of including their perspectives. The speakers who are listening are thus constituted as witnesses. Lorraine returns to talk with Emma about the meanings she makes from hearing these responses.

LORRAINE: What's it like to hear this?

EMMA: It's like she has already achieved what we are talking about. Having people already share her unconditional love has made a little difference.

LORRAINE: What has this little difference done for you?

EMMA: It has made me stronger. I can honor her life. But mainly, what we were talking about in talking with the kids, maybe that becomes a possibility. That keeps her very much alive. It doesn't make the loss less or the pain go away, but it makes it like she is still there too. And look how much she is still alive. 'Cause all these people now know her too and so her story doesn't end. That is what we want – for our stories to continue and to not end. And with your help, we just created that.

LORRAINE: As a mom, we want this for our babies. Of course.

EMMA: It gives her life meaning and it diminishes the hardship and the pain that she suffered. Because she has created a beautiful memory for others.

LORRAINE: Can the pain that she suffered, and the hardships she had, stand for something?

EMMA: Yes, because, it enables her story to be told. And it enables connections.

LORRAINE: It is tremendously meaningful to bring Sophie here. As for your willingness to talk about her, when I asked if you wanted to talk about her, you didn't have to.

EMMA: Yes, I was very scared of this. But what I feel is overwhelming and making it hard to breathe. This is my life now and I want to honor her. If I hide this (the tears and pain), then I am hiding her. This is the love for her I don't get to share. Really, that's what this pain is...because I cannot touch her and hold her.

Emma's final statement is intriguing. It contains again a clear reference to the pain of loss but it is also a statement of hopeful meaning. It is, too, an example of the aspect of meaning-making that Hibberd (2013) refers to as constructing a "purpose in life" (p. 678) and as an event that bears on "life significance" (p. 679). Emma does not want to hide the pain, because it is testimony to the implicit meaning that an exclusive focus on the sense of loss would leave as absent. Again, we do not consider that the idea of dual tracks captures this sense that the meaning that can be made is part of the same thing as the sense of loss. She is describing what are two sides of the same coin, rather than separate tracks that we must choose between, focus on separately, or oscillate between.

The meanings that can be spoken into life in such conversations, however, are not just products of individual cognitions. They exist in the context of relations between people and between groups of people. Emma is conscious of this context when she speaks of the need to act in transgressive ways in relation to the conventions that silence talk about suicide. This domain, in which conventions are specified, and often policed, is the territory to which we will turn next. It is the realm of political struggle, where meanings are pulled in different directions.

127

CHAPTER 6

The Politics of Death

There is always a politic in any domain of human expression, because, whenever human beings are involved, some form of power relations pertains. Therefore, this must be so for the practices and discourses that govern how death is handled and how grief is defined. Saying so does not have to mean that everything can be reduced to political issues. Human life contains many other things than power relations – for example, much of biology and physiology exist without the same power structures that shape relationships. Accounting for power in relationships does mean, however, that there are often struggles that take place over whose version of events is to be recognized, whose preferences are acted upon, or whose influence over what will happen comes to dominate (Foucault, 1978). That is our starting place for this chapter.

To be clear, we are not talking about electoral politics here but about the influences that people exert upon each other, knowingly or not, to shape events and discourses as they would desire them to be. In the process, people try to influence each other. That is the basis of power – the exercise of influence. It becomes much more complicated than that, however, as attempts to exert influence become patterned and systematized, to the extent that they are barely recognizable as flows of power, because they are assumed to be realities and taken for granted as just how things are. Often in the institutional context, or when they are defined by the state, they become so striated (Deleuze & Guattari, 1987) that they can be referred to as hegemonic grief (Lebel, 2011). The word "hegemonic" refers to social patterns of domination that are achieved without coercion. Striated means grooved and often the patterns of grieving are repeated so often that it feels like they are the way a person has to go about it. When such social patterns hold sway over personal decisions, we can talk about these patterns as hegemonic.

To get at power in these terms, we need an analytic framework to apply. It is not so easy to get at, because even competing analytical frameworks can be subject to struggle and debate over which version will be used. Some analyses might be based on a liberal humanist account of power relations (see Monk, Winslade, & Sinclair, 2008) in which flows of power are measured in terms of personal influence, often amassed on the basis of wealth, position, education, or charisma. By contrast, other analyses are based on a structuralist analysis of relations (ibid.) between large groups of people and the individual expression of power seems trivial. A Marxist analysis might be like this, for instance. We do not believe either of these approaches are adequate, however. In this chapter we will apply a poststructuralist analytical framework, drawing especially from Michel Foucault's (1978) analytics of power in the modern world (see Monk, Winslade, & Sinclair, 2008, for a full account in relation to counseling), together with some concepts drawn from Gilles Deleuze to showcase how these ideas influence conversations about death and grief.

To highlight the ways in which power exerts influence on a person facing death, a story may help.

Lorraine first met Janet when she was admitted to a hospice program. She was a very youthful-looking 58-year-old woman, who had been struggling for two years with pancreatic cancer. Lorraine first met her with her husband of twelve years, Hank, as he wanted to also provide some history and enlist Lorraine's assistance. Hank explained that he was concerned about his wife and also concerned about the interactions between her and her two adult daughters.

Lorraine started by asking, "Can you give me a sense of how you have been managing?"

Janet replied with uncertainty, "It's been hard knowing what to do . . . " and her utterance drifted off.

Hank took over, "She has been receiving chemo up until a couple weeks ago and I wanted this to continue. Her doctors even thought it could still help her. Her daughters have wanted Janet to try it their way with more vitamins and juices."

Lorraine wanted to hear Janet's voice. "What have you wanted?" she asked.

Janet again prevaricated, "I don't know. Hank is right that I was on the chemo until recently, but that was really hard. I felt weak all the time and have been struggling with my stomach being upset."

"And your daughters? Are they local?" Lorraine asked.

"Yes," Janet said. "They both live in town. Christy is 32 and Samantha is 30." She added appreciation of her daughters that had not been there in Hank's comment, "They have been so good to me, bringing me things to eat and helping me dress."

Hank was quick to contest Janet's appreciation of her daughters. "I can do this, Janet. I don't like what they are feeding you. It is not helping." Turning to me, he added, "They want her to take thirty vitamins twice a day and drink juice five times a day, but it is just making things worse for her."

Lorraine asked them both, "What happens when they are here?"

It was Hank who responded, "I just ignore the whole thing, but I don't want them giving her vitamins, 'cause it's quackery and we don't know if it won't make her more sick. I figure they can be with their mom for a few hours each day, but they need to leave so things can go back to normal here."

Lorraine was conscious of the force behind what Hank was suggesting and wanted to ensure that Janet had a say here. She asked Janet, "What do you want?"

Janet was clear this time, "I want everyone to be happy and not fight. The girls are being kind and so is Hank. I wish they wouldn't argue about this."

Janet was struggling with the effects of competing discourses, each exerting a line of force upon her. She was feeling pulled between her daughters' and husband's preferences for her health. In the background it is possible to detect the dominance of medical power that might see alternative treatments as less viable forms of treatment. There might also be background conversations about gender, which were granting Janet or Hank or Janet's daughters more or less authority to speak. The tension was intruding on her family's peace and creating challenges for Janet and her family.

A poststructuralist account of power relations emphasizes the role played by discourse in the construction of the norms by which people make decisions and establish institutional policies or state mandates. It is interested in how particular forms of knowledge come to dominate a field of inquiry and does not assume that these knowledges are always dominant because of their objective truth value, for example the power bestowed on medical professionals to accurately treat biological conditions. In fact, truth itself often becomes a by-product of power. Particular "regimes of truth" (Foucault, 1980, p. 131) come to hold sway and become taken up as a result of a range of social forces. The rise of conventional grief psychology can be understood through

130

this lens because dominant ideas are often advanced by physicians and academics from esteemed institutions.

On further exploration, Janet expressed concerns for her daughter, particularly Christy, and wasn't sure if she was all right. She knew that Christy had been emotionally affected and was also going through divorce. Janet and Hank were questioning how much Janet could have her girls around.

"Even though the visits sometimes exhaust me, I want to have them close by," she said.

She continued to explain that this was confusing and difficult as her husband did not always approve.

Hank added, "I am just concerned as they hover and do not let her rest. I think they could be here for short periods and I could leave when they are here."

It would be tempting to suggest that Hank is being too controlling, but to do so would be exerting the counselor's power as well. It would be more useful to help Janet and Hank with questions about the practices that produce this kind of conflict. The kinds of questions that might be inquired into, therefore, are as follows.

- What practices become the norm and how are such norms established?
- How have family members been induced to internalize these norms and how do they respond to them?
- Amidst the clamor of voices around death, whose voice matters and whose is excluded?
- How are people positioned by social and cultural lines of force (Deleuze, 1988; Winslade, 2009) in the context of death?
- What stories are told or silenced before and after a person's death?

These questions both structure personal responses and are structured by them. They assume an individual who is not completely free, because they live in a social world, are shaped by cultural norms, and must use language to communicate intelligibly with others. But this person is also not just a puppet of social forces either. As a discourse user, they are always in the position of exerting some influence on the discourse they are using.

The democratic ideal we are espousing here is one in which people have a say in the construction of their own lives. They are not completely dominated and neither are they completely independent. As Jacques Derrida argues (see Monk, Winslade, & Sinclair, 2008), such a democratic vision is always deferred into the future. Hence, in a play on words that works better in French than in English, Derrida talks about the "democracy to come". It never finally arrives but it is a democracy that is to be sought nevertheless.

There are many directions we could go in this chapter and we cannot pursue them all. We shall, therefore, concentrate on the politics of the therapeutic relationship as one starting point. We shall also refer to the politics of knowledge and consider epistemological power relations within the knowledge that has developed around death and grief. Finally, we shall also consider some of the social forces at work in the contexts in which people are bereaved that exert powerful effects on them and touch back with Janet and Hank as well.

The Politics of the Therapeutic Relationship

In the hands of Michel Foucault, professional knowledge lost its innocence. Power was no longer all in the hands of the capitalist overlord or the political leader. Nor was it all associated with Dwight Eisenhower's indictment of the military-industrial complex. Foucault showed how professionals seized upon opportunities to construct the world according to their own ideas and exerted disciplinary control over aspects of people's lives. Having spent time working in the psychiatric clinic at La Borde, Foucault had a particular interest in the psychological professions. In his genealogical investigations into nineteenth-century psychiatry in France (Foucault, 1999), he traced how, at a particular moment in time, psychiatrists seized from the courts the right to say when a defendant at trial was guilty or innocent by reason of insanity. At the same time, they claimed to be able to treat such insanity. According to Foucault, they achieved this coup not so much on the basis of a strong clinical knowledge, but because of the ability to take control of discourse and shape it.

Modern psychology has inherited this legacy. Psychologists, counselors, social workers, and psychiatrists all participate in the promulgation of the privileges that accrue from this disciplinary power. As Gilles Deleuze (1988) observes, "The sciences of man are inseparable from the power relations that make them possible" (p. 74). Power influences the exchanges of discourse that take place in the counseling room when people are experiencing the suffering that grief brings. Without taking great care, it is easy for psychological professionals to become intoxicated by the privileges that accrue from this disciplinary power in every moment of their practice. Clients often look to professionals to assume this position in hope for relief from their suffering. The power exists in the right to name and to diagnose, the power to ask questions, the power to assume right of entry into someone else's intimate experience, the power to control time, to exact fees, and so on.

Professional power also exists in the forms of knowledge that professionals are trained in, believe in, and practice from. As Árnason (2000) shows, the practice of grief counseling as "emotion work", no matter how much it is performed in a person-centered way, directs people into a particular version of life. It is associated with a particular political vision, Árnason argues, that stresses the rhetoric of enterprise, freedom of choice, individuality, and personal initiative as the driving force of human action. It is embodied in a view of emotions as naturally occurring and as separate from the social contexts in which they occur. Árnason demonstrates that this view is contestable, but it nevertheless has held sway, in its political form, through the growth of a neoliberal political hegemony that has gathered force around the world (see also Rose, 1999).

At the same time, it is easy to get carried away with the analysis of this kind of power and represent it as total domination. Actually, people do have, and often exert, the power to refuse professional domination, even as they are affected by it. Freud called this refusal resistance and mistook it for a defensive reaction. He trained psychoanalysts to find ways to overcome it. In grief psychology this same charge has been levied against "denial". Sometimes, indeed, "resistance" may serve to keep "neuroses" in place, but sometimes it might also be an expression of vitality, of the will to live life on one's own terms, of desire for personal agency in the face of professional power. In keeping with the theme of this book, not being dominated into giving away this desire for agency is critical if people are going to do grief on their own terms, and craft their own response to it, rather than have it designed for them in pre-packaged stages or tasks. Let us include, by way of example, another piece of Janet's story.

A meeting took place with Janet's daughters, Christy and Samantha, along with Janet. The two daughters were upset that their mother's nurse had taken them aside that morning and talked with them about what was going on.

Christy took up the story, "She was telling us how mom might need to detach from us and couldn't do so as easily if we were around."

Sam added, "It is possible that Hank talked to her and got her to tell us that, but it is a pretty lousy thing to say."

Lorraine was careful to establish a position that did not take sides in the family politics, "Regardless of whether Hank said anything or not, what did you think she [the nurse] meant?"

Sam said, "I think she is telling us we are interfering with Mom's dying by staying close. Not that it would be helpful that we would want to do things for her."

Janet had an opinion here. She said, "I know this is hard, girls, but she might know what she is speaking about too, since she's the nurse."

Christy was insistent, "Mom, I don't want to stay away. That is just wrong. How are you going to get to the toilet or get water? I want to be with you and I feel bad when I am not here. I worry about you all the time when I am not here."

Lorraine asked, "If there was a physiological process taking place for Janet that was happening regardless of what you did or didn't do, and if this process was such that you couldn't stop or start if from happening, would knowing this make a difference?"

Sam conceded, "Yes, it would keep things in perspective. It doesn't solve anything that we are not around as much as we want to be, but it helps to think that we are not causing mom more pain or suffering."

Janet picked up on where Sam had left off. "You are not causing me pain. This whole thing has been difficult, but it is not your fault."

Janet shared how she felt confused by what was happening, but more importantly, that this was something that was always with her. She said, "I don't feel like I have a strong voice. I didn't know what I wanted in life. And now, I am facing death still not knowing what I want."

Lorraine asked Janet, "Are you feeling pulled at times about what to do and pulled also between your girls and your husband?"

"Yes," said Janet, "but this is not new. I have felt this way for a long time. It's not that I don't love any of them, but I can't make up my mind what to do."

How might a therapist respond to such expressions? This is indeed critical. If a therapist draws themselves up to full height and insists on professional authority, as it seemed Janet's nurse was suggesting, there is little chance for the client, or family, to be supported in the personal quest for agency. If, on the other hand, the therapist opens up the space in the therapy room for a democratic sharing of power, without giving away completely the experience and skills they have developed, but instead are willing to deploy these in the interests of the client, then a different kind of relationship can ensue. It can be based on a genuine partnership, on a collaboration (Paré, 2013).

In a collaborative partnership, a counselor might abandon some of the privileges that professional membership bestows and might offer to the client the opportunity to control things such as: the right to define and name problems; the right to assess and evaluate persons and situations as normal or not; the right to interpret meanings;

the right to use particular counseling techniques (including the right to ask questions); the right to set therapeutic goals; the right to give advice; the right to make life decisions; the right to suggest homework assignments; and so on. Each of these are rights that therapists have often assumed without ever asking clients for. Each is a domain of micropolitics. Each of them, therefore, can become an aspect of professional colonization if we are not reflexive about how we assume the right to exercise such power. David Paré (2013) outlines a vision of counseling performance that aims at a collaborative partnership to mitigate against the dangers of professional colonization.

Curiosity and Respect

In this section it is our intention to map out the contours of such a partnership in relation to grief counseling in particular. It begins in an attitude of respect and the practice of curiosity about the knowledge of their own life that each client has. Dubbed by anthropologist, Clifford Geertz (1983), as "local knowledge", and by psychologist, Jerome Bruner (1990; see also White, 2001), as "folk knowledge", this knowledge can be treated by counselors as trustworthy, rather than as inferior knowledge or superstition, not worthy of the respect of scientist-practitioners. When it comes to the experience of grieving, people's expertise in their own experience can be relied on more than psychological models to suggest what they will find comforting. Counselors need to develop skill not so much in diagnosing and matching people's lives to existing models, as in asking questions to inquire into how people are using the skills already at their disposal to make sense of death and its aftermath. It requires curiosity to inquire how the deceased person's influence helps, or hinders, grief. Because we had the opportunity to speak with Janet before her death, she was able to hear where some of these future influences might feature in the lives of her daughters.

Such curiosity is almost like the deliberate adoption of naiveté. It is about seeking to be informed by what the client might say in response to a question like, "Why is that important to you?" The tone of the question is important too. Such a question should not be asked in a way that demands a justification or insinuates judgment, so much as out of genuine interest. It might be directed at the content of a client's emotional experience but might also focus on their cherished values and beliefs.

Asking these kinds of questions is a skill that can be practiced and developed too. One way to know that one is accessing such skills is to

135

experience being repeatedly surprised by what people say. Surprises are the key to hearing little moments of differentiation (in Deleuze's terms). If everything seems predictable, then the chances are that a counselor is not hearing enough exotic detail yet in what a client is saying. Here is how Janet, Sam, and Christy started to develop this.

Janet started by explaining her difficulty in speaking her mind, "Yes, but this is not new. I have felt this way for a long time. It's not that I don't love any of them, but I can't make up my mind what to do."

Her difficulty seemed to flow from the family politics. Lorraine therefore asked, "Can I ask you and the girls a few questions about the future too?"

They all nodded in agreement.

Lorraine continued, "Imagine a time down the road and look back to now. What might you want to say about how you knew that you wanted everyone to get along?"

Janet had something to say now, "I hope we can talk about how I really value peace. They are family and I want them to get along."

Lorraine turned to Sam and Christy, "Is this a value that your mother has always stood for or is this something new?"

Christy was the first to respond, "She has been this way for a long time. She has told us time and time again that you can catch more with honey than with bees."

Lorraine was curious, "What did that statement mean to you?"

It was Sam who answered this time, "She wants us to be nice and not sting or hurt. That has always been true. When she was first going to marry Hank, she asked Christy and I if we could get along for her sake."

Lorraine pursued the political point, "When you look back on this time from somewhere away in the future, would you say there are some things your mom has done that are consistent with who she has strived to be?"

Christy and Sam both readily agreed.

Lorraine's questions seek to honor the value of Janet's role in the family politics. In the process, Janet is able to articulate and embrace her position as an advocate for peaceful relations, rather than as a personal deficit. In the shadow of death, this exchange later takes on extra significance for Sam and Christy. Ethical practice also involves taking deliberate care to forestall the possibility of domination by going beyond the basic standard of ethics that is usually embodied in codes of ethics. This might mean treating many more moments than is legally required as opportunities for clients to exercise informed consent. For example, a counselor might regularly ask a client whether the conversation is going in the desired direction or addressing the topics the client would prefer to address. It might also mean asking permission to inquire into a particular topic, rather than assuming the right to ask. Finding ways to check out whether a counseling conversation is experienced by a client as helpful is also important to remaining client-centered. It might involve intentionally taking a one-down position and asking a client to inform the counselor, rather than looking for opportunities to pass on one's own accumulated wisdom, professional, or personal.

The Politics of Knowledge about Grief

The field of grief psychology and professional knowledge about how to work with the bereaved is a sub-category of a professional discipline. Because this knowledge impacts on many practices and gives shape to the performance of grieving, it can be referred to in Foucault's terms as a "regime of truth". Many people come to see a counselor with the stages of grief and the search for closure already in their minds. Professional knowledge about grief has infiltrated lay knowledge to a considerable extent. Evidence of this lies in the frequency with which knowledge about stages of grief appears in popular television shows or movies and is replicated in news media.

137

It is also not uncommon for counselors to be asked to work with a young person whose parents are concerned that they "have not grieved yet", say, over the death of a grandparent, usually because the young person has not cried the requisite amount of tears. In such cases, the young person may be fine in their own mind, but may not have satisfied the adult's expectations about the experience of distress in grief. Pressure may have been brought to bear upon the young person to perform emotional expressions to fall in line with what Foucault called the confessional norm. The idea of the need to do "emotional work" to process grief lies in the background here.

If counselors take up the task of inquiring into the experience of loss and take for granted the knowledge that is being referenced by the parents, it is likely that the young person's experience will be colonized. Their own experience will count for less than the disciplinary power that is overlaid onto it. In the most egregious examples, if the young person resists these efforts and insists on being fine, the risk is that they will be consigned to a pathological category. There may, for instance, be a reference to the young person as "in denial". This pathologizing designation will then become a lens through which a person is viewed. Such a designation is as powerful as it is difficult to resist.

The alternative to a counselor exploiting the advantages of disciplinary power lies in a practice founded on a different kind of spirit in which what someone says about their own experience is taken more seriously than conventional disciplinary knowledge. This might mean listening for the expressions a person uses that affirm identity beyond the individual self in a sense of belonging to a community of people who have something to say about what is of value to them. This break with the individual self and affirmation of the communal self is what leads to the political expression of what a particular bereavement means. It may involve protest about a situation, assertion of a perspective, or rejection of a designation.

An example comes from an Australian study into the experiences of parents of young persons who had died in car accidents (Breen & O'Connor, 2010). This study honored the participants' private and sometimes public resistance to both the dominant knowledges about grief (which tended to be short-term, stage or task based, jargon-riddled, and pathologizing). These parents found that the dominant models of grieving were imposed on them (often by family or friends, if not by professionals) and departures from these models were policed. They felt silenced and yet gained more of value from peer support from others who had experienced similar losses, and some of them drew strength from working actively in social and political resistance to existing medical and legal frameworks. These parents were advocates on behalf of a principle of justice for their children's sake.

A similar example arose from the tragic shooting of twenty elementary-aged school children and six adults at Sandy Hook Elementary School on December 14, 2012 in Newtown, Connecticut. Many of the parents whose children were killed came together to launch The Sandy Hook Promise (http://www.sandyhookpromise. org), an education and advocacy organization aimed at ending gun violence and supporting mental health early intervention programs toward this end. It is another place where grief is channeled into political advocacy to give continued meaning to the lives of the young children who died. At the press conference announcing the newly formed organization one month after the death of his son Ben, David Wheeler said the following:

My wife and I have spent the last month tasked with being the best possible parents for our surviving son, Nate. But what we have recently come to realize is that we are not done being the best parents we can be for Ben. If there is something in our society that needs to be fixed or healed or resolved, it needs a point of origin. It needs parents.

(Stableford, 2013)

Counselors should support such attempts to exercise agency on their own behalf of children, and understand it not as pathological, but as a brave effort to craft their own responses to grief.

Social Forces That Exert Influence on the Practice of Grief

The politics of grief extend beyond the politics of therapy itself, however. They also frequently include points of connection with other social and political forces with which death becomes intertwined. When this happens, the meaning someone makes of death and the process of grieving become bound up with these social and political forces. Counselors, therefore, need to be alert for the lines of force (Winslade, 2009) that run through the personal aspects of grieving and impact on the meaning of the death.

The anthropologist Barbara Myerhoff was studying the lives of members of an elderly Jewish community in Venice Beach in California in the 1970s and 1980s. She was concerned about the invisibility of this community and began conducting life history seminars to help increase their visibility to themselves and to "enhance reflexive consciousness" (Myerhoff, 1992, p. 232). Reflexive consciousness referred to a sense of folding the consciousness of community back on itself so that members of that community could become more intentionally aware of it. Myerhoff called the ritual performances she witnessed "definitional ceremonies" (p. 234), because she understood them to serve the purpose of "collective self-definitions specifically intended to proclaim an interpretation to an audience not otherwise available" (pp. 234–5).

While she was doing the life history seminars, an event transpired that revealed the political character of this work. A member of the community, Anna Gerber, aged 86, was struck by a bicyclist and died from her injuries. As Myerhoff wrote:

The youth who hit her was reported to have said in defense of himself, "I didn't see her." His statement outraged the old people, for Anna had been directly in front of him. Clearly it seemed a case of "death by invisibility".

(Myerhoff, 1992, p. 265)

The outrage was expressed in a protest march, complete with a mock black coffin and placards reading, "Save our seniors", "Life not death in Venice", "Let our people stay", and so on. The march was led by two blind men and included people using walkers, while all the participants wore bright clothing to make themselves visible and to not "look poor or pathetic" (ibid.). Marchers were heckled by young people and the elders "spoke up sharply" (ibid.) in response. The march ended at a synagogue where the elderly people refused to be divided into males and females (another form of political protest) and held a memorial with prayers for Anna. Afterwards, they returned to their community center where a celebration was held for another community member who was turning 100.

Myerhoff noted the existence of a series of "reflecting surfaces" (p. 268) that made the event definitional for the members of the community. One was the presence of news media, which helped make them visible in a way they had not been previously. They "exploited signs of their fragility" through the use of canes and walkers but presented themselves as "strong presences" (ibid.), for example in the way they dressed. They laid claim to "moral superiority" despite their "structural inferiority" (p. 267). They made a public show of being "angry but not defeated" (p. 267). They were quite literally "making a scene" (p. 266) to get their message across.

Myerhoff comments on the effects of this event for the community members. She notes how they changed their position in their world. Local politicians took note of their concerns and acted upon them. The elderly people actually became stronger in their sense of community solidarity, because they had expressed their grief in a way that both honored Anna and made them proud to be members of a community with her. They were angry not as an expression of a stage of grief, but as an expression of a desire to bring about change.

The challenge for therapists is to help people identify such processes with the people who consult them. In Barbara Myerhoff's example, the political expression evolved organically and she managed to hold it to the light. In other contexts it might only become clear through careful conversation. Let us now examine some other situations where grief and political lines of force mingle.

Lorraine asked Janet, "Down the road, when your girls are speaking about how you have been a supportive peaceful force, what do you hope this would mean to them?"

Janet responded, "I know they will continue to remember. Sam can get hot-headed and I don't want her telling off people at work, as I know how much she likes working at the school. I hope she would remember to be a little more patient and kind."

Lorraine continued, "And if she or Christy were to tell this story about you as a way of introducing you to the people in the future – that you are a woman who supports peace and people getting along – what might it mean to you?"

Janet thought carefully. "I don't know," she said. "I haven't thought about this much, but I would hope they would find something of mine that is useful to them."

The Politics of Military Deaths

One context in which lines of force exert powerful influences on grieving is the military context. For example, Udel Lebel (2011) traces several shifts that have taken place in the experience of grief in Israel for families who have someone killed in battle. In the early years of Israel, says Lebel, private family grief was commonly taken up in relation to a hegemonic state requirement to grieve within specified nationalistic parameters. Families that made the "supreme sacrifice" were expected to align their expressions of grief to fit a national "regimen of bereavement" (p. 354), through which their personal experience was appropriated to bolster a national agenda. Loss was converted into sacrifice, and family members were expected to behave in emotionally restrained ways (avoiding crying in public, displaying public decorum, and so on). This expectation was backed up, according to Lebel, by a panopticon effect promulgated by the military and the government with the connivance of the media.

Lebel then traces how the dominance of this ethic shifted as a result of social protest by family members of soldiers who had died. Parents abandoned their observation of the required restraint and began behaving in ways that did not meet official expectations, in part because of growing public dissatisfaction with the performance and behavior of the IDF (Israel Defense Force). Again, the expression of grief was encompassed by a meaning that had a social force behind it, but this time it was a counter-force, rather than a state-sanctioned force. The point is that the expression of grief is often more than just a private, personal experience. The personal is inevitably bound up in the political to some degree. Therefore, the crafting of grief frequently needs to involve the bereaved in the crafting of a political stance.

The Israeli example links with other examples of a similar nature. In Britain, a ritual developed around the repatriation of the bodies of soldiers who had died in Iraq and Afghanistan that centered on the town of Wootton Bassett (Jenkings, Megoran, Woodward, & Bos, 2012). This town lay close to an airforce base where all bodies repatriated from these two wars landed in Britain and were taken to the coroner's office in Oxford before being released to their families. Jenkings et al. (2012) point out that, until a change of policy in 1991, British soldiers who died in foreign wars were buried where they died, rather than being repatriated. A ritual developed in the town in which people lined the main street of Wootton Bassett in silence as the vehicles drove by. Some were family members of the dead, some were civilians, and some were military personnel. Among the latter, it became commonplace to salute as the hearses drove by. The ritual arose organically and was not organized by the military or by political leaders, but it took on political significance, which grew as it began to be reported in the media. The invention of a ritual for mourning of the dead, as Jenkings et al. show, stood in for political support for the war. This became clear when a controversial Islamic leader planned to organize a march through the town to commemorate the non-British Muslim dead in these wars as well. Once again, grief was not just a private experience. It became bound up in political debate about the wars themselves.

The boundaries between what is public and what is private are frequently disturbed by the grief of bereaved persons. It was one of the points of concern about the intrusiveness into the private domain by paparazzi after the death of Princess Diana. It is only when they are disturbed, however, that we become aware of the fact that such boundaries are established by an unspoken political consensus. In other words, the boundaries are an artifact of discourse. Sometimes, people deliberately transgress against this consensus to make a public (and therefore political) argument out of an otherwise private experience of grief. Such was the case with Cindy Sheehan (Murray, 2012) who in 2005 used her personal grief over her son's death to express her opposition to the Iraq war. She expressed her emotions over her son's death very publicly and demanded, as she camped outside George Bush's ranch in Crawford, Texas, to know from the U.S. president, "For what noble cause did my son die?" The question was rhetorical and Cindy Sheehan has been described as using "grief as a mode of public argument" (Murray, 2012, p. 14). Although some

142

were shocked that she did so, it can be said that she created, through protest, an added meaning for her son's death and her own grief.

In an article on the development of the "New Dawn" organization in Iceland, Árnason, Hafsteinsson, and Grétarsdóttir (2004) trace how the experience of grief in Iceland has been shaped by both recent and long-standing political narratives. On the one hand, grief is associated with a long history of loss from an ancient glorious past and, on the other hand, with the production of a modern neoliberal self, untrammeled by the former burdens of the nation state and making public what was once a more private experience. Ánarson et al. argue that the institution of grieving as an "ongoing private project" involves "turning yourself into a subject of liberty and [making] responsibility a personal endeavor" (p. 342). This is a political move in the sense that it fits with the development of a new right agenda of privatization of public assets and the downsizing of the welfare state.

Klass and Goss (2003) argue that the function of cultural narratives about grief is political in another specific sense. These narratives, they say, police grief and maintain the cultural frameworks in which people are allowed to express their grief. These cultural narratives exert pressure on individuals to make their cultural actions conform to the larger cultural narrative. They cite examples from contexts as widely different as Maoist China and Wahhabi Islam. In both instances, they illustrate how individual experience is channeled so that it can conform to collective grief narratives and thus legitimize political narratives.

Janet unfortunately did not live long past the conversation above with Lorraine and her daughters. She took a sudden turn for the worse and slipped into a coma. During this time, her daughters continued to be by their mother's side as much as they could and Hank remained uneasy about it. He spoke about how he hoped his life would return to normal and that he would be relieved when Janet was free from suffering. He struggled to find compassion for her daughters, but he felt he had been protective of Janet till the end.

Christy and Sam did share one last conversation with Lorraine after Janet's death. During this conversation, they both expressed the distress they felt at feeling separated from their mother in her final days. There had been one particularly bad incident just following Janet's death, when Hank had threatened to call the police to get Christy to leave her dead mother's side and "to get out of his house". Luckily, this threat was not actualized and the hospice workers were able to defuse the situation, but it still had been very painful for both Christy and Sam. During the conversation with Lorraine, they spoke

143

about their mother as a woman who was willing to make peace, even when it was under threat. They both agreed that Janet would have wanted them to stand down to Hank, rather than having things become more out of control or have the police involved. This was a place of solace.

Disenfranchised Grief

Another way in which social discourses exert an influence on the way people grieve is through the establishment of norms about who is entitled to show their grief in public. Those who are not so entitled have been referred to as experiencing "disenfranchised grief" (Doka, 1999). The difference between those who are expected to show their mourning and those whose public shows may be frowned upon is a difference in entitlement. The implication of the concept of disenfranchisement is that the general discourse exerts power over what is regarded as acceptable, normal, and true. In other words, entitlement is granted by dominant discourse, rather than, say, legislative fiat. Wherever the dividing line falls, some will lie outside it. Doka (1999) suggests that there are rules about "when, where, how, how long and for whom people should grieve" (p. 37). These rules may be said to disenfranchise recognition: of the person who is grieving; of the relationship between the deceased and the grieving person; and of the loss that is being grieved (Martin, 2002).

In a modern world, the frequent assumption is that those who have a close family relationship are allowed the latitude of space to grieve. There is a close relationship between the discourse of grieving and the discourse of kinship (Butler, 2004; Reimers, 2011). Such designations are frequently made manifest in employment rules about who is allowed time off work, and for how long, as bereavement leave. Others are excluded from these provisions. It means that the experiences of those who belong to cultures which honor intensity in extended family relationships are not recognized. Others who may be disenfranchised in some quarters include parents who have experienced miscarriages, unrecognized lovers, gay spouses and partners, work colleagues, pet owners, and those whose loved one died by their own hand. For example, Reimers (2011) shows how in Sweden a heterosexual kinship norm exercises hegemonic control over grieving practices and marginalizes other LGBT relationships. Importantly, however, she also documents instances of subversion of this hegemony where people are able to exert agency and resistance to these norms.

Harju (2015) uses the concept of disenfranchised grief for a different purpose to describe the experience of fans who are affected by the death of someone they admired (such as Steve Jobs), even if they are not close relatives. Judith Butler (2006), however, traces something much more contentious hiding in the "recesses of loss" (p. 22). She poses the question, "What makes for a grievable life?" (p. 20). Her answer is that it is not just a matter of personal connection but a matter of political recognition of someone as legitimately vulnerable. Those whose lives are bound up in "precarity" are not so likely to be mourned when they die. In other words, the position that a person occupies in the social world while alive, in the legitimate mainstream or on the margins of legitimacy, makes a difference to whether that person's death is recognized as grievable.

She notes that many lesbian and gay people fall outside this category, as do those who are intersexed, transsexual, and transgender. She also refers to American soldiers fighting in foreign wars as grievable, while those whom they kill are not. Those who are made "other" by either social or military violence are scarcely accorded the status of being human by a dominant humanistic discourse and, therefore, their lives are not recognized as grievable. She cites, by way of example, a San Francisco newspaper as not accepting obituaries of a Palestinian family killed by Israeli troops, lest doing so cause offense. In this way, the politics of the social norm insert itself into what is often regarded as the privatized world of grief.

So what is the response that counselors might make to someone who seeks consultation about grief that they may experience as disenfranchised? According to Neimeyer and Jordan (2002), disenfranchised grief amounts to an empathic failure, which suggests that addressing the problem lies in the counselor providing the empathy that has been missing. They rightly caution against attributing to the disenfranchised a deficit condition in the person who is experiencing it. We believe, however, that providing someone with an experience of counseling that is animated by nonjudgmental empathy is useful but not sufficient.

If we were to recognize disenfranchised grief as symptomatic of normalizing judgment (Winslade, 2013) based in dominant discourse, then another step beyond empathy is suggested. It is the step of turning the judgment back on itself. Normalizing judgment is the term developed by Michel Foucault (1978; 1999) for the ways in which people are more likely to be judged in the modern world for whether their actions are normal or abnormal, rather than right or wrong. There are hundreds of ways in which people can be assigned deficit conditions if they transgress such norms, and disenfranchised grief is one of these. The step of turning a judgment back on itself entails inviting people to deconstruct the dominant discourse itself and examine the work it has been doing. For example, someone whose grief has been disenfranchised might be asked, "What is the assumption that is being made about you and your experience by the lack of recognition you have been offered? What do you think of that? Is it fair or not?" This last question actually invites the person who has been subject to social judgment to judge the judgment.

As Harju (2015) asks rhetorically, "Who gets to say whose grief is legitimate? Who gets to say which type of grief is allowed and socially sanctioned? Who gets to say when grief is real, or indeed, enough?" (p. 125). These are legitimate questions that bespeak a spirit of social critique. If we are to help people craft a response to the challenges of grief then, such questioning is needed of the specifications that dominant discourse lays down. That is what it means to intervene in the politics of one's own subjective experience. We believe that grief counseling needs to entertain an openness to the possibility of protesting hegemonic meanings. Disenfranchised grievers may often be interested in protesting their own disenfranchisement. Such a desire too deserves an empathic response. Counselors, therefore, need to be prepared to respond to this and facilitate their clients in decision-making about how they might express the desire to protest against ways in which they are not recognized as living grievable lives.

What we have not yet addressed is the language in which modernist discourse specifies that we should think about time and how this impacts on death and the stories of grief. This too is a particular domain of political influence. This is the subject we shall turn to in the next chapter.

CHAPTER 7

Elastic Time

The novelist John Berger has his main character in *Here Is Where We Meet* (2005) engage in a series of meetings in different locations in Lisboa with his mother. This is not remarkable in itself except that his mother has been dead for fifteen years. Their meetings take place in his dreams. They are vivid meetings in which different moments of his life from boyhood through to old age (long after she is dead) are concertinaed together in succession. His mother teaches him things about life and scoffs at his idiosyncrasies. Toward the end of his meetings with her, Berger comments, "After the death of mothers, time often doubles or accelerates its speed" (p. 54).[1]

In this brief sentence, Berger alerts us to a different sense of the passing of time. He alludes poetically to the elastic experience of time, rather than to the straightforward categorization of units of time as it is measured. To appreciate time in this way, we need to step out of the world of conventional knowledge and into the way time is sensed in multiple ways. Berger is suggesting that death interrupts our experience of time and throws us into a different sensibility where time can speed up or slow down.

Berger is not the first or the only writer to talk in this way. Gilles Deleuze (1990) traces the way in which Lewis Carroll (1865) treats time as elastic in the classic story of *Alice's Adventures in Wonderland*. Amidst the dreamlike absurdities that mark Carroll's text, Deleuze teases out an almost hidden sense along which the logic of the plot flows. Even nonsense words convey a sense and absurd actions make sense if we suspend our usual modes of logical thought. The novel transgresses our usual logic of causality and inhabits a world of effects,

1 This sentence is reproduced with permission from Vintage Books from John Berger's *Here Is Where We Meet*.

or what Deleuze refers to as a logic of "quasi-causality" (p. 33) where the linearity of cause and effect cease, while the paradox of timelessness opens to the continuity of becoming. There are a number of ways in which Deleuze analyzes Carroll's use of language, but here we are most concerned with Carroll's use of time.

Chronos and Aion

Deleuze elaborates on two particular ways of thinking about time. Each of them is "complete and excludes the other" (p. 61). Drawing on ancient Stoic thought, one of these he calls *chronos* and the other is *aion*. *Chronos* is the conventional way in which we conceptualize time as divided into the past, the present, and the future, as well as into minutes, hours, and days. There is, however, another sense, another logic, another discourse, in which time can be conceptualized and Gilles Deleuze refers to it as *aion* (p. 61). In this logic (Foucault might call it a "regime of truth", 1980, p. 131, or Wittgenstein, 1953, a "language game"), the past, the present, and the future are not marked off into tidily separate categories. They are fluid, flowing backwards and forwards into one another. The past flows into the present and the future is implicit in the now. Deleuze references the recognition of this reading of time to "the greatness of Stoic thought" (p. 61) and alludes to the parable of the tortoise and the hare as a representation of this sense in narrative form.

In this chapter, we want to explore the ways in which death disrupts our usual sense of how time is carved up as *chronos* and throws us into a different world of understanding the passing of time as *aion*. Rather than setting these two "readings" (p. 61) of time into conflict or competition with each other, Deleuze's account invites us to hold a dual appreciation for what each sense of time makes possible. As he does with regard to other aspects of living, Deleuze advocates for multiplicity that enhances life, rather than for reductive simplicity.

The Event of Death

When someone dies, an event takes place, even what Deleuze calls a "pure event", and an event can be thought of as a "singularity". Deleuze (1990) explains:

Singularities are turning points and points of inflection; bottlenecks, knots, foyers, and centers; points of fusion, condensation, and boiling; points of tears and joy, sickness and health, hope and anxiety, "sensitive" points.

(p. 52)

What distinguishes an event from a mere accident is the sense we make of it. There is not any difference in the thing itself, in what took place in the time of now, measured as units of *chronos*. What happens in the now is rendered into and registered as an event, or as a singularity, by the sense, or the mode of thought, in which we think of it. Thus, when we grieve, we do not just grieve the moment of death of a loved one, or even the causes of that moment – we grieve a much fuller sense of how a person's life stretches out in our memory. In doing so, we collapse our sense of time from the usual way in which it is measured and calculated. We construct a narrative of a person's life, and this narrative dances before our eyes in the immediacy of our sense of *aion*. It is in the collapsing of time into this narrative that we defer to cultural patterns, or to discourses that enable the making of sense of how one life is part of the larger tapestry of life. As Deleuze suggests, we sense "an eternal truth" (p. 53).

As a person passes through the foyer of death, they may be said to step outside their existence in time as *chronos*. The event of death happens in the now of *chronos* but the now quickly passes into history and a sense of the person's death begins to form in the logic of *aion*. We can pass from one sense of time to the other at moments when the two readings of time "resonate" (Deleuze, p. 53). This happens at critical moments of "fusion, congelation, boiling, condensation, coagulation, and crystallization" (p. 53).

To illustrate the fluidity of time where we have our feet in many time zones simultaneously, we wish to offer some pieces of transcript from a conversation between Daniel and Lorraine. In this conversation, Daniel tells how his deceased grandmother has flowed seamlessly between the past (in various retrospective versions of events), has accompanied him over the course of many years, and moves with him into a future where she can take up residency in his life. It is notable that Daniel's grandmother lives in both a sense of *chronos* and in *aion*.

```
DANIEL:  I'd like to introduce you to my grand-
         mother Ann.
LORRAINE:  Ann. Did you have a special name that
           you called her?
```

DANIEL: Grandma.

LORRAINE: Grandma. Would it be ok if I also called her that?

DANIEL: Yeah, absolutely.

LORRAINE: Alright. And was Grandma your mom's mom, or dad's mom?

DANIEL: My dad's mom.

LORRAINE: Can you give me a sense about who Grandma was to you?

DANIEL: My Grandma had Alzheimer's disease when I was born. She was diagnosed right before I was born. My relationship with my grandmother, my experience was that she was very reliable, she was never mean or difficult. She was always very pleasant, calm, and like non-fuss. And so I felt very safe with her. My mother and I spent a lot of time going to visit her.

LORRAINE: Before she had Alzheimer's, before you were born, what do you know about the kind of woman Grandma was?

DANIEL: She was very different from what I've been told. She was very, very anxious. Very strict. Very demanding and "passive aggressive". And very much lived through her son or daughter and their accomplishments...so a difficult person to deal with. And that's the story I get from both my father and my mother. But that was not my experience, because that's not who she was anymore when I was a child.

LORRAINE: So you got to have a different kind of grandma. So when you were growing and you were a young boy, what kinds of things did you notice that might have been different from how your parents experienced her?

DANIEL: Well she lost her inhibitions for one thing. So she would say things that were like a little bit...Like she called me a

handsome little bugger once. She had for-
gotten what the word bugger meant. So she
would do things like that. She was just
very tender with me, that's how I would
describe her, very tender.

LORRAINE: So when you were little, what was
that like to have a grandmother who was
tender with you? What was that like for
you?

DANIEL: [pause] It's beautiful.

What is *Chronos*?

The modern science of time has taught us how to measure time and
to allocate different chunks of it for different activities. It is associated
with the logic of causation that governs modern science, business,
and politics. Under the influence of capitalist economic discourse, we
have learned to calculate a value for time and to put a price on our
own or others' time. We can even make a profit from our operations
in the economy of time and find ourselves with the surplus value that
we call leisure time.

Modernist thought has revised the conventional discourse about
time in this way to fit with an economy organized along the lines specified by the version of capitalism that currently dominates. Modernist
reforming zeal has generally been unenthusiastic about maintaining
a sense of the past. The modernist hero Henry Ford famously sought
to free himself from history, when he declared in an interview with
the *Chicago Tribune* that:

History is more or less bunk. It's tradition. We don't want
tradition. We want to live in the present and the only history that
is worth a tinker's damn is the history we make today.

(May 25, 1916, cited in Andrews, 1993, p. 408)

We are also invited by a series of humanistic psychologies and
popular culture texts to live in the now and thus to escape both our
influences from the past and our anxieties about the future. In modern life, time is routinely allocated to clearly demarcated categories so
that there is no blurring of the boundaries between the past, the present, and the future. But the most important sense that is celebrated

in the modern world is the sense of *now* as freedom from the clutches of the past. The now does not collude with our future or the horrors of anticipation, but only focuses on the exacting moments of what is right before us.

Daniel's story is impacted by a particular variation produced by Alzheimer's disease as it changes how a person once was. It divides time into before and after the diagnosis, at which point a person changes, often having lost bits of themselves. In this instance, it was the irony of this particular disease that what was lost made a new relationship possible between Daniel and his grandma and even how this was witnessed by his mother as well.

```
LORRAINE: When Grandma was tender with you and
          uninhibited, what do you think it was like
          for your mom to witness that?
DANIEL: It was really special for her.
LORRAINE: Do you have a sense about how then
          your mom's story shifted, or did it shift
          maybe?
DANIEL: Yeah, oh it did. In the years before
        she died, my mom and I were her points of
        contact, and we were who she remembered.
LORRAINE: What do you think shifted for your mom?
DANIEL: What shifted for her was she saw that
        she was becoming someone different. And
        that it was really important to her that
        her children were connected to their
        grandmother, whenever possible.
LORRAINE: When your mom's story started shift-
          ing about who Grandma was, who her mother-
          in-law was, how do you think that she took
          that back to your father?
DANIEL: I have no idea. When my grandmother
        got ill, my parents' marriage started col-
        lapsing. In the years before she died, my
        father really avoided my grandmother. The
        whole thing was really scary for him.
```

In our conventional sense of *chronos*, a deceased person, and often the person with Alzheimer's disease, has run out of time. This finite (or definitive, perhaps even definitional) sense of time constitutes the reality that we are enjoined by Freud (1917) and most of modern psychology (including grief psychology) to accept. Family members speak about being witness to those who have Alzheimer's disease or dementia as accepting a thousand deaths as they see a person slipping away. The dead, and those who cease to be vibrantly alive, must be consigned to the past. We must change our verb tenses when we talk about them. They are people who *were* and any sense that they still *are* must be regarded as a slip of the tongue, a lapse into an expression born of familiar habit, rather than of deliberate intention, lest concern may grow that a speaker is not connected to reality or is delusional. *Chronos* dominates the logic of mental health, including when it is assigned to grief psychology.

We who are alive are now separated from the dead by a curtain that is drawn across the past – a curtain that keeps separate the distinct categories of *chronos*. The veil of time is drawn across the gap between the living and the dead. We and the deceased exist literally in different time zones and not ones that we can negotiate by turning our watches forward. We, the living, live in the present while they, the dead, live beyond the veil. There are assumptions built into this sense of time that have consequences for the meanings we make of our lives. It is not easy, however, to get a handle on these assumptions, because they are so familiar. They are discursive assumptions that fit precisely into the category of things we take for granted and view as so natural as to be beyond the influence of cultural patterns of thought. They are, we assume, simple realities of life. However, a little deconstructive reflection loosens their natural authority. We can hear the tension between these realities in what Daniel says next.

> DANIEL: My Grandma was nice and kind. I've been scared to share my stories with my father, because I think it would scare him.
>
> LORRAINE: If you were to tell your father about the kind and tender grandmother that you have, what do you hope he would hear?
>
> DANIEL: [pause] That she's remembered, that she's still part of my life. And the way that I remember her is just as valid as any other way of remembering her.
>
> LORRAINE: So it might crack open a little bit of a space?
>
> DANIEL: It might. My thing is I do talk to my grandmother, and I don't think my dad

would understand that. But I talked to
her, since I was really little. And since
I was very little, I have felt some of her
presence, since she died.

One assumption is that time, as it is measured objectively and scientifically, has a mortgage on the real and the subjective experience of time is potentially either illusory or psychotic. This includes the struggle that Daniel faces against there being one "true" version of his grandma, because his differing version of her lives in a different construction of time and reality. Modernist thought has been very particular about the regularization of the measurement of time. *Chronos* has been specified as never before in relation to the movement of the earth. Atomic clocks, and even our cell phones, allow us to insert very precise leap seconds as required to ensure that our time sequences match precisely the rotation of the earth and its movement around the sun.

The Greenwich mean has been chosen as the arbitrary point of origin for our measurement of longitude and the establishment of time zones. In this way, the dimension of time is intimately connected with our measurement of spatial dimensions. We can be exact about knowing the time, if we coordinate with the Greenwich mean. But actually the choice of Greenwich was not just arbitrary. It was a highly relative decision. Greenwich was chosen as a result of the power relations that had established the British Empire's pre-eminence on the earth, as well as the power relations that govern the world of science. The strength of the British scientific community, the requisite number of physicists and academic journals to recognize the decision, and the existence of a scientific narrative that could sustain the idea were all part of the installation of Greenwich as the point of origin for time for the entire world and for eternity. Greenwich mean time is thus arbitrarily relative to the social conditions out of which it emerged. It is no less useful because of that. We would only have to travel to a different planet, however, to notice that our division of time into minutes, hours, days, months, and years is also relative to the perspective on life given by living on the planet earth. On Mars, an earth day makes no simple natural sense. The point is, as Foucault maintained, that knowledge emerges out of, and is often constrained by, regimes of truth; that is, by ways of thinking buttressed by dominant discourses that are sanctioned by power relations. *Chronos* is thus always, to an important degree, bound within cultural limits.

154

What is *Aion*?

At times, however, we also need to call upon a different logic to make sense of our experience of time. In this different sense, time is not so bound by the distinctions of modern definitional categories and is noticeably more fluid. Deleuze calls this logic of time *aion* rather than *chronos*. He argues that people do not have a singular logic through which they negotiate their experience of time. Like many other things, time is more usefully thought of as multi-storied. It is a different sense of time that enables Daniel to have an ongoing relationship with his grandmother.

LORRAINE: So when you talk to her, what's your sense about her response?

DANIEL: Hovering.

LORRAINE: What difference would that hovering make for you?

DANIEL: Well, when I was really little, and when my parents broke up, I took refuge in my Grandma and I would talk to her. So it was a comfort. It was a bit unnerving, because I was not taught to expect this kind of experience. But, it was very natural at the same time.

LORRAINE: So is this right, that you had a sense of a companion in her?

DANIEL: Yeah, and it comes and goes. At certain times in my life it's been stronger than others. But yeah, absolutely.

LORRAINE: If you were to call on her, would she be there for you?

DANIEL: Uh hum. Yes.

LORRAINE: And if you were to call on her, would she offer you any particular guidance at that time? Or is it different than that?

DANIEL: It's different than that, because what was most important about our relationship was with us. So I experience her as a wordless presence.

LORRAINE: So what is that, how would you describe that wordless presence?

155

DANIEL: I would just describe it as . . . [tear-
fully] . . . it just feels a certain way. It
feels like I'm walking into her spirit.
Like I'm protected. Like I'm held, held
tenderly.

LORRAINE: What is that like for you to be held
tenderly in her presence? What does that
enable you in life to do?

DANIEL: [tearfully] It helps me to feel.

LORRAINE: And to feel quite deeply?

DANIEL: Yes.

In this sense, the lives of the dead continue to have "duration" in time as *aion*. Daniel's grandma is right beside him, almost as if she is alive, holding him tenderly. "Duration" is the term articulated and elaborated by the philosopher Henri Bergson and adopted by Deleuze (1990). Noting that "it is not easy, in thinking of time, to escape the image of the hour-glass" (p. 26), Bergson asserts that to exist means to endure, to have duration in time. This duration is marked by a ceaseless movement of variation, of change, of a grand-mother's love for her grandson. It involves life and living beings in constant "invention, the creation of forms, the continual elaboration of the absolutely new" (p. 20). Duration through time is not, how-ever, "merely one instant replacing another" (p. 14). It is thus not just about the now or about the reading of time as *chronos*.

It instead involves the accumulation of memory "continually swell-ing with the duration which it accumulates: it goes on increasing – rolling upon itself, as a snowball on the snow" (p. 12). But Bergson is particular about how he thinks about memory. It is not so much a matter of "putting away recollections in a drawer, or of inscribing them in a register" (p. 14). It is rather a process by which the past "in its entirety, is prolonged into [the] present, and abides there, actual and acting" (p. 24). As Deleuze would argue later, Bergson postulated a difference between two senses of time, which Bergson referred to as "concrete time" and "abstract time" (p. 29).

So what is this reading of time as *aion*? For a start, it is recognized and represented in many languages by a different verb form. Time in the infinitive form is not marked for the present, the past, or the future. Rather, it is called non-finite. It need not be "infinite but may only be infinitely subdivisible" (Deleuze, p. 61). Deleuze talks about this version of time being sensed as a "pure straight line, at the sur-face, incorporeal, unlimited, an empty form of time independent of all matter" (p. 62). When we pass into the mode of thought that grants a sense of *aion*, the past, present, and future exist in a fluid relation to each other. The past is never completely gone. It continues in the now. The future too influences and creates the present. There is in fact a flow of time between the three domains of time that *chronos* has designated as real. We have a sense of this flow, rather than just a sense of living in the now. If this sense of time is "incorporeal" and "independent of all matter", then it may be assumed to be indifferent to the real, and to realism.

It seems thus a particularly appropriate place to nurture a sense of personhood that is not incorporated in a live body so much as in a life. Whereas, in a sense of the present, of *chronos*, a person's life may be deceased, in *aion* there persists, or perdures, a sense of a person living on in an incorporeal way as narrative, as having mattered in the corporeal past and of continuing to matter in the future. Indeed, in this sense, there is no reason why a person's life may not continue to accumulate new ways in which it might matter that were not available at the time the person was alive. In this way, a person's life, and purposes, need not be contained in the finite time in which they were incorporated as a body. Thus Daniel explains how his dead grandmother has been a comfort to him following the unexpected death of a dear friend. He is able not only to call on his grandmother's love in his life, but extends that love to his deceased friend as well.

157

> LORRAINE: When your friend died recently, how was your grandmother's presence holding you at that time?
>
> DANIEL: Well he died quite suddenly, tragically. At first, I don't think I felt her when that happened. I've had conversations with him, more recently, and I felt her presence when I'm having these conversations with him.
>
> LORRAINE: What's his name?
>
> DANIEL: Jack.
>
> LORRAINE: Tell me what Grandma loves about Jack?
>
> DANIEL: His heart.
>
> LORRAINE: Would she have recognized his tenderheartedness?
>
> DANIEL: Oh, yeah.

LORRAINE: Would she be holding his tender-
heartedness? So what's that like for you to
know that love is being extended to Jack?

DANIEL: It feels less lonely.

LORRAINE: Is it less lonely for Jack, or is it
less lonely for Daniel, or both?

DANIEL: Both. I hope so.

LORRAINE: Jack is someone who would have liked
that warm love?

DANIEL: Oh, yes. Most definitely.

In the logic of *aion*, the meaning of the death of a loved one opens up to a different kind of reading and that is why it is important for the practice of grief counseling. It means finding new avenues for a continuing relationship or even finding a new purpose for a relationship, as is seen between Daniel's grandmother and friend Jack. Rather than maintaining a sharp division between the present and the past, the logic of *aion* allows for a sense in which the past lives on in the present. Deleuze talks about how an event, like a death, "runs along the entire *aion*" (p. 64). A person who is no longer alive may be said to live on in our minds in a certain sense – the sense of *aion*. This is what Daniel is telling us. Not only does his grandma live on for him, but she has a new timeless purpose for Daniel and now for Jack.

LORRAINE: Daniel, is Grandma's love limitless
for you?

DANIEL: Yes. No question.

LORRAINE: Ok. When you see yourself stepping
into the next day or the next week or the
next month, tell me how you would like to
carry Grandma's love with you?

DANIEL: I'd like to be less fearful of that connection, because it's always been, maybe
when I was really little it didn't feel
not-normal, but as I got older, it did.

LORRAINE: So when you say you would like to be
"less fearful", fearful of...?

DANIEL: That vulnerability and that intimacy of
my grandmother offered.

LORRAINE: Would you be then embracing it more?

DANIEL: Yeah.

The Timelessness of *Aion*

This is the sense in which events are connected to meanings. At the risk of stretching a point, we might link Deleuze's distinction between these two ways of sensing time to Jerome Bruner's (1986) distinction between the dual landscapes of action and consciousness or meaning. Bruner proposes that these two landscapes are connected to an understanding of what constitutes a well-formed narrative. Maintaining a sense of *aion* can be considered necessary for the formulation of the thematic elements of meaning-making that give life (or a narrative about a life) its sense of continuity and significance. To hold onto this sense of continuity, we need to somehow escape the sense of the present and the awareness of *chronos* that it represents.

This sense is not completely different from what happens when someone we are close to goes away on a trip. While the person is gone from our presence, we hold a sense of their significance until they return and in the meantime allocate a place for this person to live in our consciousness. In this way, the person remains alive for us, even without constant reminders of their presence.

This sense of holding someone alive in mind, even without the person's immediate presence, is a skill we learn as children. Jean Piaget (1977) called it "object permanence". It develops along with an infant's ability to have a sense of a bond of relationship with a parent. When a mother or father goes out of the house, the child learns to manage the anxiety about the person's absence from meaning that the loved parent is gone forever. We even make this object permanence into the game of peekaboo. Young children enjoy the repeated surprise of this game, as they laugh at the contrast between absence from sight for a few seconds, followed by sudden reappearance. The game is instructive as well as playful and it might be argued that the child is learning rudimentary elements of a sense of *aion*. The sense of relationship that a child is learning to trust is sustained across the gaps in presence. In other words, the child learns that they do not need to live entirely in the now. Instead they can hold a memory across the boundary between the past and the present. The same can be true of re-membering a deceased person's ideas or stories. We continue to draw on this "object permanence" to capture pieces of the relationship in the past to act as a timeless platform on which to stand.

159

```
LORRAINE:  I was thinking about what it's like
           for you to be the holder of a story of your
           Grandma as being kind and tender?
```

DANIEL: Special. Sacred.

LORRAINE: How did your grandmother choose you to give that story to?

DANIEL: Maybe I chose her.

LORRAINE: Was there a mutual choosing?

DANIEL: Yeah I think so. I've seen videos of me when I was an infant, and the look on her face when we were together.

LORRAINE: What was that look?

DANIEL: Just wonderment. Just joy.

The experience of grief can be thought of as testimony to this sense of *aion*. Were it not that we still had a sense of relationship that transcends the now, we would not perhaps experience the difficulties of loss. But neither would we be able to hold onto a sense of relationship through any of the challenges that a relationship inevitably sustains. Each hiccup experienced primarily through a sense of the now would spell the end, and could not be matched by what memory of the past can offer. In any relationship, we have learned to carry forward a sense of close connection across the gaps in immediacy of presence. When someone dies, we continue to do the same. What changes is that the sense of relationship is no longer, or at least not so easily, refueled by new experiences of immediacy. Through our sense of *aion*, however, we carry forward a sense of the other that now relies more on memory than on constant refueling in the now. As we shall see, however, holding close a sense of *aion* can also mean the repeated refueling of memory with new experiences. The next few comments in the conversation speak to this sense of how the memory of the past not only refuels the now but becomes infused with it.

LORRAINE: Over the years, have you talked with your mom about how you keep Grandma alive?

DANIEL: Yes and no.

LORRAINE: Which parts have you spoken of?

DANIEL: [pause] Actually you know what, I have, I really have. I shared a poem that I wrote with my mother about my grandmother. It was really about her being with me and some of the images that I hold onto, and the feelings that I hold onto between my Grandma and me. I shared that with my mom,

and I talked to her about sharing it with
my dad, but haven't done this yet.

LORRAINE: When you shared it with your mom,
what was that like?

DANIEL: It felt like I was inviting her in.

LORRAINE: Inviting in your mom and your Grandma?

DANIEL: Yeah, absolutely. Both.

LORRAINE: Was that space for you kind of a
sacred space?

DANIEL: Pretty much. It's the same sacred space
that has always been there between me, my
mother, and my grandmother.

LORRAINE: So is that a very strong place?

DANIEL: Yes. Definitely.

It is not uncommon for people to be in relationships that ebb and flow in an interstitial dance between constructions of time and place – the past, the present, and the future all rolled into one simultaneous frame. As a relationship accumulates memories, it may be said to develop a stronger sense of *aion*. Connections between people do not just rely for their meaning on a sense of immediacy or on what is happening in the now. They also rely on the ways in which the present is layered with memories of the past. Too heavy an insistence on the primacy of *chronos* might devalue the richness that lies in the appreciation of a sense of *aion*.

Cultivating an Aesthetic Sense

In light of our theme of treating the encounter with death as the subject of aesthetic design, rather than passive suffering, it seems appropriate to consult someone who writes about art. The articulation of aesthetic values in André Malraux's (1978) work is relevant in this regard. He makes a series of comments about the relationship between art and death and, in the process, introduces an important distinction that we want to highlight. Echoing Deleuze's sense of *aion*, Malraux remarks that, "Time flows – perhaps towards eternity; assuredly toward death. But destiny is not death" (p. 630). Instead, Malraux conceives of such destiny in the act of artistic creation, which represents a "defense against fatality" (p. 631). "All art is a revolt against man's fate", he claims (p. 639). It is in this resistance toward death that "a man becomes truly Man only when in quest of what is most exalted in him" (p. 642).

161

While we are not all great artists able to resist the fate that death brings us through painting or sculpting a masterpiece that lives on long after our physical bodies, we do all have an aesthetic sense, especially if we cultivate it. It therefore seems appropriate to extend Malraux's argument to everyone. We are all capable of considering our lives as works of art and of cultivating an aesthetic sense through which we might make judgment calls about who we are becoming. In doing so, perhaps like the artist who creates a work of art, we leave a mark on the world. We thus create something that death does not obliterate and, in this sense, resist death and become more fully agentic.

In this vision, counseling those who are touched by death amounts to a practice of cultivation (or entering life into culture). In conversation, counselors can invite forth an aesthetic appreciation of the process of becoming someone that a dying person has crafted and which a bereaved person is left to appreciate and to continue to cultivate. That such cultivation can continue to be crafted after death is an instance of what Malraux was referring to, albeit in a narrower context. It is the crafting of questions that brings the love of Daniel's grandmother close to him and closely interweaves this with the stories of his mother as well. This crafting is most notable in the following excerpt, where Daniel speaks of the ways in which his deceased grandmother becomes the presence of love and strength during his parents' divorce.

162

> DANIEL: My grandma died and my father left almost at the same time. So it was a big loss at that one time. And I had to start taking care of the other people in my life.
>
> LORRAINE: So how did Grandma guide you at that time? In that big life change?
>
> DANIEL: Her presence told me, "It will be ok."
>
> LORRAINE: What did she know about you, that maybe other people might not have known, that she was able to see that for you?
>
> DANIEL: She saw promise. And a lot of beauty and joy and life.
>
> LORRAINE: So when she saw those things, when you were just a little one, did that give her knowledge about what would unfold in your life?

DANIEL: I think it gave her faith. We're a tough stock.

LORRAINE: Ok. So you're tough, yeah?

DANIEL: There's tough stock on both sides of my family. Like, we live forever despite ourselves. And, yeah, we have a stubborn will to survive.

LORRAINE: But your grandmother, it wasn't just stubborn will, was it also stubborn will of love?

DANIEL: Absolutely.

LORRAINE: Yeah, so has that stubborn stock been influenced differently in what she infused in it for you?

DANIEL: Well, there's certainly the tenderness that she brought to it. And my mother's very tender too. So we were very similar that way.

LORRAINE: So for your mom, what's your sense about what it is like to kind of melt into the warmth of her mother-in-law, at a time that her life was also changing?

DANIEL: I think it was a refuge for her too. After my grandmother passed away, my mom always took me to see other elders we knew there. So we continued the tradition of going to the original old folks' home that my Grandma lived in, and visiting the parents of some family friends, and so they became grandparents of mine as well.

LORRAINE: Did your grandma open the door for your mom to have a different story about what grandparents could offer?

DANIEL: Yeah. It was so special for her to have my grandmother.

LORRAINE: Do you have a sense about how that made a different life for you, Daniel?

DANIEL: [pause] It gave me a connection to the past that is very much alive and yeah, it's hard to articulate. It's definitely

163

more rich. I know what it's like to have
a grandparent who's absent. And so I know
what it's like to have a grandparent who's
very there, even though we say she's not
all there [because of her Alzheimer's dis-
ease], she was there.

LORRAINE: She was there. And totally present
with you.

DANIEL: Oh absolutely.

LORRAINE: If she had words or non-words that
she wanted to offer others who hear about
her, what gift do you think she would
bring to that?

DANIEL: Listen to your ancestors. Open your ears
to your ancestors. And, that's what I've
done within my life, I've been blessed
with all this.

We often hear how someone has, in the end, "lost" a battle with
cancer. Even if they are credited with having "fought" this battle for
a long time, the final conclusion is assumed to be decisive. Or we
hear, as Daniel referenced, how a person with Alzheimer's disease
is "no longer there". But we question why the story need be told
in this way. We would argue that it is the assumptions of time as
chronos that are at work here. If we switch to thinking about the same
person's life in terms of *aion*, suddenly all of the person's life comes
into view, not just the immediate fact of their death. As a result,
death does not win out completely, as long as we re-member a life as
a work of art and continue to cultivate an aesthetic sense in which it
may be admired as such.

Practice Implications

So far, in this chapter we have outlined ideas that are complex and
can take some effort to grasp. We are now ready to explore the implications of these ideas for therapeutic practice. It is time, in all senses
of this word, to go there.

In the first place (notice how we have many linguistic markers of
time), if our thinking were completely governed by the immediacy
of *chronos*, then it would make sense in grief counseling to emphasize the facts of the here and now. We would enjoin clients to accept

this reality as quickly as they can turn their faces toward it, assigning the event of death and the pain associated with grief to the past. We would ourselves use past-tense verbs when talking about the deceased to underline the "reality" that the person has gone. We would select out for recognition and empathy anything the client says that suggests movement toward the acceptance of the death as final. Any utterance that the client makes that hints at a gap between the present, in which they live on alone, and the past, in which the deceased and the bereaved lived in some form of relational connection, would be welcomed as movement toward a positive therapeutic outcome. And we would encourage the saying of a final "goodbye" and the letting go of a sense of relationship. These would not be viewed as harsh interventions but as compassionate attempts that offer healing.

All of this makes good sense, if we are thinking of time in terms of *chronos*. If it sounds familiar, it may be because many of the grief counseling conventions give form to these kinds of assumptions. In Deleuze's terms, the virtual aspect of these assumptions is actualized in the living out of the implications of the death of a loved one.

Neither are we suggesting that this reading of time is irrelevant. Everyone does have to live in the immediacy of the present. There are some realities that do have to be accepted. For example, a corporeal sense of the deceased as an embodied, living presence is no longer available. There are many things to let go of and even say goodbye to. Bank accounts have to be closed. Property has to be dispersed. People have to be notified of the death. Perhaps dinner has to be eaten alone. The deceased person can no longer consume food, for example, because they have moved from a corporeal to an incorporeal existence.

The problem, however, is that this reading of time has often been overplayed. Doses of modernist realism have been presumed to be the best tonic for every grief symptom. Saying "goodbye" has been taken to heart as a statement of talismanic significance. "Letting go" of a sense of relationship has been totalized to the extent that clients are assumed to have to let go of everything. The reading of time as *chronos* has thus been privileged over the reading of time as *aion*; realism has overruled virtual realities.

What is lost if we insist too strongly on these assumptions drawn from *chronos* is the value that can be accessed in the relationship with the deceased, if we think in terms of *aion*. Let us dwell there for a while and draw some contrasts.

White, in 1989, pointed in this direction in the title of his article, "Saying hullo again". The word "again" suggests the sense of duration that Deleuze wants to retain from Bergson. "Again" suggests a sense of time as moving forward and creating new opportunities. "Saying goodbye" is no longer final, if there is a chance to "say hullo again". Instead time becomes fluid and can be sliced in a variety of ways. Each slice becomes a new opportunity to either say goodbye or say hullo again. Perhaps this is one way of making sense of what Friedrich Nietzsche (1974) referred to as the "eternal return".

The anthropologist Barbara Myerhoff's concept of "re-membering" picks up on the same idea that Bergson stressed when he spoke of memory, or a sense of duration, as a critical component of consciousness. It is necessary, he argued, for the development of *élan vital* (Bergson, 1911), or a vital force. Myerhoff (1992) noticed how the holding of a deceased person in memory as an ongoing member of a community benefited the bereaved. They could continue to actualize the deceased's meaning in their own lives and in the life of their community. They could incorporate the values and actions of the deceased in their own identities, so that the person's death would not be for nothing. Myerhoff showed how responses to the death of a person could be taken up by a community in ways that were enriching, rather than depressing.

If something is enriching and enlivening, and strengthens a grieving person's sense of identity and purpose in life, then we would argue that it has important therapeutic value. To access this potential value, however, we need to think of time in terms of *aion*. This move requires us to shift from conventional chronological thought to a more fluid emphasis on the past, present, and future as flowing into each other. Grief gives us the opportunity to contemplate the life of the person who has died, not just their death. A person's life stretches over many territories and to conceptualize it is to select from it, to set in train some particular narrative. That is what Barbara Myerhoff noticed in an elderly Jewish community in Venice Beach in California.

So how might we make use of this sense of *aion*? One place to start is by asking a bereaved person to engage in conversation about the life of a deceased loved one, as they have known it. Rather than starting with, "Tell me how you have been feeling about the loss" or "How did your loved one die?", it is preferable, we believe, to start grief counseling with questions like these:

- Tell me about this person who died.
- Introduce them to me.
- In what ways do you re-member them?
- What is it like to know them?
- In your memory of them, what stands out?

166

Such inquiries are not invitations to say goodbye. They are more like invitations to keep someone alive in memory, or to "say hullo again". They embody a sense of duration. Notice how they are intentionally constructed to allow the past to flow into the present. There is no insistence on rapid movement into the past tense. You might even say that some of these ways of talking are "unrealistic", and we would agree, as long as what is real is restricted to what appears so from the perspective of *chronos*. From the perspective of *aion*, however, they make much more sense.

The central argument we are making in this chapter, then, is that grief counseling could benefit considerably from reading time as *aion*. There is no need to jettison *chronos* either. It is perfectly possible to entertain multiple readings of time in forming meanings. In fact, according to Deleuze, we do this all the time. As counselors, therefore, we can certainly talk with people about the experience of loss, the breaches in relationship that the death of a loved one brings, and the discontinuities of living that must be negotiated. But we need not stop there. There is much to be gained by inviting bereaved persons into a different reading of time informed by a sense of *aion*. In this reading, the past flows into the present. A person's life stretches out in memory. A relationship continues to pulsate, even beyond the grave, like Berger's relationship with his mother years after her death, and like Daniel's relationship with his grandma. In this domain of experience, a person's life approaches the quality of being timeless.

167

As we re-member a person who is no longer alive, we can repeatedly bring them into the present and update their existence. Such an existence may now be incorporeal in the Stoic terms that Deleuze articulates, but it is nonetheless real and can have perfectly real effects in the life of the living. For example, when a woman becomes a mother for the first time, she might come to know her own dead mother in a new way. The selection of memories that populate her story of her mother's life might alter and form a different narrative. She might even have a sense of her mother guiding her in the formation of her own identity as a mother. This sense may give her comfort, if we talk about it in a careful way, instead of overburdening it with a sense of yearning or painful loss.

The Crafting of Grief

Now let us return to our theme of crafting the process of the grief experience, rather than just suffering through it. We have been at pains in this chapter to stress the multiplicity of the possible readings of time. If *chronos* and *aion* are both necessary, yet represent different readings of time, then it must be possible to become skilled at moving between them. Such movement allows a person to make choices about where to situate different moments of grieving. It is here that an aesthetic sensibility can be fostered. There are no formulaic rules for which reading of time to use. The choices to be made are aesthetic ones. As we grieve, we intuit them as we move through them.

As therapists, it is also useful to think in terms of crafting. The crafting of particular questions and other responses also assumes one or the other reading of time. We are not advocating a wholesale rejection of questions based on *chronos*, but we are advocating a greater emphasis on *aion*, and the asking of many more questions that assume this reading of time. There is much therapeutic value that can obtain through appreciating the life of the deceased, through saying hullo again, through valuing the continuity of a relationship, and through updating memories in the light of new events in life.

168

CHAPTER 8

Embracing Fragility

The Gift of Damocles

Paula has advanced cancer, and knows she does not have long to live. When things became increasingly difficult for her to care for herself, she moved in with her daughter Megan. Paula has been receiving chemotherapy and other cancer treatments, but they have come at a huge cost of energy and painful side effects. She is finding that her memory is not as sharp as it once was and she can no longer see out of one of her eyes. Her daughter, Megan, invites Lorraine to hold a conversation with Paula to help her give definition to her living during this part of her life. This chapter will be built around the conversation that ensues between Paula, Megan, and Lorraine.

169

What we aim to show here is how to craft a conversation in the shadow of death that is still about the affirmation of life. It still seeks to craft something beautiful and sustaining in the face of impending death. There is no need to divert energy into the grim losses that death brings. The painful aspects will do their own work soon enough. They need to be acknowledged but we see no great importance in focusing exclusively on these aspects. What seems more important to Lorraine is to find stories that can represent for Paula the legacy that she might want to live on after her death. This becomes all the more precious as Megan has recently discovered she is pregnant with what will be Paula's first grandchild. Megan's presence in this conversation means that she gets to bear witness to these legacies and thus to have them made available to her, and through her to others, including her future child. In other words, there is a particular relational exchange that is at work here.

As this conversation develops, the presence of death hovering nearby is palpable. It lends an urgency to the task. It allows some things to be said that would otherwise not so likely be spoken.

Some of the beauty that emerges can be appreciated because of its contrast with the ugliness of illness. This is the gift that death can offer when it sharpens our sense of what matters and renders life more precious. This is the gift of Damocles.

In 1961, John F. Kennedy made a speech to the United Nations in which he mentioned the sword of Damocles. He referred to the threat of nuclear annihilation as a sword of Damocles hanging over all of us. The thread that holds this threat over our heads, Kennedy warned, could be cut at any moment, perhaps by accident or by a hasty or irrational decision.

Kennedy's reference was to the story made popular by the Roman orator, Cicero, who told of the courtier, Damocles, a prominent advisor to Dionysius, a fourth-century B.C. Sicilian ruler. When Damocles, so the story goes, made comment about how fortunate Dionysius was to be so powerful, Dionysius invited him to switch places. Damocles quickly accepted the offer. But Dionysius also arranged for a giant sword, held only by a slender thread, to be placed over Damocles' head. The power of the ruler to act was there, but along with it came constant peril. The sword could fall at any moment. In this chapter, we shall examine the extent to which we all live with Damocles' predicament, and not just because of the threat of nuclear annihilation. We all live with the anticipation of death and we never know when the sword might fall.

170

The Imminence of Death

For Paula, the moment when the sword might fall is imminent. Lorraine begins talking with Paula and Megan by inquiring about how life has been for her living with the illness. This is the second time they have spoken together and Paula was recently hospitalized.

> LORRAINE: So since I've last seen you, you've had an ambulance ride, you've had time in the hospital, you've had some chemo treatments...And you've had some time in a rehab center. [Paula nods.] That's a lot, Paula. So how has this been for you?
>
> PAULA: It's been...A lot of it's a blur. You know I kind of remember the hospital stays, but I don't...But I feel like, no, I've got to go through it. So...
>
> LORRAINE: Not easy, just the same.

There is no avoidance of the unpleasant aspects of the cancer and its treatment. These are acknowledged, because a focus on the imminence of death inevitably raises the question of its anticipation. Many people, although importantly not all (think of the deaths of young children, for example), are afforded the chance to contemplate the implications of death, both for themselves and for their loved ones, in the period before death occurs. Even without a death sentence or a life-threatening illness, we all live with the knowledge that one day we will die. This knowledge becomes even more poignant as it starts to move from being a primarily virtual knowledge to a knowledge of the imminence of death.

Hearing the footsteps of death marching implacably nearer need not become the sole focus, however. The period in which these footsteps can be heard also represents another opportunity to craft a response to the presence of death in our lives. Hence, it would be remiss of a therapist to not address it. Paula's speech is uncertain and her memory faulty but she still refers to places where life has meaning for her, especially in her relationship with her family.

Lorraine turns soon to sources of comfort that Paula speaks about in the face of the unpleasantness of chemotherapy. These comforting thoughts are openings to another story of relational possibility. This emphasis on the relationship theme has been a touchstone we have revisited repeatedly through previous chapters. It is no less important here before death than it is in bereavement. The questions we shall address are, therefore, better formulated as relational questions, rather than just as individual questions. The approach of death is not just about how an individual inside themselves might make sense of the hovering presence of death, but also about how relationships might be constructed through this time. What sort of exchanges might be crafted? What allocations of responsibility might be made to the dying and the living? What stories might guide our responses to each other? What social and biological lines of force might be expected to pull us into familiar ruts of thinking and how do we respond to these? In what ways might we craft an aesthetic response, an ethical response, to these challenges? These are the kinds of questions that, for us, circle around this topic.

171

LORRAINE: And since you've been here with Megan
and Nathan [Megan's husband], how is this
for you now? Are you settling in? What are
you finding?
PAULA: I find it's comforting.

LORRAINE: What's comforting about it?

PAULA: The fact that I'm here with Megan.

MEGAN: Aw, it's comforting for me too, to be able to come home from work and be here with you.

The Gifts of Relationship

What has been comforting for Paula then lies in the relationship with her daughter. Lorraine hears this as an opening into a conversation about their relationship and about the gifts that are ushered in alongside the tragedy of death. If we are going to stress the ways in which relationships can be a more useful resource than requiring an individual to face up to death on their own, then it is important to capitalize on such openings and flush out what other storied threads are available at times of great change. But "comforting" is a general concept. It is not very specific. It needs to be opened up with curiosity into some stories.

LORRAINE: So...can I ask you two a couple of questions? Because last time we talked, we talked about a whole bunch of different things. And I'm just wanting to follow up, would that be ok?

PAULA: Yeah.

LORRAINE: Ok. So one of the things I remember talking about was your crocheting and knitting, and how you had been showing Megan how to do this.

PAULA: Yeah.

LORRAINE: How is she coming along as a student?

PAULA: Well, we haven't done any more.

MEGAN: We have the pink...you did a blue baby blanket, and then I have the pink one.

PAULA: I did a blue one?

MEGAN: You did a blue one a while ago, and I have that up in the closet in a bag. I am just about done with the pink one, but you have to help me and we can do that in the next week or so, do a trim on it. Because I want to do a trim, in a different color, like white.

LORRAINE: Now is this crochet or knit?

MEGAN: Crocheting. She can do both but she's taught me how to crochet.

LORRAINE: Ok. Well I remember one of the things you were telling me about the crocheting was that you thought that it might bring patience for Megan sometimes. Do you remember?

PAULA: It might. It's a very calming type of thing, a hobby.

LORRAINE: Yeah, I remember you saying that you were hoping she would find it that way as well. And I remember you were telling me about growing up in England and some of the stories there. Do you remember any of those?

PAULA: Not really.

LORRAINE: Tell me again where you grew up.

PAULA: I grew up in Reading.

LORRAINE: In Reading. And when did you learn how to crochet and knit?

PAULA: Gosh, I can't remember...I remember a teddy bear I had, had a hat on. And he had a half-moon. Wish I had that teddy.

MEGAN: But who taught you to crochet — was it your mom or your grandma?

PAULA: My grandma.

MEGAN: And what was your grandma's name?

PAULA: Umm...Mary.

LORRAINE: And so when you crochet now, or in your lifetime, would you think of your grandmother?

PAULA: Yeah.

LORRAINE: Yeah? And what was that like for you?

PAULA: It was wonderful.

LORRAINE: What was wonderful about it, Paula?

PAULA: Just um...the fact that she, she liked that I crocheted. I think that was neat.

MEGAN: Because it's something she taught you. And then she saw you learning it.

PAULA: She saw me doing it.

LORRAINE: We were talking a little bit about your future grandkids also, and your hope that they might crochet as well.

Bestowing Legacy

In the questions Lorraine asks lie some implicit assumptions. One is that Paula still has things to teach her daughter (here they are about how to crochet). Paula's identity, therefore, cannot be totalized by her suffering. She is not just a patient (literally, one who suffers) but is still spoken into a position of agency (one who acts and has gifts to bestow). But the knowledge of how to crochet and, by implication, her identity, does not just belong to her alone. It is constituted by Lorraine's questions as an aspect of legacy that is passed down through generations – from Mary to her granddaughter, Paula, and then to Paula's daughter, Megan, and on to future grandchildren. Out of the sense of comfort has now grown a consciousness of a skill passed down through generations and this case, there is something tangible that is being passed in the blankets and other items made by Paula. The version of time accessed here is that of *aion*. They step into a timeless storyline. Paula is implicitly invited to draw comfort from her participation in this line. She is thus invited to face death, not through an emphasis on her owning her own life like a piece of property, but through her consciousness of something bigger than her – in this case a female line, defined by a particular skill. Her own death is not so much the final end of her ownership of property but a plot event in an ongoing multi-generational narrative. Lorraine seeks to extend this narrative.

LORRAINE: If they [Megan and her children] were to do that, what's your sense about how that would connect them to you?

PAULA: I think it will connect them to me in the sense that without...without it, they wouldn't get to crochet.

LORRAINE: I'm imagining somewhere off in the distant future, if they were crocheting, let's say they learn how to do these skills, like you've taught Megan to do, would you like stories told about you as they're crocheting?

PAULA: Yeah, I wouldn't mind that.

LORRAINE: Any ones in particular? Things that you would want them to know about who you are and things you've done in your life?

PAULA: Not really, just... [laughs]

MEGAN: I think you're so humble and modest. But one of the most amazing things to me, one of the things that I would want them to know is how patient and kind and sweet you are, you know. And how you are just so easygoing.

PAULA: That has to come from somebody else.

LORRAINE: Oh, so what if Megan told that story?

PAULA: That would be okay. [Megan laughs.]

LORRAINE: That would be okay with you.

MEGAN: I see! You wouldn't be telling stories about yourself, "I'm so great because..."

LORRAINE: Because that would be bragging, wouldn't it?

PAULA: It would.

MEGAN: And she's humble. But I mean, just growing up, whenever I was different, or I wanted to dye my hair, or I...

PAULA: I let you.

MEGAN: You let me. You wanted me to be who I was.

PAULA: Right.

MEGAN: Whereas some parents were very strict and controlling and so then I think their children went and wanted to do bad things more.

PAULA: Right.

MEGAN: But you were never like that. I say you have the patience of a saint. You really do. [Paula is smiling.]

LORRAINE: Is that okay for her to say that?

PAULA: Yeah.

LORRAINE: Do you see that in yourself sometimes?

PAULA: Yeah.

LORRAINE: Yeah. I suspect with what you have had to endure, within the last couple of years, that that patience has been tested. [Paula laughs and agrees.]

Here the practice of crocheting is paired with the sharing of conversation, which allows for the telling of stories. Such storytelling is then enacted through the allusion to some stories of parenting. Because Paula's articulation is not very strong, the telling of these stories needs to be picked up by her daughter. Humility and cancer both make it easier for these stories to be told by Megan and thus they too, like the skill of crocheting, are shared across generations. However, it is clear from her smiling and laughing that Paula appreciates the stories that are emerging of her parenting qualities. At this moment, Paula and Megan are sharing memories of years previously that are, in a sense, being re-lived, re-membered, and re-constituted in conversation. Along with them, something else is being re-constituted. It is the sense of family membership. This too is an aspect that is potentially comforting in the face of death. Implicitly, the message is that death does not have to be faced alone, but in the context of family connections.

Bequeathing Personal Qualities

Before going any further, however, let us admit to a certain bias. It is the bias of an attitude that seeks to emphasize a sense of vitality in life, rather than a sense of morbidity. We are seeking to privilege responses that promote a sense of possibility, rather than acquiescing to pain and the tragic circumstances of death. What has been called anticipatory grief, therefore, is not just a time in which the pain of grief is siphoned off, so as not to be experienced quite as intensely later. It is a time of unique possibility for living, and potentially a time of seeking beauty in the relational exchanges that might transpire. Therapy in this context, then, might be about finding such virtual moments of beauty and actualizing them (as Deleuze might say).

In the conversation with Paula, such a moment is initiated by her daughter Megan.

> MEGAN: But it's so strange – honestly, my friends complain more over small things like a running injury. I complain more over a running injury than she complains about her life. Not to say you can't complain, but you just usually don't. If she does, it's temporary – over something very small. But not what you would expect, not what I would expect.

LORRAINE: So how would you explain that, Paula?

MEGAN: Yeah, how do you explain that?

PAULA: Well, I don't know.

MEGAN: Do you think it's part of your basic temperament or is it something you've learned?

PAULA: I think it's part of my basic temperament.

LORRAINE: Mm. Do you ever feel like hauling off and punching somebody? [Paula shakes her head.]

LORRAINE: No? Do you ever feel like chewing somebody out?

PAULA: No. [smiles]

LORRAINE: So has this helped you in how you parent?

PAULA: I would say so, yeah.

LORRAINE: And how you face obstacles in life...Like cancer?

PAULA: Yeah.

LORRAINE: Yes, okay. So patience has been a friend...for your whole life.

PAULA: It has.

Lorraine may have been curious about these moments of family history, but it is not necessary that she knows what Paula and Megan are referring to. No doubt there are multiple instances of family life all collapsing into a single reference here. As Deleuze suggests, in the mode of thought that is animated by *aion,* the past and the present collapse into one line. The future too is part of this line, because they are speaking about Paula's personal qualities in the context of thinking about her future grandchildren, who might learn about her through being told about these character strengths. This too makes it easier to face the approach of death, to know that one will still be part of the future in a family and that one's personal qualities may not go to the grave and be lost forever. In the last exchange of this segment, Lorraine invites Paula to make a link between the personal quality of patience, which she has exhibited throughout her life and her parenting, and her current struggle with cancer. It is as if patience is summoned to her side. It is needed as a resource that might help her handle the cancer and the treatments for it.

Next, patience is treated in the same way that crocheting was. Paula's personal qualities, like her practical skills, are located in an intergenerational line.

LORRAINE: Were there other people in your immediate family, like your parents or your
grandmother, who helped grow that patience
that you now have?

PAULA: I think the patience came from my
grandmother.

MEGAN: Your grandmother Mary?

PAULA: Yeah.

LORRAINE: She was a patient woman?

PAULA: She was very patient.

LORRAINE: So how did you notice her patience?

PAULA: I just noticed a lot of things happening
and she was instrumental in seeing them
through. Very instrumental.

LORRAINE: So was she also a woman who got things
done?

PAULA: Yes.

LORRAINE: And is that similar to Paula? Paula
is a woman who gets things done in life,
do you think?

PAULA: I think so [laughs].

178

Two things are worthy of note here. First, an intergenerational sense
of membership is being constituted. Paula is thus invited again to see
herself as part of something larger than herself as an individual. Second,
personal values and character are treated as legacies that can be passed
down, rather than as something that dies with a person. Implicitly, Paula
is invited to think of her contributions to the intergenerational line as
having a past and, therefore, a future. Death need not stop this legacy
from continuing, particularly since her pregnant daughter is listening to
this conversation. In this sense, the meaning of her life does not all go
to the grave with her. Through the ongoing line, it continues to resonate
into subsequent generations. Many people find this very comforting.

Actualizing Vitality and Resisting Death

In his book entitled *Foucault*, published after the death of Foucault,
Gilles Deleuze (1988) comments on the death of Michel Foucault:

We can no longer even say that death transforms life into destiny,
an "indivisible and decisive" event, but rather that death becomes

multiplied and differentiated in order to bestow on life particular features, and consequently truths, which life believes arise from resisting death.

(p. 95)

Let us pause for a moment to consider the implications of this statement. It is a carefully worded utterance that conveys some aspects of poststructuralist thought in relation to death. Notice his rejection of the idea that death is a singular event. In Deleuze's terms, it is a multiple event. Appreciating such multiplicity requires that we seek out the subtle places of differentiation, through which each person's experience is different and universal prescriptions fail to capture a sense of the particular moment. Accordingly, Lorraine does not seek to isolate Paula's impending death in Paula's own experience, but to constitute it in a line of multiple lives and deaths, as part of a generational line of becoming.

Notice too that death, in Deleuze's terms, does not convey a final moment of a single "destiny" that renders a life meaningful. Instead, he argues that, like any event, a death can be divisible in a number of ways. Even if we were able to isolate a single frame to represent the moment of death, that frame is actually part of a moving picture. The drama of life is more like a movie than a snapshot. It can be spliced in different ways. As we divide a person's life up in different ways, as we edit and juxtapose scenes, we create different meanings. This is no less true after someone dies than when the person was alive.

179

Deleuze goes further and claims that such differentiated meanings "bestow" something on life. They enhance the vitality of living. We now have a paradox. Death, which is about the stopping of life, has an important role to play in enhancing the living of life. The final phrase is important too. Whereas many approaches to death and to grief urge us to *accept* the finality of death, Deleuze is suggesting that we *resist* death and that doing so will enable us to glimpse further truths about life. Resisting death then is necessary to affirm life.

The phrase "resisting death" is chosen by Deleuze in reference to the pioneering Enlightenment biologist, Marie-François Xavier Bichat, who died in 1802. Bichat (1923) is famous for the following definition of life: "Life consists in the sum of the functions, by which death is resisted" (p. 10). Bichat was a scientist who believed that life owed its spark to a vital principle, one that was later called the *élan vital*. There is a long history of this idea that goes back to ancient philosophy and was part of Stoic thought. In the present day, vitalism has been generally discredited, but Deleuze retains some elements of it. We need not buy into all of the vitalist beliefs to respond to death by affirming life. Our interest in this book is in how conversations with those who have encountered the death of a loved one, as well as conversations with those who are facing death, might be conducted in a way that affirms life. To resist death in Deleuze's terms must mean resisting the "dogmatic images of thought" (Deleuze, 1994, p. 129), the taken-for-granted discourses, the dominant stories, through which the meanings of death have been conveyed to us.

Intergenerational Legacies

In the conversation with Paula, the intergenerational line has another addition in the next segment. Megan begins this process and Paula is able this time to speak more eloquently until she runs into some lapses in memory.

MEGAN: But going back to getting things done. Your mom was a single mom for part of the time.

PAULA: My mom was the type that, she had a two-story house, that had little square windows in it. And I remember she would take down the netting off the windows, because everybody had netting. And she would wash the netting by hand. Dry it off on a clothes line, iron it, it had to be ironed. Everything had to be ironed, everything had to be done and done.

MEGAN: And she worked.

LORRAINE: Did she work?

PAULA: Forty hours a week.

LORRAINE: What kind of work did she do, Paula?

PAULA: It's funny actually, she worked at a bowling alley, and she made sandwiches. She worked at Fairmile... [pause] I've got to remember.

LORRAINE: It's hard when the memory goes into those spots, isn't it? [Paula nods.] It's like you can almost feel it there but it's not accessible.

PAULA: Right, right. But um, she worked at Fairmile, was it Fairmile? I think. I can't remember the name. She wanted to do a man's job, because she wanted a man's pay. Which is typical of her. And she got it.

MEGAN: Did she? [Paula is wiping tears.] That didn't happen back then.

PAULA: That didn't happen back then. It was refrigerator doors, and her boss said, you can't lift that! And she said, oh yes I can! [laughs] And she did.

LORRAINE: So you come from a long lineage of women who were patient and spunky and got things done.

PAULA: Yeah.

LORRAINE: So how do you see those qualities in your daughter?

PAULA: I see them in Megan because Megan tends to not lay down and take anything. She fights for everything.

LORRAINE: She must be great with the kids at school, huh?

PAULA: I would imagine. Because from what I've heard over the months, her kids love her.

LORRAINE: And those same qualities of being willing to be an advocate and stand up for what's right, how does that help her, in life you think, in terms of her relationship with her family, with her husband?

PAULA: I think it will help her, or does help her, in that she gets a different perspective.

LORRAINE: If she were telling those stories to your future grandkids, they were all hanging out and crocheting together, and she's telling the stories about how their grandmother is a humble woman, a woman of great patience, would they also be hearing stories about how you're a woman that got things done?

PAULA: I would think so, yeah.

Resisting death here aligns with resisting narrow gender specifications in the workplace. Paula is proud of her mother's stand against patriarchal constructions. She is proud to think of herself as a part of a matrilineal line that includes her daughter. This time, a political strand is woven in (or perhaps crocheted in) to the intergenerational line. Moreover, the imminence of death can be said to bestow something extra (as Deleuze suggested) to Paula's and Megan's sense of what is important. Counseling at this time, we would argue, is valuable to the extent that it does actually bestow something extra on a person's life and skillful and compassionate counseling actually uses the imminence of death to enhance the vividness of what is bestowed. As Lorraine asks her to extend this legacy out into her daughter's life, it is enhanced again. Both of them now can share this legacy: for Paula in the knowledge that what has been important to her will continue; and for Megan in the knowledge that what she does will always be connected to her mother and death need not separate her from it. Future conversations with as yet unborn grandchildren are foreshadowed too, and Paula gets an inkling of her life beyond her own death.

The conversation then returns to the life Paula has before she dies.

Populating the Membership Club

> LORRAINE: I'm just thinking about what lays ahead for you, and I'm thinking about how do we support you in a way that you would like. Have you thought about that?
>
> PAULA: I haven't really thought about it. Um...I suppose I just um, people around my bed...[laughs] I don't know.
>
> LORRAINE: You like having people with you?
>
> PAULA: Yeah.
>
> MEGAN: Even when she was in the hospital, for the almost three weeks, somebody was there twenty-four hours a day. Mostly dad, dad was with you, he spent the night there almost every night.
>
> PAULA: Oh.
>
> LORRAINE: So you had people sitting vigil with you to make sure that you were getting the love that you deserve.
>
> PAULA: I must be.

LORRAINE: So that's something that continues to be important to you.

PAULA: Yeah.

LORRAINE: And if you were in a position, down the road, where you couldn't tell your stories, how would you want Megan to kind of keep you close?

PAULA: Um...not be morbid in my stories. I think that mostly have some humor. I still believe humor is the best medicine.

MEGAN: And that's why you married dad.

PAULA: Yeah.

MEGAN: Because you get it every day whether you want it or not [laughs].

PAULA: [laughs]

LORRAINE: How many years you've been married? Like fifty years?

PAULA: About forty-five.

LORRAINE: So you've probably heard one or two jokes over again, right?

PAULA: Yeah, but he's always got a twist on them. He's very intelligent. I think that's his downfall, in a lot of ways. And he's extremely honest, which I don't think is a bad quality.

LORRAINE: Yeah. So what's your sense about what it means for Megan that you have been her mom?

PAULA: Um...I don't know. That I have been her mom?

LORRAINE: Yeah. Do you think it's been a good thing to Megan that you have been her mom?

PAULA: Yeah. Because there's so many moms I know, I think of, oh my god, if Megan had another mom, she'd stand no chance. They're just not nice people. But I keep that to myself.

MEGAN: I think if I had one of those other moms, that I could have just chosen the first guy that came along to get married to. And I think that I didn't and I waited until I was older, until I found exactly what I

183

was looking for, because I knew how much you loved me, and you were so kind and patient and all of those things.

LORRAINE: And why was that the best for her?

PAULA: Because I think if she had had children too young, she wouldn't have, she wouldn't have learned as much as she has.

MEGAN: I wouldn't have been the mom that I will be when my child is born.

LORRAINE: How old were you when Megan was born?

PAULA: Twenty-five.

LORRAINE: And your son? What's the age difference?

MEGAN: Eight years.

LORRAINE: And how do you want him to hold you close to himself in story? What would be important for him to know about his mom?

PAULA: Um...I think Glen, in a way Glen's closer to me, because he doesn't say much. And I don't really say a lot. So I think that we have a bond that is close.

LORRAINE: It's unspoken?

PAULA: Unspoken, yeah.

LORRAINE: So for him, would it be important to continue to notice that bond, do you think?

PAULA: Yeah.

LORRAINE: You must worry about him, Paula.

PAULA: Yeah.

LORRAINE: Are there things that you want Megan to do to kind of help keep your memory and that bond close for Glen?

PAULA: Um...Just that, I don't know, that she or he talks about me.

LORRAINE: That would be important?

MEGAN: With a little bit of humor.

PAULA: Yeah. Has to be humor in there.

MEGAN: Well, Nathan has made a promise to make sure that we always look out for Glen.

PAULA: Good.

MEGAN: It's completely different but just like we will always look out for his [Nathan's]

> brother. He will be our responsibility and
> live with us at some point. And so with
> Glen, we are always going to make sure he
> has a place. And you know, that we regularly
> visit him, he's coming out here next week.

In recent years, there has been a strong interest in the literature on grief in continuing bonds. Here is a conversation, then, that actualizes these bonds before Paula dies, in the hope that these will continue in memory after the person's death. Lorraine continues to talk to Paula, not as an individual facing death but as a member of a family network which might sustain her in the period before death and re-member her after she dies. This biological event of her death will impact on numerous others – her daughter, husband, son, son-in-law, and future grandchildren, not to mention countless others. Rather than a lone event, the assumption is that people handle death more courageously when they hold each other close. When death is approaching, one thing it bestows is urgency in such conversations. The presence of death can serve to bring people closer and to enable important things to be said that might otherwise be put off until another day.

185

Another example of such a special exchange happens in the next segment.

> LORRAINE: Megan, I asked your mom about what
> she thought it meant for you to be her
> mom. How is that for you? What has it
> meant to have Paula as your mom?
> MEGAN: It's been the best thing in my life.
> Like, dad is a really good father, and
> he loves me and he's fun and everything.
> But sometimes he can be unpredictable.
> Mom is predictable. She was always there
> when I came home from school. Always just
> somebody you could count on and somebody
> who really cared. Whereas other parents,
> sometimes they'll ask how is your day,
> but they're just asking out of obligation,
> they're not really listening. And through-
> out my whole life, even as a child in high
> school, I would talk about something that

now I realize must not have been as interesting to her, but she got into my world and wanted to know about it. And asked questions and we'd sit at the table talking for hours.

PAULA: Two hours and three hours.

MEGAN: And it was about stuff that, now that you know I'm a high school counselor and I guess it's different with my students. But they talk about these things and I think, gosh that's just not so important. And I have to really pull myself in and pay attention. It is important to them. Mom was just right there. She didn't have to try to act interested or ask those questions, she just did. I could not have picked a better mom in the whole world.

PAULA: Aww.

MEGAN: Like my very best friend.

LORRAINE: So will you hold this bond with her, in honoring this for now until forever?

MEGAN: Well, every day she'll be a part of what I do and part of how I live my life. You know, I didn't realize as much until this conversation today that it would come back to your mom and your grandma Mary. And I told you, Mary is the name that we want for our child. But, you know, I'll always honor that by trying to be...If I can be half the mom she was, I'll be an amazing mom. By remembering that patience and that kindness and that connection.

LORRAINE: So what's this like when you hear Megan talking about what it's been like to be parented by you? How is that for you?

PAULA: It's how I want every child to be parented.

MEGAN: It's how every child deserves to be parented, but not every child is.

PAULA: Right, exactly.

LORRAINE: But you succeeded.

PAULA: Yeah. Megan did fine, everything wasn't perfect I'm sure. But overall...if I look back, if I just scan my life, I scan it and it is very, very good.

LORRAINE: The overall scan is a good scan? You see good things when you look back. And that includes your kids?

PAULA: Yeah, definitely.

LORRAINE: It includes your grandmother, it includes your mom, it includes crocheting?

PAULA: My whole life, yeah.

LORRAINE: As you scan them back, I'm wondering how we scan them forward too. About how we kind of keep those present, just in the chance that you're not here, can we keep those also present so that you are here, in an odd kind of way, if that makes sense?

PAULA: Yeah.

LORRAINE: I'm wondering what that would be like for Megan, if she were to have that scan of your life then.

PAULA: I think it would help her. Rather than trying to bury it, you know like, ignore it.

MEGAN: Exactly.

LORRAINE: An important distinction, right.

PAULA: Yeah. And it doesn't mean that I have to be brought up every second, because that would get on my nerves.

LORRAINE: Okay. So there's comfort there. Has that helped you face what you have had to face with the treatments?

PAULA: It's something that I felt that I'm going to have to face anyway, so what does it matter whether it's bad or it's good...It's going to happen anyway.

LORRAINE: [to Megan] I was thinking about how much your mom's taught you throughout your life — about patience, about crocheting, about how to be an advocate, and how to face obstacles. And I was wondering if the way she has sat with the prospects of dying has also been one of the things that she's teaching you about.

MEGAN: Yeah, it's always been my biggest fear, losing people I care about. Even though we haven't been married a year, I already think about losing Nathan. And I told him, I need to go first.

LORRAINE: There's rules, apparently [laughs].

MEGAN: And the whole thing just has been very frightening to me, since I was 16 or younger and I don't know why, but through this you have, without doing anything, just being yourself, given me strength. I remember when you were first diagnosed, for two weeks I was so upset. Even going to the grocery store was tough. Or making myself go for a run was tough...But you adjust. And then I started looking at all of the positive things. I think what I've learned from you is you don't dwell on the...

PAULA: What you can't change.

MEGAN: Right. You look at all of the stuff you do have and all of this time we've had has been such a gift. Having you here, living with us, is such a gift.

PAULA: Right.

MEGAN: I never thought I would have been able to do it. But I have because of you. And that's one thing I've thought about. I'm not stuffing it away, I'm able to work, I'm able to be a wife to Nathan, I'm able to do all those things, but it's because of your example, you know. I don't think I would be doing as well with things if I wasn't your daughter.

PAULA: Aw, that's nice to hear.

MEGAN: But it's the truth. It's the truth.

LORRAINE: Even when you feel like you can't remember things, or you feel like you're different now, because your mobility has been impacted...did you realize that you're still teaching so much?

PAULA: Uh, I didn't really think about it. You know, I just...

LORRAINE: You just do.

PAULA: Just do, yeah.

LORRAINE: It's funny that you just kind of keep teaching and keep parenting, right. Even in the face of hardships.

PAULA: Yeah. I feel like my energy wouldn't be so low if I...see there it's gone again.

LORRAINE: When the thoughts come and go, what's that like for you?

PAULA: Well, it's like I think of something, and then all of a sudden I go back to thinking about it, and it's gone.

LORRAINE: It has slipped away to someplace different?

PAULA: Yeah, and I can't figure out where it's at.

LORRAINE: And that's been going on for a little bit, huh? [Paula nods.] Does it then come back around and reappear, that thought? Or does it just slip off...

PAULA: Yeah, that thought might come back later, the next day or...

LORRAINE: Do you ever write them down?

PAULA: Yeah, I have.

LORRAINE: Does that help?

PAULA: Yeah, but only when it's important enough.

LORRAINE: What I hear you telling us too, of what's important, is just being able to have people with you.

PAULA: Yeah.

LORRAINE: That's one of the most important parts. So you don't have to do this whole process by yourself.

PAULA: Right.

189

Notice how Lorraine does not avoid making reference to death and to illness. Nor does she just focus on the positive things in life. Her references to these things are gentle, however, rather than harsh. She talks about "this whole process", about the "prospect of dying", refers to "the chance that you're not here" and invokes the future in which

Paula might be "in a position, down the road, where you couldn't tell your stories". Paula is invited to talk about these things in the context of what is comforting and also invigorating without the need to be blunt or rude in how the question is posed.

The Fragility of Life Is the Mother of Beauty

So let us go back and consider the ways in which a death might actually become a multiple, rather than a singular, event. Modernist science has attempted to specify the singular time of death, through linking it to the ceasing of the heartbeat, or to the moment the brain stem ceases to function. It is commonly represented in movies by the flatlining of a heart monitor. However, the organs of the body do not all shut down at the same time. It is not uncommon, for example, in the discourse of death to hear some people being described as "brain dead" when they require the assistance of a breathing machine to stay alive. Paula's memory, for example, is failing her and this means that others sometimes have to carry that function for her.

Moreover, even when a moment of death is certified, the process of generating the meaning of a death continues through a series of further events (autopsies, funerals, memorials, newspaper eulogies, coroners' investigations, the reading of wills, murder trials, and so on). In her conversation with Megan and Lorraine, Paula gets to participate in some of the ways in which her life will continue to be knitted into to the fabric of her family's life. Paula is granted a glimpse of the future where she continues to play a part.

Each of these events, including the conversation we have just witnessed, has the potential of adding something to the significance of the event of death. Each of them provides another slice in the animation of truth about a life and a death. Each of them also potentially enhances the life of the dying person or the deceased in the minds of those who survive them. The life of a person who has died may thus be said to perdure in our memories of them. Depending on what we re-member, the life of a dying person might continue to become in particular ways. It is not unreasonable then to argue that lives and relationships, which are continuing to acquire new meanings, are, therefore, not necessarily complete at the singular moment of death. Their significance can continue to multiply.

There is another sense too in which we believe death might accrue multiplicity. Philosopher Todd May explores this sense in his (2009) book on death. May argues that human life is shaped by the knowledge of the certainty and inevitability of death and also by the

190

uncertainty of exactly when it might happen. This knowledge stays with us right through our lives. He does not insist that other animals might not have or might not evolve similar knowledge, although it seems that many animals live without this knowledge. They might grieve, but they do not live with knowledge of death as a constant companion.

Todd May goes on to point out how awareness of the fragility of life and of the sword of Damocles hanging over us all contributes to a sense of poignancy and urgency in life. It sharpens our sense of the significance of each other's achievements and projects. We see this in Paula's conversation with her daughter and with Lorraine. It focuses on making life all the more valuable, rather than on facing its annihilation. Even something like crocheting takes on a spiritual significance as it is fed into a story of patience and calmness in the midst of the maelstrom of life. As Todd May says, because life is fragile, "We take care of it, we look after it, we concern ourselves with it in ways that we would not were it not fragile" (p. 85). He, therefore, poses the question of how "one might live a fragile life" (p. 87).

His answer is a question of ethics, in that it addresses the question of how to live a good life, a satisfying life, a worthwhile life. Todd May argues that living in the knowledge of the fragility of life helps us make the choices that lead to such a life. Living with the knowledge that death might come at any moment underlines the preciousness of the time that we have. It emphasizes that death can either enhance or diminish the meaning of the life we have lived. And it leaves us, argues May, with the need to choose. He says, "Death is the ultimate source of both the tragedy and the beauty of a human life" (p. 113). Without the beauty of the moments we treasure, there would not be any sense of tragedy at their loss. Without the possibility of a tragic end, we would not be able to appreciate the beauty of such moments. Perhaps this is why some people who are facing a terminal diagnosis report an enlivened zest for life. Death gives us the gift of vulnerability and the knowledge of it allows us to shape our lives into something worth living.

This was the gift of what Dionysius gave to Damocles. It was at the same time a threat of a mortal end and a knowledge that sharpened the importance of choices about how to live. If we were to live in the daily knowledge of life's fragility, then we might be moved to ask ourselves what at any moment is most important, or most valuable, or most meaningful, and we might be more likely to choose those things. On this account, it is the fragility of life that is the mother of beauty and purpose.

191

This is a paradox, of course. But it need not be a contradiction, as Todd May also shows. It is better described in Gilles Deleuze's terms as a "doubling" of the meaning of death. Michael White articulates a similar sense of paradox, or doubling, in his description of the "absent but implicit" (2000). It is a way of listening that turns meanings on their head. For example, White talks about someone who is experiencing despair. He suggests asking this person about what they might be despairing of. Such a question flips the meaning over. To answer it, one must recognize that the experience of despair must exist in implicit contrast with the hopes that the same person at other times might have embraced. The question inquires into these hopes, rather than dwelling on the despair. It opens up a line of inquiry that was not at first apparent, but it is not a jarring disjuncture. It actually follows from what the speaker has just said.

Thinking of death in terms of the fragility of life and using this sense of fragility to sharpen what someone finds meaningful similarly flips the meaning over. It emphasizes the rich possibilities of life. It affirms the vibrancy of life, rather than the tragedy of death. It is the kind of differentiation that opens onto a sense of multiplicity, in Deleuze's terms. The meaning of death no longer lies just in its tragic aspect. It also affords us a view of what is beautiful and precious. We surmise that this is what Deleuze was suggesting when he claimed that death "bestows" something on life.

The implication of this idea for grief counseling is that it suggests some different lines of inquiry. For those who are facing imminent death and for those who are grieving the death of a loved one, we would argue that it is therapeutic to seek out just what it might be, in each particular instance, that death bestows upon life. It is not that we should ask people in such blunt terms, "What does death bestow upon your life?" To ask such a question would be crass. We can, however, listen for and inquire into the particular possibilities for uniquely poignant conversation that might become possible in the imminence of death or in its aftermath. Paula's focus is on how the things that matter to her continue for her children and grandchildren. With a focus on personal identity as a product of relational exchange, rather than of internal essence, we might ask before someone dies, "At this time, what is important for you as friends or family members to talk about, or to perform?" We do not think there are universal prescriptions for what might be exchanged at this moment, as Ira Byock (1997) claims that one must confess love and transgressions or ask forgiveness to die well. Indeed, the question just mentioned might often be redundant. It may be more useful to listen to what people are saying to each other and ask appreciative or elaborative questions to enhance the beauty of the moment.

After someone dies, a relationship shift clearly takes place. The voice of the deceased may continue to echo but this person is not able to add further to the conversation without the assistance of the living. The responsibility for the relationship shifts primarily to the bereaved. In such circumstances, how then might death have something to bestow upon life? The answer to this question may vary considerably. A wise counselor, however, will have such a question hovering in their mind and will continue seeking out the beauty that may lie amidst the pain and the unpleasantness of dying. The combination of urgency and the consciousness of fragility that surfaces at such times will likely help produce such moments of sparkling beauty.

This chapter brings to a close the major points of focus we want to emphasize in this book. It remains to bring these points together and reiterate them one more time. That will be the purpose of the final chapter.

193

CHAPTER 9

Reinvigorating Hope

At this stage of the book, it remains to bring together the major themes we have touched upon and to ask what they all aim to achieve. The title of this chapter begins to speak to this purpose. When Freud titled his 1917 article "Mourning and Melancholia", he was concerned to separate grief responses from what was then called melancholia and is now more commonly referred to as depression. The reason for doing so was presumably because it was easy to mistake grief for melancholia. Perhaps it still is, as is reflected in the debate circling around the *Diagnostic and Statistical Manual of Mental Disorders, Fifth Edition* (DSM-V) and the removal of grief from descriptions of major depression. Regardless of the label, it is certainly possible to become mired in grief to the extent that life loses its sense of vitality and value.

The most common response in counseling has been to help people move toward an acceptance of "reality" in the hope that this reality will "gain the day" (as Freud put it) and to return to fully functioning, productive citizenship. The question that is begged is, "Which reality?" This is a complicating question that was scarcely in sight in Freud's day, but you have to have blinders on not to be aware of it now. Is it the reality affirmed in research by the calculation of probabilities? Is it the reality of duty expounded by conventional morality? Or is it the virtual reality that Deleuze was reaching for in Todd May's (2005) question, "How might one live?" These are the epistemological questions we have explored in the early chapters of this text and that return again in considering our final statement of purpose.

To our way of thinking, the emphasis on accepting the reality of death as some kind of affirmation of rational realism and then moving to pick up the reins of life as a now bereaved person is, as commonly conceived, an awkward and clumsy exercise that crams people's experiences into prefabricated models. We are concerned that it can sometimes exacerbate the pain that people are experiencing and we doubt that this insistence is necessary. The challenge then is to specify a different approach. That is what we have been reaching for in this book.

To address this challenge, we believe, requires that counselors embrace a version of reality (from among the competing versions available) and embody it in their practice. Our hope is that it is possible to find, in the many forms of grief that people experience, moments of vitality and the affirmation of cherished values. George Bonanno's (2009) research found, for example, occasions when bereaved people experienced joy and laughter, and not just unrelieved sadness. Such moments are more than just real. They are invigorating and they make living worthwhile. The task of finding and bringing these moments forward into the light is founded on asking questions that concentrate on generating new, finely nuanced realities, not just accepting existing ones.

What Is Hope?

In seeking a therapeutic approach based on the expression of hope, we are conscious of the need to separate hope from optimism. Vaclav Havel (1993), after the fall of communist Czechoslovakia, made a clear distinction between hope and optimism when he claimed that hope is not the same thing as optimism. Optimism, said Havel, is being convinced that all will turn out well. To hope is to believe that something makes sense, whether or not it turns out well. Havel's claim is attuned with the postmodern shift from *accepting an already given reality* to *making an as-yet-undetermined meaning*. This is the experience that we believe opens up moments of vitality, and even beauty, in the face of death. The story of a death is often experienced by those who survive the death of a loved one as an example of when things do not "turn out well". Hope lies then not in the real enough circumstances of death, but in the ways that people make meaning of events. This statement indicates where the bulk of our questions need to focus – that is, on meaning generation, rather than on accepting reality.

Not just any meaning will do, however. To become hopeful requires the choice of meanings that are sustaining in the face of sometimes harsh challenges. Neither does "sustaining" refer to transient emotions, but actions that are anchored in values and community. Seeking happiness is not enough. What sustains people through difficult circumstances is richer and more complex than that.

Neither does hope lie in certain kinds of persons. It makes no sense to speak about "hopeful persons", as if some people have the necessary genes and others do not. As with other personal qualities (resilience, loving kindness, prudence, and so on), falling back on an essentialized explanation is a mistake, because these qualities are produced in relations between people, rather than originating in the heart of the individual. Hope is not a commodity that can be amassed, even though some modern forms of capitalism have tried to turn such personal qualities into private property and have linked them to entrepreneurial projects (Lazzarato, 2014). Hope is more like a by-product of the narratives by which we are governed, or by which we govern ourselves.

It is more accurate, therefore, to talk about hope as something people do, rather than as something they are. As Kaethe Weingarten (2010) has explained, hope is best thought of as a verb rather than a noun. If hope is produced within a narrative framework, then the challenge for counselors is to enhance the possibility that a bereaved person can access the story. This happens through the kind of inquiry that persists in asking people who are grieving to make meaning of experience and to do so not so much in isolation, but in the fertile relational soil where actions grow.

Hope is also invigorated by breaking out of a solely individual focus. If we can do hope, then we can do it for each other (Weingarten, 2010), not solely for ourselves. For this reason, it makes sense for the bereaved to be asked to imagine what the deceased might say. Responses to such questions double the voice of meaning-making, because the respondent is speaking as him or herself, but is incorporating the voice of the deceased within the response. In this sense, the dead get to live again, in modified form, through their voices being heard when someone else speaks. Weingarten calls this vicarious hope. It is quite common, then, to generate a sense of hope through accessing it in someone else and folding it into oneself.

Assumptions That Form the Foundation for the Crafting of Grief

For a final time, let us visit a conversation in which Lorraine illustrates the practice of grief counseling. We shall use it to highlight the assumptions and practices we have emphasized through the different chapters of this book. This is a conversation that took place with a woman whose husband had died many years previously. The conversation shows how she has continued to keep his stories alive for herself and for their sons.

196

Assumption One

Grief is a relational experience. It is experienced in the relationships between people, and there are always at least two people involved. Hence, it makes sense that a grief counseling conversation should begin with an introduction. The example below suggests there are others besides Nancy who might become players in the conversation. She speaks of those who can lay claim to the stories of her deceased husband.

> LORRAINE: So, where I like to start, Nancy, is to get a sense of who your husband is and I'm wondering if you would just introduce him to us, as a starting point.
>
> NANCY: Sure. His name, I like how you said "introduce him" because he's still here. So Robert is my husband's name, my late husband's name, and he died at age 49, two weeks short of his 50th birthday. And it was a sudden death from a heart attack. He was a family doctor and grew up in Pennsylvania. He was very bright.

197

Assumption Two

Generating meaning about someone's life begins in the past, when he was alive. It will move eventually into the present and the future. The first concentration, however, is on the relationship between the deceased and bereaved before the death. Grief counseling involves noticing the little moments that can become part of a person's present and future identity, even after they are deceased. These moments are informed by collecting memories to give shape to the stories through which a posthumous relationship remains viable.

> LORRAINE: So can you tell me, when you first met Robert, what pulled you to him? What did you notice about him?
>
> NANCY: We met at a Heroin Detox program where we both worked. He was coming from a training program in Ohio, and I was coming from a training program in Florida. He was really

tall, six foot four, and had really beautiful curly brown hair. And I remember I walked by him, and I just thought, he looks really interesting and it was an immediate attraction, he was just handsome. And he had on this white sweater that later, after he died, I kept.

LORRAINE: So initially you noticed, hey here's this really nice-looking man who's quite tall. And then, as you got to know him, what kinds of things about who he was as a person did you appreciate in those early days of the relationship?

NANCY: Well he introduced me to a lot of things that I do today...He tuned in to public radio. We used to listen to public radio, and I didn't know anything about it, about how important it was to be informed about politics. And he taught me about being adventurous.

LORRAINE: What do you think he saw in you that he knew that adventurousness was something that he could solicit?

Assumption Three

People usually enjoy, as Nancy does here, talking about memories of the person who died. It is more than simple reminiscence, however. It brings to life the relationship between the bereaved and the deceased. In the following excerpt, the sense of relationship is enhanced by asking Nancy to speak his lines, as well as her own.

NANCY: He was a big journal writer. He kept journals through his whole life. So one time I found his journals, and I looked at the part where it talked about where we met. It was like I got to hear his voice.

LORRAINE: And what did he write about?

NANCY: My bright green eyes. I'm not sure when he wrote it, but he talked about the kind of person I was and we used to spend time talking and just getting to know each other. Our time together initially was really short, it was a month we had in New York at the same time.

LORRAINE: So when did you and he realize that this was something more then?

NANCY: He went back to Ohio to finish his medical program, and I went back to Florida to finish my training program. He came to visit me on a long weekend, and I think we knew when we parted that there was something there. He asked for my phone number, and I just somehow knew he would call. If my brother were here, he would tell you how I jumped like twenty feet in the air when he called. I was so excited. Robert was scheduled to become a surgeon, and was headed to start the process. After being with me in Florida for about a month, he told the surgeons whom he was supposed to work with, who had handpicked him for the surgery training, that he had found his mate, which would impact on his moving. So that's when he decided, in a really spiritual kind of way, that we were going to stay together.

LORRAINE: Over the years of being with him, what kinds of things did he know about you?

NANCY: [pause] He knew I had had some hard times in my life. I remember he was really fascinated with how people change their lives. That was something he would tell people.

LORRAINE: And what was he proud of, do you think?

NANCY: I think that I had changed a cycle, you know a cycle that had been going on in my family, and I was probably the first to do

199

it. So I think he was proud that it could be done, that I was an example for him that people could change. They didn't have to stay on that path of difficulties.

LORRAINE: So what do you think it meant for him to witness that? That even in the face of generational experiences, and generational story, you took a different path. What did that mean for him to witness that?

NANCY: There was some connection he had with it. While he didn't have childhood trauma, there was some connection to that pain, that psychic pain about being hopeless. I think he had a connection to that in some way.

Assumption Four

The values that animate people's decisions and actions are grounded in their relationships. Bringing them to the forefront of conversation, rather than a person's deficits, strengthens vitality.

LORRAINE: Was bearing witness to that a place where he had hope?

NANCY: I think so.

LORRAINE: In what way?

NANCY: [pause] I don't know. I just know that in his journals, that was something he wrote about, that he had a fascination with, how people could get better after trauma.

LORRAINE: Do you think that made a difference in the way he treated his patients?

NANCY: Oh, I know he was a good doctor, yes.

LORRAINE: So how did it impact on what kind of physician he was?

NANCY: Well, I know he connected deeply with patients. I found out, after he passed, what people thought of him. He didn't make as much money as other doctors, because he spent a lot of time, and we were already going into managed care, you know, push people through in ten minutes. He never bought into that. He would deal with people wherever they were and stay with them. I don't know if it was me, per se, but the choice of where he went to do part of his training, in New York City, so that was already there, the connection. I think he saw me being willing to do whatever it took to get better.

LORRAINE: Ok. So he saw your stick-to-it-tive-ness? Is that correct?

NANCY: Yeah, probably, that I was committed the whole way to living a healthy life.

Assumption Five

The voice of the deceased continues to live on and demand responses in the period since his death as in the following excerpt. This provides an opportunity for the living to garner strength from what might otherwise be a fleeting thought.

LORRAINE: Ok. So tell me, Nancy, since Robert's death, how has that stick-to-it-tive-ness been helpful for you?

NANCY: Well, we had a conversation in our kitchen not long before he died about what we would do, if either of us died. It was really good, because I knew what he wanted.

LORRAINE: So he gave you some instruction that was important? [Nancy nods.] So, when the unthinkable happened and you followed that instruction, what was that like for you to be able to pay attention to his words?

NANCY: It became my mantra.

LORRAINE: Can I ask what that mantra was back then?

NANCY: He said that I needed to go back to school, to get advanced training, because I would have to support the boys. So I did. I went back. I got my master's, and now I'm in a PhD program. I'm in the last stages of it. There's a lot of

> stick-to-it-tive-ness that's keeping me in
> it, because I would like to quit. But I'm not.
>
> LORRAINE: Do you find yourself calling upon his
> voice, when you feel like you'd like to
> quit?
>
> NANCY: Yeah. It's now for my boys, to see how
> hard you have to work . . .
>
> LORRAINE: So what would Robert say about what
> kind of role model that you are offering
> to your sons?
>
> NANCY: It's all been very hard but today they're
> my strongest advocates. They would say,
> "Mom, you have to finish, because we did
> not move across the country for you to
> quit. You can't. You've got to finish."

Assumption Six

The performance of meaning around memories takes place in the context of family and community relationships, not just in individuals' minds. As Lorraine and Nancy speak, other family members are folded into the stories.

> LORRAINE: How is it that you've become such a
> channel for their father, do you think?
>
> NANCY: I wish that they could be part of this
> conversation too. I'd love to hear their
> thoughts about it, because both of them
> are different, how they've incorporated
> his death. But they both had so much of
> him in them.
>
> LORRAINE: What have you done or said that has
> fostered that relationship for Robert to
> be in each of the boys?
>
> NANCY: I'll remind them of how some of their
> strengths come from their father.

Assumption Seven

Each of us is multi-storied. We are always, therefore, more than any one person's memory can contain.

LORRAINE: So your boys have had different
    fathers in many ways, to respond to the
    differentness in them.
NANCY: Right, yeah. There's nothing he loved more.
LORRAINE: He loved being their father?
NANCY: He did and he responded to each of them
    in a different way. He worked with our
    older son to learn about astronomy, which
    is something to this day he loves. He
    would spend time with our younger son and
    taught him about sports.

Assumption Eight

There is nothing about a narrative conversation that is only focused
on the positive. Pain still needs to be acknowledged and meaning
made from the challenges that death brings. However, pain and emotional distress always exist in the context of other narratives that also
deserve acknowledgment.

NANCY: There are times when I really just feel
    for the boys. The pain...
LORRAINE: You hurt with a sense of loss for them?
NANCY: Because they would have had such a great
    dad. Their lives were rich — good memo-
    ries, good role model. There's nothing
    that soothes that.
LORRAINE: We ache for our children, don't we?
NANCY: [She nods and is tearful.] Yeah.
LORRAINE: When you think about them having a
    sense of their father with them, what hap-
    pens to that ache?
NANCY: I guess it's more soothed and I have to
    become almost spiritual, like there's a rea-
    son. The boys have done some of the activi-
    ties that they used to do with their father.

Assumption Nine

The sword of Damocles that hangs over all our lives reminds us of mortality and the brevity of life. Paradoxically, this awareness gives life a

sense of poignancy and urgency that can enhance a sense of beauty in people's responses to harsh and painful events. Counselors need to be willing to inquire into the aesthetics of grief to bring these moments to life, and invite agentic responses, as we see Lorraine doing below.

> LORRAINE: Have you made meaning of his death for you?
> NANCY: My life would have been so different.
> LORRAINE: Were there gifts to you in his death?
> NANCY: Yes. There were. To not take life for granted, treating people always with the utmost respect. To really just be aware that things can change on a dime. Life just...You have to really embrace it, enjoy it, you don't know.
> LORRAINE: What would Robert say about this?
> NANCY: He would be happy for me that this appreciation of our fragility is a part of my happiness now. That sounds kind of odd, but it feels like I am more loving in some ways because of this. I don't take things for granted.

Assumption Ten

The relationship between the bereaved and the deceased continues in the time after a death, as it did here for Nancy and Robert. Through his legacies, he is assumed to still be influential for Nancy, to still have benefits to bestow on her and messages to convey. By making them visible below, they become a further basis for action.

> LORRAINE: Has this been one of Robert's legacies, to say that there's a vibrancy in life?
> NANCY: Yes. And grace. Grace with his death.
> LORRAINE: Where are the times in your life, on a day-to-day basis, when you stop and notice the grace and appreciation of vibrancy that are Robert's legacies?
> NANCY: All kinds of places. Just when I see someone on the street, I smile at them, and I make sure that they know there's

204

just some connection. I want people to know that there's a lot of good, I don't know. There's just, I'm not sure how it exactly fits, but I think it does.

LORRAINE: Is that smile, something that reminds you of Robert?

NANCY: Yes, exactly. I want them to feel his love too.

LORRAINE: When you love somebody else in passing, Robert's love will go into that moment?

NANCY: Yes, yes.

Assumption Eleven

Counseling can also provide an opportunity for the bereaved to notice the possibility of incorporating the memory of the deceased into current life by introducing him to new members of a membership club. Nancy has introduced Robert to her new husband since he died. Nancy explains below how her current husband, Jerry, has come to appreciate Robert's connection in the family.

LORRAINE: What would Jerry say that he really appreciates about Robert?

NANCY: Oh, he would tell you about when we moved from here to Vermont, he had to pack up, because I had not put Robert's things away. There were a lot of things. We lived in Vermont for one year for Jerry's job. When we got back here, Jerry went through all of Robert's things, so he got to know who Robert was. And his response was, that he was such a powerful man and that he was tough competition. Jerry thought that, because Robert had been an incredible man, it's like he knows him. Jerry and I live on the property that Robert and I bought. Jerry says he's in awe of where we live; it's an incredible place. I have wondered if Jerry would rather live elsewhere, but he says there's a real spiritual thing

here at our home; that there's a feeling
of Robert there.

LORRAINE: So what's that like for you to be married to a man who, not only makes space for
Robert, but reminds you of his presence?

NANCY: It's wonderful. I was very lucky. When I
married Jerry, one of our good friends who
knew Robert too, said, just right before
the ceremony, "Some women are lucky if they
marry one good man – you get two." That's
my reason to remind me to be grateful.

LORRAINE: Do her words fit for you?

NANCY: Yeah. It fits that I am grateful. Sometimes
I don't always understand why it happened.

Assumption Twelve

Memories are often helped to stay strong through association with
things like clothing that carry a sense of the deceased as a living person.

LORRAINE: And if there weren't one specific
meaning...? There were many, for many
people...?

NANCY: Yeah. I am thinking about this now as we
are talking.

LORRAINE: Are there some yet to be discovered?

NANCY: Yeah.

LORRAINE: Would that be an okay thing for you?

NANCY: Yeah. It's not, we talk about him not
dying, it's like he's not dead; Robert's
somehow still very much a part of my life.
I think of him every day.

LORRAINE: And so you have clothes of his. Do
you wear any of his clothes?

NANCY: I don't anymore. I had kept his socks,
because they had a nice smell, and so
I put them in a bag, so that the smell
wouldn't go away, so I could pick it up
and smell his socks. I know that sounds
kind of weird, but it was comforting. I
also had a t-shirt that had his body odor.

LORRAINE: You said there was a white sweater that was important?

NANCY: Yeah, I kept his sweater. It's the sweater that he wore when I first fell in love with him. He also wore another sweater that I really liked. A friend had made it for her father. It was one of his favorite sweaters that he wore when he used to write.

Assumption Thirteen

Re-membering need not be solely focused on the past. It can move into the present if a counselor invites a person to engage in time travel, where stories exist in a sense of aion. Nancy has talked about Robert in the past when he was alive, and has spoken of her ongoing relationship with him since his death. Lorraine's next question brings her sense of him right into the present moment.

LORRAINE: What's it like for you to talk about him now?

NANCY: I think that his story is really powerful, and that it's important that I speak about him.

Assumption Fourteen

It is not unusual for a bereaved person to articulate a sense of the deceased almost facilitating a connection with other people who have experienced similar events. With the help of the subjunctive questions, the deceased loved one's voice is reconstituted momentarily through the bereaved person speaking about what the deceased would say.

NANCY: I was at the dentist to get my teeth cleaned, and the dental hygienist's husband had just recently died young too. I told her about Robert and how I continue to think about him every day. I now have a connection with other women or men who have lost someone. You don't have it unless

you've gone through it. I said to this
woman, "You know have joined the club that
nobody wants to belong to, but yet we do."

LORRAINE: Is that one of those Robert legacies
as well, to say, there will be people
along the way that you get to comfort?
Would he like that?

NANCY: He definitely would. He'd want me to do
that — to be comforting to another person.

Assumption Fifteen

Speaking through the subjunctive, the deceased person's voice can
be enlisted to address the future. The deceased can even be invited,
through the living, to give advice to others. This amounts to an
embodiment of hope.

LORRAINE: Ok. Let me just ask you one more
question. Is there anything that he would
want, if he was to give words of advice
to everybody in the room, do you have a
sense about what kinds of words of advice
he might give them?

NANCY: Well I think of his t-shirt that he used
to wear. His favorite t-shirt, that said,
"Don't smoke, be bright, die anyway." I
think that says a lot. It's like, enjoy
life, because it's not about being too
rigid, but take care of your health, even
though he died young at 49.

LORRAINE: So he'd have given a message to
people — life's short, enjoy some.

NANCY: To the fullest.

Assumption Sixteen

Grieving is governed by power and privilege embedded in everyday
relationships. However, in the conversation with Nancy, we do not
notice overt illustrations of this. Nancy, in some ways, has been fortunate to not have to struggle against dominating discourses that sanc-
tion some grief as legitimate and other forms as not. Nancy has been

encouraged to re-member Robert by those around her – her children, her current husband, and her community. Not everyone is so fortunate. Some lives are not recognized as grievable, which steals away agentic responses from the bereaved. Some people are disenfranchised by rituals, and even by conventional psychological practices, from the chance to grieve or to re-member. To be clear, however, this does not mean that Nancy has it easy or has not encountered considerable pain. To resent her position as a bereaved person because others are disenfranchised would be churlish and helps no one. Like everyone else, Nancy still has to transgress against the modern discourse of death to find moments of beauty and agency.

An Aesthetic Approach

The approach to death and grief we have emphasized throughout this book is based in an aesthetic sensibility. We believe that counselors need to foster in their practice such a sensibility to help those who are living with grief. It is the ethos that Michel Foucault (1986) articulated as the "care of the self". It does not mean matching client responses to a predetermined model, or taking care to avoid professional "burn out" and "compassion fatigue", so much as facilitating the achievement of agency in charting a course through the valley of the shadow of death. For each of us, this will be slightly different, even though we also draw from common cultural resource banks. We have chosen the concept of crafting to stand for this ethos. It carries with it connotations of what the ancient Greeks called *techne*, active and intentional production of what it means to be bereaved, or to be dying, or both.

To emphasize this point is by no means to ignore the pain, sometimes profound and debilitating pain, that is created by death. It does, however, mean that pain can be mitigated with comforting meanings derived through the crafting of resonant stories and relations between the living and the dead. The sense of a relationship continuing, albeit in modified form, is a key part of this mitigation that can address the profound yearning for connection that often accompanies grief. This assumption of the continuity of a relationship is less abrasive and harsh than the assumption of the sudden cut-off and the requirement of completion at the moment of death. Counselors, however, need to do more than noticing or acknowledging continuing bonds. They need to ask questions that provide scaffolding for the building of a relational edifice on this foundation – one that builds a way forward to interweave stories of the dead alongside the living. It is the willingness to step into a new kind of conversation that can be infused with stories of vitality and love.

As we have noted, we do not believe there is anything to be gained by an insistence on "objective" reality. Nor does reality have to be built into a model of "normal grieving". Helping people find, or create, other pathways through grief that are based on remembering the past, connecting it to the present, and shaping the future is much more invigorating. It is these pathways that require the kind of aesthetic sensibility that gives people at least momentary glimpses of beauty. When these moments are glimpsed, the air seems bright and clear and contains some hints of sweetness. Death presents some of the most challenging aspects of life and achieving these glimpses of beauty need not be left to chance. They must be constructed out of memories and dreams. If this is achieved, a counseling conversation can uplift the anchoring pain of grief that otherwise weighs heavily. Counselors and those who listen well can craft moments of lightness, ever so gently, through the application of curious questioning that seeks the beauty in grief.

210

References

American Psychiatric Association (2013). *Diagnostic and statistical manual for mental disorders, fifth edition*. Washington, DC: American Psychiatric Association.

Anderson, H. (1997). *Conversation, language, and possibilities: A postmodern approach to therapy*. New York, NY: Basic Books.

Andersen, T. (1991). *The reflecting team: Dialogues and dialogues about the dialogues*. New York, NY: Norton.

Andrews, R. (1993). *The Columbia dictionary of quotations*. New York, NY: Columbia University Press.

Ariès, P. (1974). *Western attitudes toward death: From the Middle Ages to the present* (P. Ranum, Trans.). Baltimore, MD: Johns Hopkins University Press.

Ariès, P. (1981). *The hour of our death*. Oxford, UK: Oxford University Press.

Árnason, A. (2000). Biography, bereavement, story. *Mortality, 5*(2), 189–204. DOI: 10.1080/713686003

Árnason, A., Hafsteinsson, S. B., & Grétarsdóttir, T. (2004). New dawn: Death, grief and the "nation form" in Iceland. *Mortality, 9*, 329–343. DOI: 10.1080/13576270412331329830

Attig, T. (1996). *How we grieve: Relearning the world*. New York, NY: Oxford University Press.

Attig, T. (2000). *The heart of grief*. New York, NY: Oxford University Press.

Attig, T. (2001). Relearning the world: Making and finding meanings. In R. A. Neimeyer (Ed.), *Meaning reconstruction and the experience of loss* (pp. 33–54). Washington, DC: American Psychological Association.

Bakhtin, M. (1981). *The dialogic imagination* (C. Emerson & M. Holquist, Trans.). Austin, TX: University of Texas Press.

Bakhtin, M. (1986). *Speech genres and other late essays* (V. McGee, Trans.). Austin, TX: University of Texas Press.

Bartlett, F. C. (1932). *Remembering*. Cambridge, UK: Cambridge University Press.

Baumgartner, B., & Williams, B. (2014). Becoming an insider: Narrative therapy groups alongside people overcoming homelessness. *Journal of Systemic Therapies, 33*(4), 1–14. DOI: 10.1521/jsyt.2014.33.4.1

Berger, J. (2005). *Here is where we meet*. New York, NY: Vintage Books.

Berger, P., & Luckman, T. (1966). *The social construction of reality: A treatise in the sociology of knowledge*. New York, NY: Doubleday.

Bergson, H. (1911). *Creative evolution* (A. Mitchell, trans.). New York, NY: Henry Holt.

Bernecker, S. (2008). *The metaphysics of memory*. New York, NY: Springer Science.

Bertman, S. (2014). Communicating with the dead: Timeless insights and interventions from the arts. *Omega, 70*(1), 119–132. DOI: 10.2190/OM70.1.j

Bichat, X., & Gold, F. (1923/2015). *Physiological researches on life and death.* San Bernardino, CA: Ulan Press.

Blythe, K. (2010). Love and loss: The roots of grief and its complications. *Counselling & Psychotherapy Research, 10*(1), 75–76. DOI: 10.1080/14733140903226446

Bonanno, G. A. (2009). *The other side of sadness: What the new science of bereavement tells us about life after loss.* New York, NY: Basic Books.

Bowlby, J. (1961a). Processes of mourning. *The International Journal of Psychoanalysis, 42*(4–5), 317–340.

Bowlby, J. (1961b). Childhood mourning and its implications for psychiatry. *American Journal of Psychiatry, 118,* 481–498.

Bowlby, J. (1963). Pathological mourning and childhood mourning. *Journal American Psychoanalytic Association, 11*(3), 500–541.

Breen, L. J., & O'Connor, M. (2010). Acts of resistance: Breaking the silence of grief following traffic crash fatalities. *Death Studies, 34,* 30–53. DOI: 10.1080/07481180903372384

Bruner, J. (1986). *Actual minds: Possible worlds.* Cambridge, MA: Harvard University Press.

Bruner, J. (1990). *Acts of meaning.* Cambridge, MA: Harvard University Press.

Burks, S. (2005). Making sense of the death that makes no sense: A review of the book, "After suicide loss: Coping with your grief". *Death Studies, 29*(5), 459–463. DOI: 10.1080/07481180590923788

Burman, E. (2008). *Deconstructing developmental psychology* (2nd Edn.). London, UK: Routledge.

Burr, V. (2003). *An introduction to social constructionism* (2nd Edn.). London, UK: Routledge.

Butler, J. (2004). *Precarious life: The powers of mourning and violence.* London, UK: Verso.

Butler, J., & Athanasiou, A. (2013). *Dispossession: The performative in the political.* Cambridge, UK: Polity Press.

Byock, I. (1997). *Dying well.* New York, NY: Riverhead Books.

Carroll, L. (1865). *Alice's adventures in wonderland.* Mineola, NY: Dover Publications.

Clark, A. (2014). Narrative therapy integration with substance abuse groups. *Journal of Creativity in Mental Health, 9*(4), 511–522. DOI: 10.1080/15401383.2014.914457

Costello, J., & Kendrick, K. (2000). Grief and older people: The making or breaking of emotional bonds following partner loss in later life. *Journal of Advanced Nursing, 32,* 1374–1382.

Cottor, R., & Cottor, S. (1999). Relational inquiry and relational responsibility. In S. McNamee & K. Gergen (Eds.), *Relational responsibility: Resources for sustainable dialogue* (pp. 163–170). Thousand Oaks, CA: Sage.

Currier, J. M., Irish, J. E. F., Neimeyer, R. A., & Foster, J. D. (2015). Attachment, continuing bonds, and complicated grief following violent loss: Testing a moderated model. *Death Studies, 39,* 201–210. DOI: 10.1080/07481187.2014.975869

212

Davies, B., & Harré, R. (1990). Positioning: The discursive production of selves. *Journal for the Theory of Social Behavior, 20*(1), 43–63.

Deleuze, G. (1988). *Foucault* (S. Hand, Trans.). Minneapolis, MN: University of Minnesota Press.

Deleuze, G. (1990). *The logic of sense* (M. Lester, Trans.). New York, NY: Columbia University Press.

Deleuze, G. (1993). *The fold: Leibniz and the Baroque* (T. Conley, Trans.). Minneapolis, MN: University of Minnesota Press.

Deleuze, G. (1994). *Difference and repetition* (P. Patton, Trans.). New York, NY: Columbia University Press.

Deleuze, G., & Guattari, F. (1977). *Anti-Oedipus: Capitalism and schizophrenia* (R. Hurley, M. Seem, & H. R. Lane, Trans.). New York, NY: Penguin.

Deleuze, G., & Guattari, F. (1987). *A thousand plateaus: Capitalism and schizophrenia* (B. Massumi, Trans.). Minneapolis, MN: University of Minnesota Press.

Denborough, D. (1996). *Beyond the prison: Gathering dreams of freedom.* Adelaide, Australia: Dulwich Centre Publications.

Denborough, D. (Ed.) (2006). *Trauma: Narrative responses to traumatic experience.* Adelaide, Australia: Dulwich Centre Publications.

Derrida, J. (1976). *Of grammatology* (G. Spivak, Trans.). Baltimore, MD: Johns Hopkins University Press.

Doka, K. J. (1999). Disenfranchised grief. *Bereavement Care, 18*(3), 37–39. DOI: 10.1080/02682629908657467

Epston, D., & White, M. (1992). *Experience, contradiction, narrative and imagination.* Adelaide, Australia: Dulwich Centre Publications.

Foucault, M. (1969). *The archaeology of knowledge* (A. M. S. Smith, Trans.). London, UK: Tavistock.

Foucault, M. (1973). *The birth of the clinic* (A. M. Sheridan Smith, Trans.). New York, NY: Vintage Books.

Foucault, M. (1978). *Discipline and punish.* (A. M. Sheridan Smith, Trans.). New York, NY: Vintage Books.

Foucault, M. (1980). *Power/knowledge: Selected interviews and other writings.* New York, NY: Pantheon Books.

Foucault, M. (1982). Afterword: The subject and power. In H. Dreyfus & P. Rabinow (Eds.), *Michel Foucault: Beyond structuralism and hermeneutics* (pp. 199–226). Brighton, UK: Harvester Press.

Foucault, M. (1986). *The care of the self: The history of sexuality, Vol III.* New York, NY: Pantheon.

Foucault, M. (1989). *Foucault live (Interviews 1966/84)* (S. Lotringer, Ed., J. Johnston, Trans.). New York, NY: Semiotext.

Foucault, M. (1999). *Abnormal: Lectures at the Collège de France 1974–1975* (V. Marchetti & A. Salomoni, Ed., G. Burchell, Trans.). New York, NY: Picador.

Foucault, M. (2000). *Power: Essential works of Foucault, 1954–84 (Vol. 3)* (J. Faubion, Ed., R. Hurley, Trans.). New York, NY: The New Press.

Foucault, M. (2010). *The government of self and others: Lectures at the Collège de France, 1982–1983* (F. Gros, Ed., G. Burchell, Trans.). Basingstoke, UK: Palgrave MacMillan.

213

Frankl, V. (1939/1963). *Man's search for meaning: An introduction to logotherapy.* New York, NY: Simon and Schuster.

Freedman, J. (2014). Weaving net-works of hope with families, practitioners and communities: Inspirations from systemic and narrative approaches. *Australian & New Zealand Journal of Family Therapy, 35*(1) 54–71. DOI: 10.1002/anzf.1044

Freud, E. (1960). *Letters of Sigmund Freud* (T. Stern & J. Stern, Trans.). New York, NY: Basic Books.

Freud, S. (1957). Mourning and melancholia. In J. Strachey (Ed. & Trans.), *The standard edition of the complete psychological works of Sigmund Freud* (Vol. 14, pp. 237–259). London, UK: Hogarth Press. (Original work published 1917.)

Gall, T. L., Henneberry, J., & Eyre, M. (2014). Two perspectives on the needs of individuals bereaved by suicide. *Death Studies, 38*(7), 430–437. DOI: 10.1080/07481187.2013.772928

Geertz, C. (1973). *The interpretation of cultures.* New York, NY: Basic Books.

Geertz, C. (1983). *Local knowledge: Further essays in interpretive anthropology.* New York, NY: Basic Books.

Geraerts, E., McNally, R., & Jelicic, M. (2008). Linking thought suppression in recovered memories of childhood sexual abuse. *Memory, 16*(1), 22–28.

Gergen, K. (1989). Warranting voice and the elaboration of the self. In J. Shotter & K. Gergen (Eds.), *Texts of identity* (pp. 70–81). London, UK: Sage.

Gergen, K. (1994). *Realities and relationships.* Cambridge, MA: Harvard University Press.

Gergen, K. (1999). *An invitation to social construction* (2nd Edn.). Thousand Oaks, CA: Sage.

Gergen, K. (2009). *Relational being: Beyond self and community.* New York, NY: Oxford University Press.

Godel, M. (2007). Images of stillbirth: Memory, mourning and memorial. *Death Studies, 22*, 253–269. DOI: 10.1080/14725860701657159

Gorer, G. (1965). *Death, grief, and mourning in contemporary Britain.* London, UK: Cresset.

Gremillion, H. (2003). *Feeding anorexia.* Durham, NC: Duke University Press.

Guilfoyle, M. (2014). Listening in narrative therapy: Double listening and empathic positioning. *South African Journal of Psychology, 45*(1), 36–49. DOI: 10.1177/0081246314556711

Hadot, P. (1995). *Philosophy as a way of life: Spiritual exercises from Socrates to Foucault.* Oxford, UK: Blackwell.

Hagman, G. (2001). Beyond decathexis: Toward a new psychoanalytic understanding and treatment of mourning. In R. A. Neimeyer (Ed.), *Meaning reconstruction and the experience of loss* (pp. 13–32). Washington, DC: American Psychological Association.

Harju, A. (2015). Socially shared mourning: Construction and consumption of collective memory. *New Review of Hypermedia and Multimedia, 21*(1–2), 123–145. DOI: 10.1080/13614568.2014.983562

Havel, V. (October 1993). Never against hope. *Esquire*, 65–69.

Hedtke, L. (2012a). What's in an introduction? In R. A. Neimeyer (Ed.), *Techniques of grief therapy* (pp. 253–255). New York, NY: Routledge.

Hedtke, L. (2012b). *Breathing life into the stories of the dead: Constructing bereavement support groups.* Chagrin Falls, OH: Taos Institute Publications.

Hedtke, L., & Winslade, J. (2004). *Re-membering lives: Conversations with the dying and the bereaved.* Amityville, NY: Baywood.

Hedtke, L., & Winslade, J. (2005). The use of the subjunctive in re-membering conversations. *Omega, 50*(3), 197–215.

Hibberd, R. (2013). Meaning reconstruction in bereavement: Sense and significance. *Death Studies, 37*, 670–692. DOI: 10.1080/07481187.2012.692453

Hockey, J. (1990). *Experiences of death.* Edinburgh, UK: Edinburgh University Press.

Ikonomopoulos, J., Smith, R., & Schmidt, C. (2015). Integrating narrative therapy within rehabilitative programming for incarcerated adolescents. *Journal of Counseling & Development, 93*(4), 460–470. DOI: 10.1002/jcad.12044

Jenkings, K. N., Megoran, N., Woodward, R., & Bos, D. (2012). Wootton Bassett and the political spaces of remembrance and mourning. *Area, 44*(3), 356–363. DOI: 10.1111/j.1475-4762.2012.01106.x

Jones, E. (1955). *The life and work of Sigmund Freud* (Vol. 2). New York, NY: Basic Books.

Jordan, J. R., & McIntosh, J. L. (2011). Grief after suicide: Understanding the consequences and caring for the survivors. In J. R. Jordan & J. L. McIntosh (Eds.), *Suicide bereavement: Why study survivors of suicide loss?* (pp. 3–17). New York, NY: Routledge.

Klass, D. (2001). The inner representation of the dead child in the psychic and social narratives of bereaved parents. In R. A. Neimeyer (Ed.), *Meaning reconstruction and the experience of loss* (pp. 77–94). Washington, DC: American Psychological Association.

Klass, D., & Goss, S. (2003). The politics of grief and continuing bonds with the dead: The cases of Maoist China and Wahhabi Islam. *Death Studies, 27*, 787–812. DOI: 10.1080/07481180390233380

Klass, D., Silverman, P., & Nickman, S. (Eds.) (1996). *Continuing bonds: New understandings of grief.* Philadelphia, PA: Taylor and Francis.

Klein, M. (1940). Mourning and its relation to manic-depressive states. *The International Journal of Psychoanalysis, 21*, 125–153.

Kübler-Ross, E. (1969). *On death and dying.* New York, NY: Macmillan.

Labov, W. (1997). Some further steps in narrative analysis. *Journal of Narrative and Life History, 7*, 395–415.

Lazzarato, M. (2014). *Signs, machines and subjectivities* (Bilingual Edn. English/Portuguese) (P. D. Oneto, Trans.). Sao Paolo, Brazil: n-1 publications.

Lebel, U. (2011). Panopticon of death: Institutional design of bereavement. *Acta Sociologica, 54*(4), 351–366. DOI: 1 0 .1 1 7 7/00016 9 9311 4 220

Lindemann, E. (1994). Symptomatology and management of acute grief. *American Journal of Psychiatry, 151*(6), 155–160. Sesquicentennial Supplement. Originally published September 1944.

MacKinnon, C. J., Smith, N. G., Henry, M., Berish, M., Milman, E., Körner, A., Copeland, L. S., Chochinov, H. M., & Cohen, S. R. (2014). Meaning-based group counseling for bereavement: Bridging theory with emerging trends in intervention research. *Death Studies, 38,* 137–144. DOI: 10.1080/07481187.2012.738768

Madsen, W. (2007). *Collaborative therapy with multi-stressed families.* New York, NY: The Guilford Press.

Maisel, R., Epston, D., & Borden, A. (2004). *Biting the hand that starves you: Inspiring resistance to anorexia/bulimia.* New York, NY: Norton.

Malraux, A. (1978). *The voices of silence* (S. Gilbert, Trans.). Princeton, NJ: Princeton University Press.

Mann, S. (2006). How can you do this work? Responding to questions about the experiences of working with women who were subjected to child sexual abuse. In D. Denborough (Ed.), *Trauma: Narrative responses to traumatic experience* (pp. 1–25). Adelaide, Australia: Dulwich Centre Publications.

Martin, T. L. (2002). Disenfranchising the brokenhearted. In K. Doka (Ed.), *Disenfranchised grief: New directions, challenges, and strategies for practice* (pp. 233–250). Champaign, IL: Research Press.

Maslow, A. (August 1970). Editorial. *Psychology Today,* 16.

Maugham, W. S. (1949). *A writer's notebook.* Garden City, NY: Doubleday.

May, T. (2005). *Gilles Deleuze: An introduction.* Cambridge, UK: Cambridge University Press.

May, T. (2009). *Death.* Durham, UK: Acumen.

McNally, R. J. (2005). Debunking myths about trauma and memory. *Canadian Journal of Psychiatry, 50*(13), 817–822.

Mencken, H. L. (1956). *The American language: An inquiry into the development of English in the United States.* New York, NY: Alfred Knopf.

Middleton, D., & Brown, S. (2005). *The social psychology of experience: Studies in remembering and forgetting.* London, UK: Sage.

Middleton, D., & Edwards, D. (1986). Joint remembering: Constructing an account of shared experience through conversational discourse. *Discourse Processes, 9*(4), 423–459.

Middleton, D., & Edwards, D. (1990). *Collective remembering.* London, UK: Sage.

Monk, G., Winslade, J., Crocket, K., & Epston, D. (Eds) (1997). *Narrative therapy in practice: The archaeology of hope.* San Francisco, CA: Jossey-Bass.

Monk, G., Winslade, J., & Sinclair, S. (2008). *New horizons in multicultural counseling.* Thousand Oaks, CA: Sage.

Murphy, S., Gutpa, A., Cain, K., Johnson, L. C., Lohan, J., Wu, L., & Mekwa, J. (1999). Changes in parents' mental distress after the violent death of an adolescent or young adult child: A longitudinal prospective analysis. *Death Studies, 23*(2), 129–159. DOI: 10.1080/074811899201118

Murray, B. (2012). For what noble cause: Cindy Sheehan and the politics of grief in public spheres of argument. *Argumentation and Advocacy, 49,* 1–15.

Myerhoff, B. (1978). *Number our days.* New York, NY: Simon & Schuster.

216

Myerhoff, B. (1982). Life history among the elderly: Performance, visibility and remembering. In J. Ruby (Ed.), *A crack in the mirror: Reflexive perspectives in anthropology* (pp. 99–117). Philadelphia, PA: University of Pennsylvania Press.

Myerhoff, B. (1986). Life not death in Venice. In V. Turner & E. Bruner (Eds.), *The anthropology of experience* (pp. 261–286). Chicago, IL: University of Illinois Press.

Myerhoff, B. (1992). *Remembered lives: The work of ritual, storytelling, and growing older.* Ann Arbor, MI: University of Michigan Press.

Myerhoff, B. (2007). *Stories as equipment for living* (M. Kaminsky & M. Weiss, Eds.). Ann Arbor, MI: The University of Michigan Press.

Nadeau, J. W. (2001). Family construction of meaning. In R. A. Neimeyer (Ed.), *Meaning reconstruction and the experience of loss* (pp. 95–112). Washington, DC: American Psychological Association.

Ncube, N. (Director) (2006). *Tree of life: An approach to working with vulnerable children* [Motion picture on DVD]. Adelaide, Australia: Dulwich Centre Publications.

Neimeyer, R. A. (1998). *Lessons of loss: A guide to coping.* New York, NY: McGraw-Hill.

Neimeyer, R. A. (2001). The language of loss: Grief therapy as a process of meaning reconstruction. In R. A. Neimeyer (Ed.), *Meaning reconstruction and the experience of loss* (pp. 261–292). Washington, DC: American Psychological Association.

Neimeyer, R. A. (2015). Meaning in bereavement. In R. E. Anderson (Ed.), *World suffering and quality of life* (pp. 115–124). New York, NY: Springer Publishing.

Neimeyer, R. A., & Gillies, J. (2006). Loss, grief, and the search for significance: Toward a model of meaning reconstruction in bereavement. *Journal of Constructivist Psychology, 19,* 31–65. DOI: 10.1080/10720530500311182

Neimeyer, R. A., & Jordan, J. R. (2002). Disenfranchisement as empathic failure: Grief therapy and the co-construction of meaning. In K. Doka (Ed.), *Disenfranchised grief: New directions, challenges, and strategies for practice* (pp. 95–117). Champaign, IL: Research Press.

Neimeyer, R. A., Klass, D., & Dennis, M. R. (2014). A social constructionist account of grief: Loss and the narration of meaning. *Death Studies, 38,* 485–498. DOI: 10.1080/07481187.2014.913454

Neimeyer, R. A., Laurie, A., Mehta, A., Hardison, H., & Currier, J. M. (2008). Lessons of loss: Meaning-making in bereaved college students. *New directions for student services, 121,* 27–39. DOI: 10.1002/ss.264

Neimeyer, R. A., Prigerson, H., & Davies, B. (2002). Mourning and meaning. *American Behavioral Scientist, 46,* 235–251.

Neimeyer, R. A., & Sands, D. C. (2011). Meaning reconstruction in bereavement: From principles to practice. In R. A. Neimeyer, D. L. Harris, H. R. Winokuer, & G. F. Thornton (Eds.), *Grief and bereavement in contemporary society: Bridging research and practice* (pp. 9–22). New York, NY: Routledge.

Nelson, H. L. (2001). *Damaged identities: Narrative repair.* Ithaca, NY: Cornell University Press.

Nietzsche, F. (1974). *The gay science* (W. Kaufmann, Trans.). New York, NY: Vintage.

Nylund, D. (2000). *Treating Huckleberry Finn.* San Francisco, CA: Jossey-Bass.

O'Callaghan, C., McDermott, F., Hudson, P., & Zalcberg, J. (2013). Sound continuing bonds with the deceased: The relevance of music, including preloss music: Overview and future directions. *Death Studies, 38,* 1–8. DOI: 10.1080/07481187.2012.712608

O'Connor, M. F. (2002/2003). Making meaning of life events: Theory, evidence and research directions for an alternative model. *Omega, 46*(1), 51–76.

Olsen, A. (2015). "Is it because I'm gormless?" A commentary on "Narrative therapy in a learning disability context: A review". *Tizard Learning Disability Review. 20*(3), 130–133. DOI: 10.1108/TLDR-03-2015-0012

Paré, D. (2013). *The practice of collaborative counseling and psychotherapy: Developing skills in culturally-mindful helping.* Thousand Oaks, CA: Sage.

Parkes, C. M. (1972). *Bereavement: Studies of grief in adult life.* New York, NY: International Universities Press.

Parkes, C. M. (2002). Grief: Lessons from the past, visions for the future. *Death Studies, 26*(5), 367–385. DOI: 10.1080/07481180290087366

Piaget, J. (1977). *The essential Piaget: An interpretive reference and guide* (H. Gruber & J. Voneche, Eds.). New York, NY: Jason Aronson.

Rando, T. (1988). *Grieving.* New York, NY: Lexington Books.

Rando, T. (1995). Grief and mourning: Accommodating to loss. In H. Wass & R. A. Neimeyer (Eds.), *Dying: Facing the facts.* (pp. 211–242). Washington, DC: Taylor & Francis.

Reimers, E. (2011). Primary mourners and next-of-kin: How grief practices reiterate and subvert heterosexual norms. *Journal of Gender Studies, 20*(3), 251–262. DOI: 10.1080/09589236.2011.593324

Root, B. L., & Exline, J. J. (2014). The role of continuing bonds in coping with grief: Overview and future directions. *Death Studies, 38*(1), 1–8. DOI: 10.1080/07481187.2012.712608

Rose, N. (1999). *Governing the soul: The shaping of the private self* (2nd Edn.). Chippenham & Eastbourne, UK: Free Association Books.

Rosenblatt, P. C., & Meyer, C. (1986). Imagined interactions and the family. *Family Relations, 35,* 319–324.

Rubin, S. S. (1999). The two-track model of bereavement: Overview, retrospect, and prospect. *Death Studies, 23,* 681–714. DOI: 10.1080/074811899200731

Rubin, S. S. (2015). Loss and mourning in the Jewish tradition. *Omega, 70,* 79–98. DOI: 10.2190/OM.70.1.h

Rubin, S. S., Malkinson, R., & Witztum, E. (2011). The two-track model of bereavement: The double helix of research and clinical practice. In R. A. Neimeyer, D. L. Harris, H. R. Winokuer & G. F. Thornton (Eds.), *Grief and bereavement in contemporary society: Bridging research and practice* (pp. 47–56). New York, NY: Routledge.

Rubin, S. S., Malkinson, R., & Witztum, E. (2012). Working with the bereaved: Multiple lenses on loss and mourning. New York, NY: Routledge.

Russell, S., & Carey, M. (2002). Re-membering: Responding to commonly asked questions. *The International Journal of Narrative Therapy and Community Work, 3,* 23–32.

Ryle, G. (1949). *The concept of mind.* London, UK: Hutchinson.

Rynearson, E. K. (2001). *Retelling violent death.* Philadelphia, PA: Brunner-Routledge.

Seidman, S. (Ed.) (1994). *The postmodern turn.* Melbourne, Australia: Cambridge University Press.

Shakespeare, W. (1998). *Hamlet (Signet classic Shakespeare edition, revised).* London, UK: Signet.

Shapiro, E. (1996). Grief in Freud's life: Reconceptualizing bereavement in psychoanalytic theory. *Psychoanalytic Psychology, 13,* 547–566.

Shneidman, E. (1973). *Deaths of man.* New York, NY: Quadrangle/New York Times.

Shotter, J. (1990). The social construction of remembering and forgetting. In D. Middleton & D. Edwards (Eds.), *Collective remembering* (pp. 121–138). London, UK: Sage.

Silverman, P., & Klass, D. (1996). Introduction: What's the problem? In D. Klass, P. Silverman & S. Nickman (Eds.), *Continuing bonds: New understandings of grief* (pp. 3–27). Philadelphia, PA: Taylor and Francis.

Smith, C., & Nylund, D. (1997). *Narrative therapy for children and adolescents.* New York, NY: The Guilford Press.

Smyth, J., & Hattam, R. (2004). *Dropping out, drifting off, being excluded: Becoming somebody without school.* New York, NY: Peter Lang.

Stableford, D. (2013). One month after school massacre, parents of Sandy Hook victims speak, urging 'real change'. *The Lookout.* Retrieved from http://news.yahoo.com/blogs/lookout/sandy-hook-school-shooting-promise-181324286.html

Stroebe, M. S., Abakoumkin, A. G., Stroebe, B. W., & Schut, H. (2012). Continuing bonds in adjustment to bereavement: Impact of abrupt versus gradual separation. *Personal Relationships, 19,* 255–266. DOI: 10.1111/j.1475-6811.2011.01352.x

Stroebe, M. S., & Schut, H. (1999). The dual process model of coping with bereavement: Rationale and description. *Death Studies, 23,* 197–224. DOI: 10.1080/074811899201046

Stroebe, M. S., & Schut, H. (2001). Meaning-making and the dual process model of coping with bereavement. In R. A. Neimeyer (Ed.), *Meaning reconstruction and the experience of loss* (pp. 55–73). Washington, DC: American Psychological Association.

Turner, V. W. (1986). Dewey, Dilthey and drama: An essay in the anthropology of experience. In V. Turner & E. Bruner (Eds.), *The anthropology of experience* (pp. 33–34). Urbana & Chicago, IL: University of Illinois Press.

Valentine, C. (2006). Academic constructions of bereavement. *Mortality, 11*(1), 57–78. DOI: 10.1080/13576270500439274

van Gennep, A. (1961). *The rites of passage.* Chicago, IL: University of Chicago Press.

Vickio, C. J. (1999). Together in spirit: Keeping our relationships alive when loved ones die. *Death Studies, 23*(2), 161–175. DOI: 10.1080/074811899201127

Walter, T. (1999). *On bereavement: The culture of grief*. Buckingham, UK: Open University Press.

Weingarten, K. (2010). Reasonable hope: Construct, clinical applications and supports. *Family Process, 49*, 5–25. DOI: 10.1111/j.1545-5300.2010.01305.x

White, M. (1989). Saying hullo again. In M. White (Ed.), *Selected papers* (pp. 29–36). Adelaide, Australia: Dulwich Centre Publications.

White, M. (1991). Deconstruction and therapy. *Dulwich Centre Newsletter, 3*, 21–40.

White, M. (1997). *Narratives of therapists' lives*. Adelaide, Australia: Dulwich Centre Publications.

White, M. (2000). Re-engagement with history: The absent but implicit. In M. White, *Reflections on narrative practices: Interviews and essays* (pp. 35–58). Adelaide, Australia: Dulwich Centre Publications.

White, M. (2001). Folk psychology and narrative practice. *Dulwich Centre Journal, 2001*(2), 3–37.

White, M. (2006). Working with people who are suffering the consequences of multiple trauma: A narrative perspective. In D. Denborough (Ed.), *Trauma: Narrative responses to traumatic experience* (pp. 25–86). Adelaide, Australia: Dulwich Centre Publications.

White, M. (2007). *Maps of narrative practice*. New York, NY: Norton.

White, M., & Epston, D. (1990). *Narrative means to therapeutic ends*. New York, NY: Norton.

Winslade, J. (2009). Tracing lines of flight: Implications of the work of Gilles Deleuze for narrative practice. *Family Process, 48*(3), 332–346. DOI: 10.1111/j.1545-5300.2009.01286.x

Winslade, J. (2013). From being nonjudgmental to deconstructing normalising judgment. *British Journal of Guidance and Counselling, 41*(5), 518–529. DOI: 10.1080/03069885.2013.771772

Winslade, J., & Monk, G. (2000). *Narrative mediation: A new approach to conflict resolution*. San Francisco, CA: Jossey-Bass.

Winslade, J., & Monk, G. (2007). *Narrative counseling in schools: Powerful and brief* (2nd Edn.). Thousand Oaks, CA: Corwin Press.

Wittgenstein, L. (1953). *Philosophical investigations*. Oxford, UK: Blackwell.

Wood, L., Byram, V., Gosling, A., & Stokes, J. (2012). Continuing bonds after suicide bereavement in childhood. *Death Studies, 36*(10), 873–898. DOI: 10.1080/07481187.2011.584025

Worden, J. W. (1991). *Grief counseling and grief therapy: A handbook for the mental health practitioner* (2nd Edn.). New York, NY: Springer.

Worden, J. W. (2009). *Grief counseling and grief therapy: A handbook for the mental health practitioner* (4th Edn.). New York, NY: Springer.

Worden, J. W. (2015). Theoretical perspectives on loss and grief. In J. Stillion & T. Attig (Eds.), *Death, dying and bereavement: Contemporary perspectives, institutions and practices* (pp. 91–104). New York, NY: Springer Publishing.

Index

Abakoumkin, A. 51, 219
absent but implicit viii, x, 105–9, 111, 116, 120, 192, 220
aesthetic(s) x, 8, 18, 19, 25, 27, 35, 36, 42, 77, 98, 161–2, 164, 168, 171, 204, 209–10
agency 9, 15, 23–24, 25, 26
aion x, 148, 149, 155–61, 164, 165, 166, 167, 168, 174, 177, 207
Alzheimer's 70, 150, 152, 153, 164
Anderson, H. 19, 211
Andrews, R. 151, 211
Ariés, P. 31, 211
Aristotle 16
Athanasiou, A. 18, 212
attachment 38
Attig, T. 67, 77, 211

Bakhtin, M. 17, 58, 84, 103, 211
Bartlett, F. 71–3, 211
Baumgartner, B. 74, 211
beauty ix, 1, 4, 8, 26, 28, 81, 108, 170, 176, 190, 191, 193, 195, 204, 209, 210
becoming viii, x, 18, 20, 21–3, 25, 26, 81, 83ff, 148, 162, 179, 211, 219
Berger, J. 147, 167, 211
Berger, P. 58, 211
Bergson, H. 156, 166, 211
Bernecker, S. 70, 211
Bichat, M. 179, 212
Blythe, K. 212
Bonanno, G. 106, 195, 212
Borden, A. 74, 216
Bowlby, J. x, 32, 36, 38–40, 45, 47, 212
Breen, L. 138, 212
Brown, S. 70, 71, 72, 73, 216

Bruner, E. 217, 219
Bruner, J. 20, 80, 135, 159, 212
Burks, S. 89, 212
Burman, E. 39, 212
Burr, V. 10, 212
Butler, J. 18, 144, 145, 212
Byock, I. 192, 212
Byram, V. 89, 220

care of the self 20, 209, 213
Carey, M. 75, 76, 219
Caroll, L. 147, 148, 212
chronos ix, 148, 149, 151–4, 155, 156, 157, 159, 161, 164, 165, 167, 168
Cicero 170
Clark, A. 74, 212
continuing bonds x, 46, 51, 52, 53, 59, 81, 108, 185, 209, 212, 215, 218, 219, 220
Costello, J. 59, 212
Cottor, R. 58, 212
Cottor, S. 58, 212
crafting ix, 7, 15, 17–18, 26, 28, 34, 81, 96, 114, 121, 142, 162, 167, 168, 196, 209
critical edge 9–10
Crocket, K. 74, 216
cultural forces 11, 13, 14, 15, 16, 17
curiosity ix, 19, 106, 113, 135–7, 172
Currier, J. 51, 212

Damocles 169ff, 191, 203
Darwin, C. 39
Davies, Bronwyn 17, 84, 213
Davies, Betty 68
deconstruct 103, 146, 212; deconstruction 105, 220; deconstructive, 25, 153

definitional ceremony 101, 139, 140
Deleuze, G. viii, x, xi, 10, 16, 21,
    24, 32, 44, 84, 85, 128, 129, 131,
    132, 136, 147–161, 165, 166,
    167, 176, 177, 178, 179–80, 182,
    192, 194, 213, 216, 220
Denborough, D. 74, 213, 216, 220
denial 12, 14, 23, 36, 43, 44, 45, 47,
    49, 95, 111, 133, 137
Derrida, J. 10, 21, 105, 131, 132,
    213
Dionysius 170, 191
discourse(s) 10, 11, 14, 16, 17, 18,
    21, 24, 25, 29, 34, 42, 47, 50, 58,
    78, 96, 103, 104, 105, 107, 121,
    122, 128, 130, 131, 132, 142,
    144, 145, 146, 148, 149, 151,
    154, 180, 190, 208, 209, 216
disenfranchised grief 144–6, 213,
    216, 217
Doka, K. 144, 213
double listening 106–7, 109, 121,
    214
DSM V 24, 194
dual process model viii, 52, 116,
    219
Dulwich Centre 74, 213, 216, 217,
    220
duration 37, 38, 156, 165, 166, 167

Edwards, D. 70, 71, 72, 216
Epston, D. 10, 73, 74, 75, 213, 216,
    220
Exline, J. 51, 218
Eyre, M. 102, 214

fabula 16
folk psychology 20, 220
Ford, H. 151
Foster, J. 51, 212
Foucault, M. 1, 10, 14, 18, 20, 21,
    23, 24, 31, 103, 128, 130, 132,
    137, 145, 148, 154, 178, 209,
    213, 214
Frankl, V. 104, 214

Freedman, J. 74, 214
Freud, S. viii, ix, 28, 29, 32, 33–36,
    37, 38, 39, 40, 41, 43, 47, 49, 51,
    133, 153, 194, 214, 215, 219

Gall, T. 102, 214
Geertz, C. 58, 135, 214
Gennep, A. van 81, 219
Geraerts 71, 214
Gergen, K. 10, 32, 58, 212, 214
Gillies, J. 68, 85, 86, 102, 104, 105,
    217
Godel, M. 77, 214
Gorer, G. 32, 214
Gosling, A. 89, 220
governmentality 24
Gremillion H., 74, 214
grief psychology viii, x, 10, 12, 14,
    18, 26, 27, 29, 31, 32, 35, 36, 37,
    38, 41, 42, 45, 47, 49, 50, 51, 52,
    56, 58, 59, 68, 70, 72, 77, 78, 81,
    102, 108, 130, 133, 137, 153
grief work 37, 49
Guattari, F. 32, 128, 213

Hadot, P. 20, 214
Hagman, G. 28, 50, 214
Hamlet 9
Harju 145, 146, 214
Harré, R. 17, 84, 213
Hattam, R. 83, 219
Havel, V. 195, 214
Hedtke, L. viii, xi, 19, 74, 78,
    95,123, 215
Henneberry, J. 102, 214
Hibberd, R. 68, 85, 102, 104, 105,
    123, 126, 215
Hockey, J. 31, 215
homicide 85, 87

identity x, xii, 24, 50, 51, 53, 58, 62,
    63, 68, 73, 75, 77, 81, 82, 83, 84,
    85, 87, 89, 92, 96, 98, 99, 101, 107,
    138, 166, 167, 174, 192, 197, 214
Ikonomopoulos, J. 74, 215

individualism 22, 23, 103
Irish, J. 51, 212

Jelicic, M. 71, 214
Jordan, J. 108, 145, 215, 217

Kendrick, K. 59, 212
Kennedy, J. 170
Klass, D. 41, 59, 69, 77, 85, 86, 87,
   103, 123, 143, 215, 217, 219
Klein, M. x, 32, 36–7, 40, 48, 215
Kübler-Ross, E. viii, x, 14, 28, 32,
   42–5, 215

Lazzarato, M. 196, 215
legacy ix, 63, 65, 66, 67, 77, 79, 81,
   89, 132, 169, 174, 178, 182
Lindemann, E. x, 32, 37–8, 40, 45,
   215
line(s) of flight 44, 120, 122, 220
line(s) of force 23, 31, 32, 84, 104,
   130, 131, 139, 140, 141, 171
local knowledge 26, 40, 135, 214
Luckman, T. 58, 211

MacKinnon, C. 67, 216
Madsen, W. 74, 216
Maisel, R. 74, 216
Malkinson, R. 67, 108, 218
Malraux, A. 161, 162, 216
Mann, S. 74, 216
Martin, T. 144, 216
Maslow, A. 63, 216
Matsushita, W. ix, xi, 1–8
Maugham, S. 80, 216
May, T. 85, 190, 191, 192, 194, 216
McIntosh, J. 108, 215
McNally, R. 71, 214, 216
meaning reconstruction 52, 68, 69,
   104–5, 211, 214, 215, 217, 219
membership 62–7, 74, 75, 76, 77,
   81, 84, 95, 96, 99, 100, 101, 134,
   176, 178, 182, 205
memory x, 8, 41, 64, 69–72, 73, 81,
   95, 120, 126, 149, 156, 159, 160,

166, 167, 169, 171, 180, 185,
   190, 202, 205, 211, 214, 216
Mencken, H. 80, 216
Meyer, C. 95, 218
Middleton, D. 70, 71, 72, 73, 216, 219
Mishima, Dr 2–4, 15
modernist 28, 44, 58, 62, 63, 71,
   80, 146, 151,154, 165, 190
Monk, G. 74, 129, 131, 216, 220
Murphy, S. 86, 216
Myerhoff, B. x, xii, 62, 74, 75, 76,
   79, 96, 101, 125, 139–40, 166,
   216, 217

Nadeau, K. 103, 217
narrative(s) 10, 15, 16, 17, 18, 19,
   23, 25, 68, 84, 86, 103, 104,
   107, 123, 143, 148, 149, 154,
   157, 159, 166, 167, 174, 196,
   203, 213, 214, 215, 218, 220;
   meta-narrative(s) 29; narrative
   conversation 203; narrative,
   perspective 15, 220
narrative practice x, 10, 220;
   narrative therapy 10, 73–7, 81,
   107, 211, 212, 214, 215, 216,
   218, 219
natural, grief as 10, 12
Ncube, N. 74, 217
Neimeyer, R. xi, 28, 50, 51, 52, 68,
   77, 85, 86, 87, 102, 103, 104,
   105, 123, 145, 211, 212, 214,
   215, 217, 218, 219
Nelson, H. L. 15, 218
neoliberal 22, 133, 143
Nickman, S. 59, 77, 215, 219
Nietzsche, F. 166, 218
Nylund, D. 74, 218, 219

O'Connor, M. 138, 212
O'Connor, M.F. 102, 103, 104, 218
Olsen, A. 74, 218

Parkes, C. x, 32, 40–2, 44, 45, 218
Piaget, J. 159, 218

223

postmodern 58, 59, 69, 71, 72–3, 195, 211, 219
poststructuralist 10, 21, 23, 104, 129, 130, 179
power x, 23, 34, 36, 70, 73, 86, 122, 129, 130, 131, 132, 133, 134, 135, 137, 138, 144, 170, 208, 213; power relation(s) 23, 24–5, 106, 128, 129, 130, 132, 154
Prigerson, H. 68, 217

Rando, T. 45, 47, 48, 49, 50, 218
re-membering viii, x, xii, 53ff, 86, 89, 95, 99, 114, 159, 166, 207, 215, 219
regime of truth 10, 14, 137, 148
Reimers, E. 144, 218
Root, B. 51, 218
Rosenblatt, P. 95, 218
Rubin, S. 52, 67, 108, 218
Russell, S. 75, 76, 219
Ryle, G. 25
Rynearson, E. 86, 219

Sands, D. 68, 86, 217
say goodbye 22, 23, 56, 109, 165, 166
saying hullo again 59, 74, 81, 109, 165, 166, 167, 168, 220
Schmidt, C. 74, 215
Schut, H. 51, 52, 108, 219
Seidman, S. 58, 219
Shakespeare 9, 84, 219
Shapiro, E. 69, 219
Shneidman, E. 62–4, 219
Shotter, J. 70, 72, 214, 219
Silverman, P. 41, 59, 77, 215, 219
Smith, C. 74, 219
Smith, N. 216
Smith, R. 74, 215
smooth 24, 25

Smyth, J. 83, 219
social constructionist x, 10, 53, 59, 217
stages of dying 11, 14, 19, 42–5
stages of grief 16, 19, 102, 133, 137
Stoic x, 20, 148, 167, 179
Stokes, J. 89, 220
striated 24, 25, 128
Stroebe, B. 51, 219
Stroebe, M. 51, 52, 108
subjunctive 78, 79–82, 95, 96, 122, 207, 208, 215
suicide x, 29, 49, 62, 63, 85, 86, 87, 89, 91, 92, 93, 111, 120, 121, 127, 212, 214, 215, 220

tasks of grieving 11, 45–7, 133
Thompson, R. 92
troubled relationships x, 97–100
Turner, V. 81, 217, 219
two-track model viii, 52, 218

Valentine, C. 11, 13, 28, 43, 219
Vickio, C. 96, 220
virtual 13, 80, 165, 171, 176, 194
vitality 109, 111, 114, 120, 133, 176, 178, 179, 194, 195, 200, 210

Walter, T. 11, 220
Weingarten, K. 196, 220
White, M. viii, x, xii, 10, 20, 59, 63, 73, 74, 75, 76, 96, 101, 105, 106, 107, 108, 125, 135, 165, 192, 213, 220
Williams, B. 74, 211
Winslade, J. viii, xi, 19, 74, 95, 123, 129, 131, 139, 145, 215, 216, 220
Wittgenstein, L. 9, 104, 148, 220
Witztum, E. 67, 108, 218
Wood, L. 89, 220
Worden, W. 28, 37, 45–7, 50, 95, 220